LESSONS FROM SHAKESPEARE'S CLASSROOM

This volume explores the relationship between the emphasis on performance in Elizabethan humanist education and the flourishing of literary brilliance around the turn of the 16th century.

This study asks us what lessons we can learn today from Shakespeare's Latin grammar school. What were the cognitive benefits of an education so deeply rooted in what Demosthenes and Quintilian called "actio"—acting? Because of the vast difference between educational practice then and now, we have not often followed one essential thread: the focus on performance. This study examines the connections relevant to the education offered in schools today.

This book will be of great interest to teachers, scholars, and administrators in performing arts and education.

Robin Lithgow was the first ever Theatre Adviser, and later the Director, of the Los Angeles Unified School District's Arts Education Branch. In that role she and her colleagues were the architects of the Elementary Arts Program, serving every one of over 550 elementary schools, with itinerate teachers in dance, music, theatre, and visual arts.

She is the daughter of Arthur Lithgow, perhaps the only person ever to have produced every play in Shakespeare's canon. She is the sister of the theatre and film actor, John Lithgow, who has kindly illustrated this book.

Routledge Advances in Theatre & Performance Studies

This series is our home for cutting-edge, upper-level scholarly studies and edited collections. Considering theatre and performance alongside topics such as religion, politics, gender, race, ecology, and the avant-garde, titles are characterized by dynamic interventions into established subjects and innovative studies on emerging topics.

Rechoreographing Learning
Dance As a Way to Bridge the Mind-Body Divide in Education
Sandra Cerny Minton

Politics as Public Art
The Aesthetics of Political Organizing and Social Movements
Martin Zebracki and Zane McNeill

Notelets of Filth
An *Emilia* Companion Reader
Laura Kressly, Aida Patient, and Kimberly A. Williams

Transcultural Theater
Günther Heeg

Lessons from Shakespeare's Classroom
Empowering Learning Through Drama and Rhetoric
Robin Lithgow

For more information about this series, please visit: www.routledge.com/Routledge-Advances-in-Theatre-Performance-Studies/book-series/RATPS

LESSONS FROM SHAKESPEARE'S CLASSROOM

Empowering Learning Through Drama and Rhetoric

Robin Lithgow

LONDON AND NEW YORK

Cover image: John Lithgow.

First published 2023
by Routledge
4 Park Square, Milton Park, Abingdon, Oxon OX14 4RN

and by Routledge
605 Third Avenue, New York, NY 10158

Routledge is an imprint of the Taylor & Francis Group, an informa business

© 2023 Robin Lithgow

The right of Robin Lithgow to be identified as author of this work has been asserted in accordance with sections 77 and 78 of the Copyright, Designs and Patents Act 1988.

All rights reserved. No part of this book may be reprinted or reproduced or utilised in any form or by any electronic, mechanical, or other means, now known or hereafter invented, including photocopying and recording, or in any information storage or retrieval system, without permission in writing from the publishers.

Trademark notice: Product or corporate names may be trademarks or registered trademarks, and are used only for identification and explanation without intent to infringe.

British Library Cataloguing-in-Publication Data
A catalogue record for this book is available from the British Library

ISBN: 978-1-032-38406-1 (hbk)
ISBN: 978-1-032-38407-8 (pbk)
ISBN: 978-1-003-34491-9 (ebk)

DOI: 10.4324/9781003344919

Typeset in Bembo
by Apex CoVantage, LLC

*This book is dedicated to
The Elementary Dance, Music, Theatre, and Visual Arts Teachers
of the Los Angeles Unified School District
and to arts educators everywhere.
Heroes.*

I was brought up at School under Mr. Mulcaster, in the famous school of the Merchant Taylors in London, where I continued until I was well instructed in the Hebrew, Greek, and Latin tongues. His care was to increase my skill in music, in which I was brought up by daily exercise in it, as in singing and playing upon instruments, and yearly he presented some plays to the court, in which his scholars were the only actors, and I one among them, and by that means he taught them good behavior and audacity.

Sir James Whitelocke, Justice of the King James I's Bench, writing about the 16th-century pedagogue, Richard Mulcaster

CONTENTS

Timeline   *ix*
Cast of Characters   *xi*
Acknowledgments   *xii*

   Introduction   1

1 Time Travel   3

2 Engagement Before Information   8

3 Angels and Eaglets   16

4 Good Behavior and Audacity: The Training Up of Schoolboy Orators   22

5 Context: The Hatch and Brood of Time: A Brief History of the English Reformation   46

6 Erasmus' Egg   54

7 The Delightful Mulcaster   75

8 Per Quam Figuram?   93

9 Erasmus Writes Colloquies   113

10 The Little Eyases: Professional Boy Actors   139

11 The Lego Snap of Learning   158

12 Conclusion   188

Appendix I: Performing the Colloquies in Latin and in English   *191*
Appendix II: Selection of Educational Drama Resources for Teachers *228*
Bibliography   *229*
Index   *236*

TIMELINE

Life of Erasmus: 1469–1536

1495–1499: Tutors English students in Paris and writes simple colloquies for practice in conversational Latin.

1599–1500: First trip to England, where he becomes friends with John Colet and Thomas More.

1500: Publishes first edition of *Adagia*.

1510–1515: Second trip to England. Teaches at Cambridge, deepens friendships, and meets Prince Henry.

1510: John Colet re-founds Saint Paul's School in London and asks Erasmus to help him to design the curriculum.

1511–1512: Publication of *De ratione studii* and *De Utraque Verborum ac Rerum Copia (de Copia)* written as curriculum for Saint Paul's School.

1518: *Colloquia familiaria* published, without permission, in Basel by the house of Johan Froben.

1522–1533: *Colloquia familiaria* augmented and published with permission, many times. Over the next century, tens of thousands of copies are purchased in England.

Life of Richard Mulcaster: 1531–1611

1561–1592: Headmaster of the Merchant Taylors' School in London. Creates a theatre in the school and regularly produces plays to be performed at court. Taught Thomas Jenkins and John Cotham.

1582: Publishes *Positions*.

1583: Publishes *Elementarie*.

1596–1608: Headmaster of Saint Paul's School in London.

Life of William Shakespeare: 1564–1616

1571–1579 (approx.): Attends the King Edward VI Latin Grammar School in Stratford.

1575–1779: Thomas Jenkins is headmaster, followed by John Cotham.

1592: First mention of Shakespeare living in London as an actor and playwright.

1509–1603: Tudor Age. The reigns of Henry VIII, Edward VI, Mary I, and Elizabeth I.

1558–1603: Elizabethan Age. The reign of Elizabeth I.

1603–1625: Jacobean Age. The reign of James I.

CAST OF CHARACTERS

Desiderius Erasmus, 1469–1536: Principal architect of Shakespeare's humanist education.

Juan Vives, 1493–1540: Early humanist, first to propose universal education.

William Shakespeare, 1564–1616: The student Shakespeare (representing his entire generation).

Richard Mulcaster, 1532–1611: Headmaster of Merchant Taylors' School who trained two of Shakespeare's grammar schoolteachers.

John Dewey, 1859–1952: 20th-century philosopher and advocate of active, hands-on learning.

ACKNOWLEDGMENTS

I want to thank my early readers, whose valued suggestions encouraged and guided me: Lisa Citron, Jill Holden, Darcy Hughes, Ray Richmond, Susan Shankin, Rob Wright, Kim Zanti, and my family. I am indebted to four intellectual pillars of my practice: Eric Booth, Brent Blair, James Catterall, and Louis Fantasia. I could not have tackled the translations of Erasmus' colloquies without the brilliance of Latinists Marisa Alimento and David Miller. I appreciate the wise leadership over the years of the Arts Education Branch of the Los Angeles Unified School District. I appreciate the supportive guidance of the editors at Routledge Press, Laura Hussey and Swatti Hindwan. I am overwhelmed with gratitude for my brother, John Lithgow, who told me I had to write this book and provided the delightful illustrations. Finally, I want to thank my husband, Tim Rudnick, for his steadfast belief in me when my own confidence waned.

INTRODUCTION

FIGURE 0.1 Young Will opens the book.

My years in education have convinced me that performing arts, storytelling, and creative language should be at the core of education. We need more of them in our schools. A great deal more. Every day. This is not because we need more actors, dancers, musicians, and writers but because we need smarter, more thoughtful citizens. We need nimble thinkers with the mental flexibility to process the daily onslaught of information provided to us in the age of the Internet. We need a population of adults for whom creative and critical thinking comes instinctively. We need to think about the education of children the way Desiderius Erasmus did six hundred years ago, when he was helping to construct the foundations of humanism and design the curriculum enjoyed by William Shakespeare's entire generation, elements of which still resonate today. For the humanists, the education of children was *for the benefit of the commonwealth*, and the curriculum they designed was far richer in the arts than has been commonly realized.

In this book we will examine two relatively short spans of time during which unimaginable changes occurred: the Reformation and the dawning of modern English language and literature. What if we could wave a magic wand and make the radical changes I would like to see in public education in the post-pandemic generation, reflecting on what we know now about how education can develop wise and healthy adults? Just as the Renaissance emerged after the Black Plague, there will soon be new cultural models that may give us an opportunity to rethink old norms. One area that is ripe for renewal is the evaluation of educational programs. My fervent hope is that the era of drill-and-kill test preparation is ending, and that the arts will lead in a new look at assessment that is authentic and supportive of lifelong learning.

There were three igniting realizations that set my course as I began this journey. First was learning that two of Shakespeare's teachers were students of Richard Mulcaster, headmaster of the Merchant Taylors' School in London, who was influenced by the early humanists and was famous for his use of drama in the classroom. The second was the common practice of students performing colloquies (brief scripted scenes) for practice in Latin. Finally it was learning about the artistry of dramatic language that was nurtured by the centuries-old study of rhetoric, or the "art of speaking well." Colloquial (conversational) language and rhetorical (elevated) language were partners in Shakespeare's education. Both involved dramatic presentation, and both contributed to the cognitive brilliance of the age.

If humanist education in Shakespeare's day in any way produced smarter and more flexible thinkers, more discerning minds, and more intelligent citizens (and it will be obvious that I believe it did), it is worth our effort to identify what elements of that education could be simulated in schools today, with a particular examination of the arts of performance.

1
TIME TRAVEL

FIGURE 1.1 Will sells tickets for a magic carpet ride.

4 Time Travel

If we could weave a magic carpet to escort us over the ocean to the late 16th century, to visit Shakespeare's classroom, what would we see? Would there be anything we would recognize?

Hardly anything. No book shelves! No blackboards! No desks! Only one classroom for students from 7 to 17! Small children admonished to speak Latin all day long! Children thrashed for speaking English, even on their way to and from school!

No girls!!

Now look closely at three woodcuts illustrating classrooms of that time. One of them is dated 1573 when the young Shakespeare was 9 years old, so if you like, you can imagine him in one of these classrooms.

In each one you see boys sitting along the walls on benches, reading or writing in something like notebooks on their laps.

(Hint: you might remember Hamlet saying, "My tables . . . meet it is I set it down. / That one may smile, and smile, and be a villain!" The notebook-like objects on the boys' laps are not textbooks. They are their "tables.")

In each picture you see an exalted headmaster sitting on something like a throne, often with a switch at the ready to apply to the backside of any misbehaving student.

FIGURE 1.2 A young student recites lessons to the headmaster in a Tudor classroom.
Source: Image courtesy, Life in Elizabethan England. See www.elizabethan.org/compendium/54.html

FIGURE 1.3 Boy reciting lessons to the headmaster in a Tudor classroom.

Source: Image courtesy, The Board of Trinity College, The University of Dublin.

Also, in each picture you see a student addressing the headmaster, reciting their daily, memorized lessons.

(I know of no research that explains the dog, but Launce's dog Crab, in *Two Gentlemen of Verona* certainly comes to mind!)

Now look at the third, most crowded, classroom, with boys lining up for their turn to address the headmaster. Here you see a second adult, an assistant called an "usher," vigorously whipping the naked bottom of a child!

(Clearly there were consequences for bad behavior.)

But what else do you see in this one? You see musical notes charted on the wall at the back of the room, with students apparently singing and one playing a keyboard. This is an indication of daily instruction in music.

In each of the pictures the seated students appear to be paying no attention at all to the student standing and gesturing in front of the teacher, or to the singing students at the back of the room. They are absorbed in their own work or in collaborative engagement with other students. This is an indication that there

FIGURE 1.4 Students reciting lessons in a crowded classroom.

Source: Woodcut from 1592 taken from a religion history book courtesy of Alamy.com.

was nothing at all unusual about the sight and sound of one of their peers performing. It might help if you knew that one student at a time presenting to the teacher was a constant practice. It went for hours every day. All day long individual students were demonstrating what Erasmus called "this endless tedium of memorization," reciting passages from Ovid, Virgil, Cicero, or another of the classical Latin writers that formed the core curriculum of the day.

But wait! There's more. We know there were other activities not shown here. In four out of five of the statutes prescribing the curriculum of that time, there were from two to four hours per week devoted to another kind of presentation: classroom performance of plays by Terence and Plautus and practice of short, simple dialogues, called colloquies. Colloquies were used to train the students in the necessary art of conversational, or "colloquial," Latin.

But whether students were performing classical or colloquial Latin, they were doing it right there in the empty space in the middle of the classroom. That was the area called the *auditorium*: the place to be *heard*.

In other words, it was a stage.

Now, if we could now bring Shakespeare's teachers back to observe a classroom in the present, here in the United States of the 21st century, would they see anything familiar?

Only in a drama class.

★ ★ ★

A Generation of Genius

Daily practice in the presentation of both formal and informal Latin was, in fact, methodical training for the mental flexibility we find today only in our most creative thinkers. In Elizabethan schools it was a requirement for success, and the evidence for this success was in the product: a generation of genius.

What was it about Elizabethan education that created such brilliant minds? There's a clue here. The classrooms that Shakespeare and his generation inhabited required daily exercise in rhetoric: in memorization and dramatic recitation of classical verse, in recognition and use of dozens of rhetorical tropes, in inventive versification of prose to poetry, and in oratorical performance. But it wasn't all rhetoric. There was also intentional training in the colloquial, conversational, informal, *non*-rhetorical Latin, which was spoken by the characters we will meet in the colloquies of Erasmus. I intend to show in this book that this overwhelming focus on each student's *presentation* or *performance* of his learning had profound cognitive benefits.

2
ENGAGEMENT BEFORE INFORMATION

FIGURE 2.1 Will holds up costume dress.

Over the course of my tenure at the Arts Education Branch of the Los Angeles Unified School District, I had many brilliant mentors. One of them, Eric Booth, gave us our mantra for all lesson design: *Engagement before information.* You need to have all your cognitive portals open before anyone can teach you anything. So in honor of Eric, I invite you to engage your imagination here before you continue reading.

DOI: 10.4324/9781003344919-3

If someone is available to read with you, perform the following two passages together. If not, read them aloud to yourself. The characters emerge pretty quickly, so play them to the hilt.

Passage 1 —A master and a servant: **Rabinus** and **Syrus**

Rabinus:	Soho, soho, rascal! I am hoarse a bawling at you, and you lie snoring still. You'll sleep forever I think. Either get up now or I'll rouse you with a good cudgel!
Syrus:	It is scarce day yet.
Rabinus:	Not to you I think; it is midnight yet to your eyes.
Syrus:	What do you want me to do?
Rabinus:	Make the fire burn, brush my cap and cloak, clean my shoes and galoshes, take my stockings and turn them inside out, and brush them well, first within and then without, burn a little perfume to sweeten the air, light a candle, give me a clean shirt, air it well before a clear fire . . .
Syrus:	It shall be done Sir!
Rabinus:	But make haste then, all this ought to have been done before now!
Syrus:	I do make haste, Sir.
Rabinus:	I see what haste you make. You go at a snail's gallop.
Syrus:	Sir, I cannot do two things at once.
Rabinus:	You scoundrel! Do you talk back to me? Take away the chamber pot, lay the bedclothes to rights, draw back the curtains, sweep the house, sweep the chamber floor, fetch me some water to wash my hands. What are you a griping about, you drone? You are a year alighting a candle.
Syrus:	I can't find a spark of fire.
Rabinus:	Flare up the ashes from last night!
Syrus:	I have no bellows.
Rabinus:	(*Aside*) How the knave thwarts me! (*To Syrus*) As if he that has you can want bellows!
Syrus:	(*Aside*) What an imperious master have I gotten! Ten of the nimblest fellows in the world are scarce sufficient to perform his orders.
Rabinus:	What's that you say, you slow-back?
Syrus:	Nothing at all, Sir.
Rabinus:	No, Sirrah, did I not hear you mutter?
Syrus:	I was saying my prayers.
Rabinus:	It was the Lord's prayer backwards then. Pray, what were you prattling about imperiousness?
Syrus:	I was wishing you might be an emperor.
Rabinus:	And I wish you may be a man made of a stump of a tree. Wait upon me at church, and then run home and make up the bed and put everything in its place; let the house be set to rights from top to bottom

	and rub the chamber pot. Put these foul things out of sight. Perhaps I may have some gentry come to pay me a visit; if I find anything out of order I'll thrash you soundly.
Syrus:	I know your humor well enough in that matter.
Rabinus:	Then it behooves you to look about you if you be wise.
Syrus:	But all this while here is not one word about dinner.
Rabinus:	Out on you, villain. One may see what your mind runs on. I don't dine at home. Wait upon me where I am to go to dinner.
Syrus:	You have taken care of yourself, but there is not a bit of bread for me to put into my mouth.
Rabinus:	If you have nothing to eat, you have something to hunger after.
Syrus:	But fasting won't fill the belly.
Rabinus:	There is bread for you.
Syrus:	There is so, but it is black as my hat and coarse as the bran itself.
Rabinus:	You dainty chap'd fellow. You ought to be fed with hay. I warrant you, Mr. Ass, you must be fed with plum cakes, must you?

Passage #2—Two wives: **Eulalia** and **Xanthippe**

Eulalia:	Most welcome, Xanthippe, a good morning to you.
Xanthippe:	I wish you the same, my dear Eulalia. You look prettier than you used to.
Eulalia:	What, do you mean to banter me already?
Xanthippe:	No, upon my word, for so you seem to me.
Eulalia:	Maybe then my new clothes may set me off to advantage.
Xanthippe:	You guess right. It is one of the prettiest suits I have ever beheld in all my life. It is English cloth, I suppose?
Eulalia:	It is indeed of English wool, but it is a Venetian dye.
Xanthippe:	It is as soft as silk, and t'is a charming purple. Who gave you this fine present?
Eulalia:	My husband. From whom should a virtuous wife receive presents from but from him?
Xanthippe:	Well, you are a happy woman that you are, to have such good husband. For my part, I wish I had been married to a mushroom when I was married to my Nick.
Eulalia:	Why so, pray? What! Is it come to an open rupture between you already?
Xanthippe:	There is no possibility of agreeing with such a one as I have got. You see what a ragged condition I am in; so he lets me go like a dowdy! May I never stir, if I an't asham'd to go out of doors any whither, when I see how fine other women are, whose husbands are nothing nigh so rich as mine is.

Eulalia:	The ornament of a matron does not consist in fine clothes or other deckings of the body, as the Apostle Peter teaches, for I heard that lately in a sermon; but in chaste and modest behavior and the ornaments of the mind. Whores are trick'd up to take the eyes of many, but we are well enough dressed if we do but please our own husbands.
Xanthippe:	But meanwhile, that worthy tool of mine, that is so sparing toward his wife, lavishly squanders the portion I brought along with me, which, by the way, was not a mean one.
Eulalia:	On what?
Xanthippe:	Why, as the maggot bites, sometimes at the tavern, sometimes upon his whores, sometimes gaming.
Eulalia:	Fie, you should never say so of your husband.
Xanthippe:	I'm sure it's too true; and then when he comes home, after I have been waiting for him till I don't know what time at night, as drunk as David's sow, he does nothing but lie snoring all night long by my side, and sometimes vomits and bespues the bed too, to say nothing more.
Eulalia:	Hold your tongue! You disgrace yourself in disgracing your husband!
Xanthippe:	Let me die if I had not rather lie with a swine than such a husband as I have got.
Eulalia:	Do you scold at him then?
Xanthippe:	Yes, indeed, I use him as he deserves. He finds I've got a tongue in my head!
Eulalia:	Well, what does he say to you again?
Xanthippe:	At first he used to hector at me lustily, thinking to fright me with his big words.
Eulalia:	Well, did your words ever come to downright blows?
Xanthippe:	Once, and but once, and then the quarrel rose to that height on both sides that we were within an ace of going to fisticuffs.
Eulalia:	How, woman! Say you so?
Xanthippe:	He held up his stick at me, swearing and cursing like a foot soldier and threatening me dreadfully.
Eulalia:	Were you not afraid then?
Xanthippe:	Nay, I snatch'd up a three legg'd stool, and if he had but touch'd me with his finger, he should have known he had to do with a woman of spirit.
Eulalia:	A new sort of shield! You should have used your distaff for a lance.
Xanthippe:	He'd have found he had an Amazon to deal with.
Eulalia:	Ah, my Xanthippe, that was not becoming.
Xanthippe:	What becoming? If he does not use me like a wife, I won't use him like a husband.

Perhaps you know a little about one of Shakespeare's earliest comedies, *The Taming of the Shrew*. Did you hear echoes of Petruchio? Could the oft-thrashed servant be someone like Petruchio's comic servant Grumio? And how about Kate? This shrew, Xanthippe, is named after Socrates' famously scolding wife. She does, in fact, get tamed at the end, although not by her drunken husband: her sympathetic friend's preaching continues with some juicy nuances. It finally gets to her and she goes home chastened. Petruchio, in fact, does compare Kate to Xanthippe, and there many other echoes in Shakespeare's comedy, including the three-legged stool, the commentary on the clothing of virtuous women, and the berating of servants. These scenes could fit right into the play and one would hardly notice.

Here are some questions I'm imagining you might have and some answers that I hope will surprise you:

Q: When were these passages written?
A: In the mid-1520s, about forty years before Shakespeare was born.
Q: They sound a bit like commedia. Were they originally in Italian?
A: No! They were written in Latin, and they were not published in translation during Shakespeare's childhood. The first was from a colloquy (or colloquial conversation) called *Herilia*, which means A Master's Commands, and the second was from one called *Conjugium*, which means Marriage.
Q: Who wrote them?
A: They were written by the greatest humanist of Northern Europe: Desiderius Erasmus.

I beg you not to slam this book shut and run for the door at the mention of that ancient sage, Erasmus. Aside from the fact that his outsized influence on modern education has not received the attention it deserves, he was, in his time, hugely famous and delightful company—a lover of good comedy. The excerpts are from two of over fifty short, scripted conversations called colloquies. There have only been two translations of his *Colloquia familiaria* published in their entirety: one by Nathan Bailey in 1725 and one by Craig R. Thompson in 1965. Bailey's are a bit spicier but Thompson's are clearer for the modern reader. These excerpts are from Bailey, but in this book I'll use Thompson's when needed, or, since they are both translations anyway, I'll take small liberties and adapt.

Q: Why on earth did a man of Erasmus' towering intellect and fame write such silly stuff?
A: They were written for schoolboys, to teach them Latin conversation (and a bit about Erasmus' views, which today we call humanism, along the way).

What fun, right? This is salty stuff for 10-year-olds. Try reading them again, imagining them performed by small boys.

I am convinced, and I hope to convince my readers, that Shakespeare performed these exact scenes, and many like them, in Latin, at the Stratford Latin Grammar School, starting at approximately the age of 9 (and, for the fun of it, I just have a gut feeling that he played the comic roles Syrus and Xanthippe). Not only did he perform them, he received training to assure that he performed them convincingly. In fact, he and his fellow students in schools all over England were on their feet at some point every day, performing. They were either performing by reciting the lessons and verses from their formal curriculum, which they had to memorize daily, or they were spouting lively dialogues like these. Either way, they were acting.

If they were following customary practice, they were also translating the Latin into English and back again, probably performing the scenes in both languages and imitating the style in their own writing. *The Taming of the Shrew* is one of the earliest plays known for certain to be by Shakespeare, and there were earlier versions of it that may well have been from the same pen. Indeed, I am personally convinced that earliest version of all was a riotously fun collaboration by schoolboys in Stratford.

The Colloquial Colloquies

I had the good fortune to win the literary jackpot in my childhood. I grew up awash in the language of Shakespeare, surrounded by actors who spoke it well. My earliest realization that live theatre is something apart from ordinary life is from the summer I turned 4. As I recall, I opened the refrigerator door one day and was shocked into momentary paralysis at the sight of my father's head, covered with blood and glowering with terror and rage, lying in a bed of lettuce. It was a *"prop,"* my mother quickly explained. He was performing the role of Macbeth at the time, and what I saw in the vegetable drawer was the severed head that Macduff carries on at the end of the play to confirm the death of the villain king. It was made of some kind of rubbery substance that had to be kept cold—thus the refrigerator.

This was the beginning of a peripatetic journey that my dad, Arthur Lithgow, took our family on as we followed him in his career establishing Shakespeare Festivals in Ohio. What a magical time it was! My siblings and I saw every single one of the plays, from the audience and from the wings, in every stage of development, again and again. Not many others on this planet can claim to have seen every play in the canon, in all stages of development, before adolescence. We knew the stories and we knew the poetry, and we knew them intimately, like old family members, so my knowledge of the text was not academic—it was family. Our dogs, birds, and even our cars were named after characters in Shakespeare: Launce, Speed, Portia the fat pigeon, and the Glistering Phaeton. My knowledge of Shakespeare, even today, is far more friendly than scholarly. Growing up in this world meant that Shakespeare was our first language. For my brother, John

Lithgow, this childhood was the foundation for a career in the theatre. For me it was just fun! But it later colored every aspect of my life in education.

All of this occurred during my years of 8 to 15. This in itself is significant, because this book will focus on exactly those formative years of Shakespeare's youth. You soak up an amazing amount of unbiased information in pre- and early adolescence.

But when I was very young it wasn't the kings and battles and lovers that held my attention. It was the *funny* people. I loved the plays! In my childish memory they were totally comprehensible. They crackled with humor. They were lively and fast-paced. In rehearsal, when actors were speaking too slowly or trying to milk a line, my dad was known to slap an egg timer on the stage and shout, "I don't care where you are in the scene, when this runs out, get off the stage!" which must have worked, because for me the theatre was a rapid fire, boredom-free zone.

For the most part, at least at first, the nuance, the insights, the intricate complexities, and the iridescent allure of Shakespeare's poetry went right over my head. British royal history was of no interest to me, and the great tragedies took awhile to unpack. But I loved the stories and I *adored* his *colloquial* characters—his clowns, his villagers, his whip-smart women who would not keep their opinions to themselves: Christopher Slye, Grumio, Gobbo, Touchstone, Feste, Peter Quince, Kate, Rosalyn, Beatrice, Mistress Quickly, Doll Tearsheet, Falstaff! What fantastic company I kept.

Now, whenever I read Erasmus' *Colloquia familiaria*, I dream in Bruegel, as his comical companions populate my imagination. It was the discovery of these entertaining scenes that Shakespeare and his generation all performed in school that set me off on the task of writing this book. I first read about them in Jonathan Bate's biography of Shakespeare, *Soul of the Age*, and, because I had a professional interest in classroom dramatics, I decided to get my hands on a copy. There it was, a moldy, disintegrating book available on the Internet. It arrived and I started reading.

> *Was it possible that nobody else had ever noticed that many of Shakespeare's most entertaining characters came straight out of lessons he was performing in Latin at his Stratford school when he was a child?*

I knew very little about Erasmus, and "dustbin of history" does not begin to describe the place where I thought that musty old intellect belonged. Musty old intellect!? He was hilarious! His *Colloquia familiaria* is a collection of playlets that Erasmus based on his conversations with common people in his daily life, including dinner guests, fishmongers, horse cheats, venal clergymen, flea-bitten kings, shipwreck survivors, abused servants, alchemists and exorcists, prostitutes, and a host of sassy, brilliant, outspoken women. I was back with the friends of my childhood.

Was it possible that nobody else had ever noticed that many of Shakespeare's most entertaining characters came straight out of lessons he was performing in Latin at his Stratford school when he was a child? Maybe so! In T.W. Baldwin's two exhaustive volumes about Shakespeare's education, *William Shakespere's Small Latine and Lesse Greeke*, he devotes only one chapter to colloquies, which were common classroom exercises at the time. He mentions, almost in passing, that someone should take a closer look at those of Erasmus, but as far as I have been able to tell, no one living and writing today, aside from myself, ever has.

Why have Erasmus' colloquies been so neglected? I think I now understand. First of all, they were used to teach *conversational*, not classical, rhetorical, Latin. Thus, in the statutes that still exist, they were not in any of the lists of required, classical readings. Instead we find them in statutes that include extracurricular activities in the weekly schedules. But it is also possible that the sometimes-questionable source of their appeal—their raunchy schoolboy humor—may have been the reason. They were perhaps considered borderline appropriate. They were written to delight young boys, not stodgy schoolmasters. We know from the receipts that copies of the *Erasmi colloquia familiaria* were purchased by the thousands and were performed in most every classroom in the realm, but, despite their popularity, some pedagogues might not have wanted to advertise them.

Shakespeare and his entire generation were being educated only a few decades away from the pre-printing press days, when schooling was still mostly oral. That realization, and more research about the classical curriculum that Erasmus designed—with its focus on physical rhetoric, or what Demosthenes called "actio"—piled evidence on top of evidence that Shakespeare and his peers attended schools rich in the performing arts. This book will explore the relationship between the emphasis on performance in Elizabethan humanist education and the flourishing of literary brilliance around the turn of the 16th century. It will also credit this same education with the nurturing of the most enthusiastic, critical, knowledgeable, and sophisticated theatre audience the English-speaking world has ever known.

The classrooms that Shakespeare and his generation inhabited required daily exercise in rhetoric: in memorization and recitation of classical verse, in recognition and use of dozens of rhetorical tropes, in inventive versification of prose to poetry, and in oratorical performance. But it wasn't all rhetoric. There was also intentional training in the colloquial, conversational, informal, *non*-rhetorical Latin, which was spoken by the characters we will meet in the colloquies.

Daily performance of both formal and informal literature was, in fact, methodical training for the mental flexibility we find today only in our most creative thinkers. In Elizabethan schools it was a requirement for success, and the evidence for this success was in the product: a generation of genius.

3
ANGELS AND EAGLETS

FIGURE 3.1 Will sneaks a peak at the audience.

> **Caliban:** *Be not afeard; the isle is full of noises,*
> *Sounds and sweet airs, that give delight and hurt not.*
> *Sometimes a thousand twangling instruments*
> *Will hum about mine ears, and sometime voices*
> *That, if I then had waked after long sleep,*
> *Will make me sleep again: and then, in dreaming,*
> *The clouds methought would open and show riches*
> *Ready to drop upon me that, when I waked,*
> *I cried to dream again.*
>
> Act III, Scene ii of The Tempest

Setting the Scene

At some point shortly before March 16, 1573, authorities were called upon to contend with raucous behavior in the company hall of the Merchant Taylors' Guild. According to the company edict of that date, there had been a play performed there by grammar school students under the direction of the headmaster, Richard Mulcaster, during the festivities of Shrove Tuesday, and the hall had been opened to the public. It must have been wildly popular, because the paying audience overwhelmed the members of the guild and grabbed all their customary seats, which were, of course, the best ones. With spelling updated for comprehension, the edict reads like this:

> Item: Whereas at our company hall plays and such like exercises, which be constantly exposed to be seen for money, every lewd person thinks himself (for his penny) worthy of the chief and most commodious place without respect for any, either for age or estimation . . . as experience of late of the tumultuous disordered persons repairing hither to see plays as by our scholars were there lately played, the masters of this worshipful company and their dear friends could not have entertainment and convenient place as they ought to have had. Therefore, it is ordained that henceforth there shall be no more plays suffered to be played in this our company hall.

This is high dudgeon indeed! But it must have soon passed, because apparently many more plays were performed there in the decades that followed. We can only assume that lessons were learned and that, subsequently, paying audiences were discouraged from shoving distinguished guild members and their dear friends out of the way.

Unruly audiences were not uncommon in Elizabethan days and were, in fact, one of the reasons that the theatres we now think of as emblematic of the era—the Globe, the Curtain, the Swan, the Rose—were forced to build outside the city limits. But why all the kerfuffle about this particular performance? It was only "our scholars." Schoolboys!

As we shall see, at that time, early in Elizabeth's reign, schoolboys provided a giant share of the theatrical entertainment for public consumption, and had been doing so for well over a century. Schoolmasters, Richard Mulcaster among them, were among the principal playwrights and dramatists of the day. Theatrical performances by school children were standard fare in towns and hamlets all over the realm for the celebration of Christmas and Shrovetide. Old men, like Polonius in *Hamlet* or Silence and Shallow in *Henry IV Part II*, would still remember their lines from roles they played as boys, decades after the applause had faded and the audience of adults had passed. Villagers would still be chatting about memorable productions years after they had been seen, the way we now reminisce about classic films, Broadway musicals, or consequential World Series games we saw in our youth. School plays were part of the social fabric of the age.

Grammar School Thespians

When my younger daughter graduated from high school, she took a semester off before going to college and went to join her sister, who was studying in Europe. She flew first to London, where she had only a few whirlwind days to take it all in before leaving for the continent. On her first day there she called me from a sidewalk phone booth, breathless with wonder. "Mom, I was just in Westminster Abbey, and there was music falling from the ceiling—the most beautiful singing I've ever heard! I thought it was angels, but then the choir door opened and out walked a whole lot of little boys!" Pesha was a California teenager and she had never heard of the Westminster Boys Choir when she stumbled onto one of their rehearsals.

In 1573 a Frenchman by the name of Claude Desainliens wrote, "Harken, I do hear sweet music: I never heard the like" and "we shall hear [in the choir of Saint Paul's] the fairest voices of all the cathedrals in England . . . and to tell the truth, I never heard better singing."

In England, the training of boys' voices for royal entertainment goes far back in history, deep into the Middle Ages. Sometime in the 12th century, probably earlier, an ecclesiastical body of musicians and singers was organized to meet the spiritual needs of the England's reigning sovereign. It still exists. Called the Chapel Royal, it is today considered the oldest continuous musical organization in the world. Traditionally it has been comprised of from twenty-four to thirty-eight men and from eight to twelve boys. Besides the Chapel Royal and the Westminster Boys' Choir there are hundreds of boys' choirs throughout Britain, the Chapel Royal only being the oldest.

No one knows when boy singers were added to the Chapel Royal or other church choirs, but they were probably present from the very beginning. Their treble voices were thought to be the closest to the voices of angels. There was a religious pursuit of this purity of tone. Churches, abbeys, and cathedrals were designed acoustically to capture it: massive sound boxes that amplified these "fairest voices." Choir schools attached to churches and training children for church choirs played a role in the pre-Reformation history of British education. They offered free education to able students. Their purpose was to assure a sufficient number of well-trained voices to supply the needs of the church. As we shall see, Erasmus himself briefly attended a song school in Utrecht, perhaps because it was an opportunity for a free education.

In England, the best of the young voices trained in these schools were pressed into service for the crown, and the Chapel Royal consistently had a small number of singers to complement the adult musicians. Their voices were, and are to this day, a thing of transcendent beauty. Boys' voices broke later five hundred years ago than they do today, evidently because there was less protein in their diet. A boy who began his service in the Chapel at the age of 7 or 8 could continue to sing sweetly until the age of 16 or 17, during which time he received an education overseen by the choirmaster.

The issue of impressment, which was essentially enforced servitude, must be seen in the context of the time. It was an accepted custom of the state, and was frequently welcomed as an honor. The crown gave writs authorizing impressment in all trades in which it had need, and grown men who were expert silversmiths, ironmongers, weavers, wigmakers, or printers could be impressed along with singing children.

That said, it must be admitted that it was poor children who filled the ranks of the choirs, not the sons of the gentlemen. The earliest choirmasters were usually almoners, the men who distributed alms to the needy. Parents whose children were impressed into the Chapel Royal may have mourned the loss of daily interaction with their small child, but they may have also welcomed the benefits. There was usually a financial arrangement made with the family, and along with a free grammar school education, students were often sent to university after their voices broke, so a seven-year stint in the Chapel Royal was a means of advancement in the world. In addition, of course, while they served, their housing, nutrition, and clothing were all provided. They literally "sang for their supper."

This strange form of servitude did not survive much past the 16th century. The impressment of children eventually led to abuses and charges of kidnapping. The writs were automatically renewed each year and not closely scrutinized, and, curiously, it was the abuse of entrepreneurs who used their royal writs to impress boys as *actors* rather than singers that contributed its demise. But that's the end of a long story, and we are only at the beginning.

In the 15th and 16th centuries the boy singers of the Chapel Royal, with their exquisitely trained voices, experienced a brief flaring of history and became a small troupe of boy actors. They were immensely popular, performing constantly at court and eventually in the public arena. Several other rival boys' companies came and went over the years, both in London and in the provinces, the most enduring of which was formed from students at Saint Paul's School. The Children of the Chapel and the Boys of Saint Paul's even competed successfully with the great men's companies of the Shakespearean era and were eventually disparaged by Hamlet as the "aery of children, little eyases, that cry out on the top of question, and are most tyrannically clapped for't," that is, squawking eaglets, who were robbing adult troupes of their paying audiences.

The boys' companies were small, usually comprised of no more than twelve actors, and for most of their history they were only seen in the halls of the aristocracy. They were a far cry from the legions of schoolboys spouting Terence and Ovid and performing comical skits in Latin. But there are two reasons to devote space in this book to them. One is that their remarkable story will reveal the vibrant thread in the weave of theatre history, leading directly to the golden age of Elizabethan drama. They spanned the century of the Reformation, and there are records of hundreds of their performances. Although we know little about the content of their plays beyond their titles, the bit we do know reveals a perceptive and witty adolescent view of the political turmoil of the time. In itself it is a fascinating and little-known history that is worth the telling, but, because it is a digression here, the telling will be referred to a later chapter.

The other reason is more germane to our topic. Boys who made up those companies came from the same society and the same education as their schoolboy peers, and their abilities were usually noticed first by a headmaster teaching singing and hearing their recitations in the earliest years of their schooling. At court they often competed with boy players from some of the prestigious grammar schools in London and other large municipalities. Eton, Westminster, Saint Paul's, and Merchant Taylors' were only a few of many schools invited to perform at court, and their schoolmasters were frequently dramatists of some renown. Indeed, we have the names of several boy actors who entered the famous adult companies directly out of grammar school. It seems fair to think that the training received in school prepared them well.

> *For most of the 16th century, theatre throughout England was almost entirely dominated by schoolboys.*

Furthermore, the culture of playacting went far beyond the classroom. Anyone who has read Hilary Mantel's *Wolf Hall* will remember that any leisure time enjoyed in the evenings by Thomas Cromwell's young nephews and clerks was filled with playmaking. The boys' companies were only the tip of a cultural iceberg that was deep and profound. In fact, for most of the 16th century, theatre throughout England was almost entirely dominated by schoolboys. As they grew up they also became members of an astonishingly vibrant audience culture, as play going was increasingly popular throughout the century leading to the Golden Age enjoyed by Shakespeare and company.

This book will closely examine the education of Elizabethan schoolboys and reflect upon the architects of that education, starting with Erasmus of Rotterdam and then looking at one (of many) of the famous playmaking schoolmasters of the Tudor Age, Richard Mulcaster.

4
GOOD BEHAVIOR AND AUDACITY
The Training Up of Schoolboy Orators

FIGURE 4.1   Swordplay.

> *As grammar schools and choir schools appeared and multiplied, they offered little islands of culture, where under the guidance of a learned master, youths were trained in speech and bearing, which are Thalia's handmaidens.*
>
> —H.N. Hillebrand

My father came by his love of language honestly. His mother, my grandma, nurtured his and my own fascination with it. This indomitable woman was my only living grandparent. She was from Nantucket, an old-school New Englander. She had lost her husband and two children to the 1918 flu, and had raised her four remaining children by working all her life as a nurse. But in her old age she spent three months of every year living with each of her four children. Our "Grammy" was not cuddly, she had a sharp tongue and we were frequently lashed by it. But she was witty and smart, and we got a taste of what she had given our dad as a child. She could recite hours of comic poetry that she had memorized in school, our favorites being Oliver Wendell Holmes' "The One-Hoss Shay" and "The Wonderful Boston Baked Beans." She entertained us with word games, puns, tongue twisters, and comic turns of phrase. She would recite to us dozens of clever riddles, but I can remember only one:

> The Queen of France gave the Duke of Northumberland a bottomless vessel to put flesh and blood in.
> (The gift? A ring!)

She also introduced us to the game Fictionary, in which a word is found in the dictionary that none of the players has ever heard of. Each player invents a definition and puts it into a hat with the real one. The hilarity of the game is in guessing which definition is right. The problem was that we always had to leave Grammy out because we could never find a word that she didn't know. Her vocabulary was inexhaustible.

Years later I came to realize something of the source of her genius. Her childhood, at the end of the 19th century, on an island cut off from the rapidly modernizing world, was probably quite similar to Shakespeare's. In a pre-radio, pre-television world, far removed from the concert halls and theatres of the mainland, her primary entertainment was *language*, and more specifically, *language that was spoken aloud to entertain, persuade, and delight*.

★ ★ ★

Before we examine the cultural, social, and theoretical underpinnings of Elizabethan education, let's look at the day-to-day schoolboy experience of Will Shakespeare and thousands of his contemporaries. Again: *engagement before information*:

If you have a chance to perform this colloquy with another (preferably an elementary school student), please have the actor playing Boy perform with his or her tongue planted firmly in the cheek. The more you know of Erasmus' sense of humor the more you will find that the appropriate attitude for our young scholar (translated from the Latin original):

Monita paedagogica (The School-Master's Admonitions)

School Master: You seem not to have been bred at court, but in a cow-stall; you behave yourself so clownishly. A gentleman ought to behave himself like a gentleman. As often or whenever anyone that is your superior speaks to you, stand straight, pull off your hat, and look neither doggedly, surlily, saucily, malapertly, nor unsettledly, but with a staid modest, pleasant air in your countenance, and a bashful look fix'd upon the person who speaks to you; your feet set close one by t'other; your hands without action: don't stand titter, totter, first standing upon one foot, and then upon another, nor playing with your fingers, biting your lip, scratching your head, or picking your ears: let your clothes be put on tight and neat, that your whole dress, air, motion, and habit may bespeak a modest and bashful temper.

Boy: What if I shall try, sir?
School Master: Do so.
Boy: Is this right?
School Master: Not quite.
Boy: Must I do so?
School Master: That's pretty well.
Boy: Must I stand so?
School Master: Ay, that's very well, remember that posture; don't be a prittle prattle, nor a prate apace, nor be minding anything but what is said to you. If you are to make an answer, do it in a few words, and to the purpose, every now and then prefacing with some title of respect; and sometimes use a title of honor, and now and then make a bow, especially when you have done speaking. Nor do you go away without asking leave, or being bid to go. Now come let me see how you can practice this. How long have you been from home?
Boy: Almost six months.
School Master: You should have said "sir."
Boy: Almost six months, *sir*.
School Master: Don't you long to see your mother?
Boy: Yes, sometimes.
School Master: Have you a mind to go see her?
Boy: Yes, with your leave, *sir*.
School Master: Now you should have made a bow; that's very well, remember to do so; when you speak, don't speak fast, stammer, or speak in your throat, but use yourself to pronounce your words distinctly and clearly. If you pass by any ancient person, a magistrate, a minister, or doctor, or any person of figure, be sure to pull off your hat, and make your reverence. Do the same when you pass by any sacred place or image of the cross. When you are at a feast, behave yourself cheerfully, but always so as to remember what becomes your age. Serve yourself last; and if any nice bit be offered you, refuse it modestly; but if they press it upon you, take it, and thank the person, and cutting off a bit of it, offer the rest

either to him that gave it you, or to him that sits next to you. If anybody drinks to you merrily, thank him and drink moderately. If you don't care to drink, however, kiss the cup. Look pleasantly upon him that speaks to you; and be sure not to speak until you are spoken to. If anything that is obscene be said, don't laugh at it. Don't reflect on anybody, nor take place of anybody, nor boast of anything of your own, nor undervalue anything of another body's. Be courteous to your companions that are your inferiors; traduce nobody; don't be a blab with your tongue, and by this means you'll get a good character, and gain friends without envy. If the entertainment shall be long, desire to be excused, bid much good may it do the guests, and withdraw from the table. See that you remember these things.

Boy: I'll do my endeavor, sir. Is there anything else you'd have me do?
School Master: Now go to your books.
Boy: Yes, *sir*.

As echoes, I could site several of Shakespeare's lecturing pedants, but here are two of my favorites. First, of course, one of the greatest send-ups of pedantry ever written is that of Polonius in *Hamlet*. Here is his endless lecture to Laertes when saying his farewell as Laertes was rushing back to his rowdy life in Paris:

Polonius: Yet here, Laertes! aboard, aboard, for shame!
The wind sits in the shoulder of your sail,
And you are stay'd for. There; my blessing with thee!
And these few precepts in thy memory
See thou character. Give thy thoughts no tongue,
Nor any unproportioned thought his act.
Be thou familiar, but by no means vulgar.
Those friends thou hast, and their adoption tried,
Grapple them to thy soul with hoops of steel;
But do not dull thy palm with entertainment
Of each new-hatch'd, unfledged comrade.
Beware of entrance to a quarrel, but being in,
Bear't that the opposed may beware of thee.
Give every man thy ear, but few thy voice;
Take each man's censure, but reserve thy judgment.
Costly thy habit as thy purse can buy,
But not express'd in fancy; rich, not gaudy;
For the apparel oft proclaims the man,
And they in France of the best rank and station
Are of a most select and generous chief in that.
Neither a borrower nor a lender be;

> For loan oft loses both itself and friend,
> And borrowing dulls the edge of husbandry.
> This above all: to thine ownself be true,
> And it must follow, as the night the day,
> Thou canst not then be false to any man.
> Farewell: my blessing season this in thee!
>
> *Laertes:* Most humbly do I take my leave, my lord.
>
> —Act I, Scene iii of *Hamlet*

And one of my absolute favorites, echoing "don't be a prittle prattle, nor a prate apace," Fluellen lecturing Gower the evening before the Battle of Agincourt in Henry V:

> *Gower:* Captain Fluellen!
> *Fluellen:* So! in the name of Jesu Christ, speak lower. It is the greatest admiration of the universal world, when the true and aunchient prerogatifes and laws of the wars is not kept: if you would take the pains but to examine the wars of Pompey the Great, you shall find, I warrant you, that *there is no tiddle taddle nor pibble pebble* in Pompey's camp; I warrant you, you shall find the ceremonies of the wars, and the cares of it, and the forms of it, and the sobriety of it, and the modesty of it, to be otherwise.
> *Gower:* Why, the enemy is loud; you hear him all night.
> *Fluellen:* If the enemy is an ass and a fool and a prating coxcomb, is it meet, think you, that we should also, look you, be an ass and a fool and a prating coxcomb? In your own conscience, now?
> *Gower:* I will speak lower.
>
> Act IV, Scene i

(When I was teaching high school I had many a ripe occasion to quote Fluellen's final line to students, and although I couldn't quite duplicate the Welsh accent, it settled many a dispute!)

There are other lecturing schoolmasters in Elizabethan plays, but as we dive into humanist curriculum, let us take a look at what we know of the life of an Elizabethan school*boy* in a Latin grammar school.

If Shakespeare was educated at all, and it's pretty obvious that he was *well* educated by modern standards, he was educated at Stratford's King Edward VI School. The fact that there is no document that exists with his name listed as a student is irrelevant. We can't prove that *anyone* attended Stratford Grammar because the statutes for that school, at that time, were lost years ago. But the statutes of many other schools in the vicinity still exist, as do records of purchases of student texts, and they show a uniformity on which we can base a reliable guess at the curriculum: what was taught from form to form and year to year. Shakespeare attended a small, rural school, where the statutes may have been applied less rigidly than they were at Eton, Merchant Taylors', or Westminster, but the salary paid to the headmaster at Stratford was a good one, an indication that the good citizens of the town valued education and paid for quality. If we take a look at some of the other graduates of Stratford Grammar—among them Shakespeare's good friend Richard Field, London printer of Latin and Greek classics—we can gather that the instruction there, under Richard Mulcaster's former student, Thomas Jenkins, was hardly less rigorous than that of the London schools.

Typically a schoolboy would have started at the age of 4, attending a petty school. Many girls, too, attended petty schools, although they seldom went any further in their formal education. In some towns, petty schools were held in private homes, and the instructors were often educated women—thus an alternative name for petty schools: "dame" schools. In smaller towns, where there were not enough students to provide an income for a petty school instructor, the little ones went to the grammar school and received their early instruction from an assistant teacher called an usher, acting as an "abecedarian." Either way, the "petties" were instructed first by the use of a hornbook, which was a small wooden tablet with lessons protected by a thin piece of transparent horn or by parchment. Lessons could be slipped under the horn and consisted of the ABCs, the Paternoster, the Apostles' Creed, the Ten Commandments, or short exercises on the Christian faith from the Catechism. From there they moved on to a primer, consisting of psalms and religious teachings in English. They were also taught the casting of accounts so that they could do mathematical functions needed in exchanging money. In the last year of some petty schools, children were taught the parts of speech and the Latin accidence, the basics of Latin grammar. This was more likely in the large cities, where many grammar schools required those skills for all entering students.

There is not a trace of evidence to tell us where Shakespeare attended petty school or by what methods he was introduced to the hornbook. Presumably there was also instruction in drawing, music, and dance, since children do not change all that much over the centuries, and we can assume that what works for preschoolers today worked for petty scholars then. Mulcaster makes much of the similarity between instruction in handwriting and drawing, so these were probably seen as one skill, and the nursery rhymes that we still sing with our toddlers today date back hundreds of years and were certainly part of the daily entertainment of little ones in the Tudor Age. It would have been only natural to introduce early learning through song, dance, and (as we shall see Mulcaster suggested) *pleasure*. There are many short, instructional rhymes to be found in our sources, and presumably they were set to melody and sung, probably with movement.

Since Erasmus, Mulcaster, and I all agree on the profound importance of those early years in preparing the mind for learning, this blank period in Shakespeare's biography is regrettable. I would love to speculate that Thomas Jenkins, fresh from the tutelage of Richard Mulcaster at Merchant Taylors', may have taken his well-documented leave from Oxford to work as an usher under Simon Hunt and teach the petties at Stratford. But I admit that is an imaginary leap taken lightly, just for the fun of it.

Either way, if Shakespeare followed the normal route, he would have started the first form of grammar school at the approximate age of 7, already knowing how to read and write in English, and there he would have remained for 8 or 9 years. For American readers, especially those not familiar with British terminology, some context may be helpful. The school year lasted about forty weeks, with time off for religious holidays (of which there were many) and several weeks off in summer. There were typically four times during the year when a student could enroll in school or matriculate to a new "form." Forms were roughly equivalent to what we in America call classes, but were more fluid. A student advanced from one form to the next by mastery, and might remain in a form for eighteen months or even two years. This system allowed for flexibility depending on the social, physical, and intellectual development of the scholar.

Except in very large schools, all the forms studied together in one room, with older children assisting younger ones. The total number of forms in a school varied from five to eight, depending on the size of the school and the number of instructors. One other clarification: grammar schools were often called *trivial* schools, which could confuse the modern reader for whom that word implies matter of little importance. They were called trivial because they focused on the medieval *trivium* of grammar, logic, and rhetoric, leaving the *quadrivium* of arithmetic, geometry, music, and astronomy for the university. However, as we shall see, elementary vocal and instrumental music were a part of the daily instruction at Merchant Taylors' and any of the many schools that prepared students well for performance.

We also don't know when Shakespeare left Stratford Grammar. Simon Hunt was the headmaster until 1575, when Thomas Jenkins took over. In 1581 Jenkins turned over the reins to John Cotham, another graduate of Merchant Taylors and Oxford and perhaps an acquaintance. Some have speculated on some pedagogical relationship between Shakespeare and Cotham. He certainly would have been familiar with him as his younger siblings matriculated through grammar school, but we do not know if he was ever his student. Late in the 17th century, when there were still folks living in Stratford who remembered anecdotes about its already famous resident, John Aubrey wrote a biography of Shakespeare and included it in his book, *Brief Lives*. The biography is brief indeed, but it includes a mention that Shakespeare "had been in his younger years a schoolmaster in the country." Cotham was from Lancaster, and there are hints that, on his recommendation, Shakespeare may have been briefly employed there as a tutor with a powerful Catholic family. That said, he would have turned 17 the year Cotham arrived in Stratford, and if he was still at the school it could have been as a senior student acting as a student teacher, or "praepositore." Indeed, if he was employed there this could also have been the source of the aforementioned quote. We are only able to state with any confidence that from the age of 11 until the age of about 16, Jenkins was his teacher.

There *is* one hint about the year he may have left in the words of a shepherd in *A Winter's Tale*:

Shepherd: I would there were no age between sixteen and three-and-twenty, or that youth would sleep out the rest; for there is nothing in the between but getting wenches with child, wronging the ancientry, stealing, fighting.

Act III, Scene iii

Well, we do know for a fact that Shakespeare did get Anne Hathaway pregnant, and there was talk of his being cited for poaching from the lands of the gentry. If these are hints of Shakespeare's own memories of those seven regrettable years, it might tell us that he left school at 16.

We have a good idea of what the day-to-day experience of a schoolboy was from several excellent sources. By far the most detailed of these are the two massive volumes of T.W. Baldwin's *William Shakespere's Small Latine & Lesse Greeke*, written in 1944. Its fifteen hundred pages go into fine detail about the curriculum, the schedules, the punishments and rewards, the publishers and purchases of texts, and the history of Elizabethan pedagogy. I've read both volumes, but the information is almost too exhaustive to absorb. More digestible, though still quite comprehensive, are Foster Watson's *The English Grammar Schools to 1660* and Cressy's *Education in Tudor and Stuart England*. There is a lot to be learned, too, by reading the works of two 17th-century schoolmasters: *Ludus Literarius or the Grammar Schoole* by John Brinsley and *A New Discovery of the Old Art of Teaching Schoole* by Charles Hoole. But a few more recent works neatly summarize all of the available information and I will rely on them heavily here since this book does not need to go into as much detail as the others. One book that I found particularly helpful was Kate Emery Pogue's *Shakespeare's Education: How Shakespeare Learned to Write*.

Most rural, non-residential grammar schools were free, funded by guilds or by the commonwealth, but students were responsible for the cost of their own materials: paper for their copybooks, candles, good quill pens and pen knives, and inks which they may have made themselves from recipes using oak gall. They also had to purchase their own texts, but these did not change much so one text could serve for all the boys in a family and perhaps be passed along to others. Girls educated at home would have used them too.

Schools varied in size, of course, but usually had only one headmaster, who taught the older students their Latin literature and perhaps some Greek. The headmaster taught the upper division and he would have had one or more assistant teachers, or ushers, to instruct the young ones with the help of older student praepositores.

According to existing statutes, the school day at most country schools was from 6:00 AM until 5:00 PM with a two hour break for lunch from 11:00 to 1:00, during which students in village schools went home to eat. They also had an hour for exercise at 3:00 PM. School was six days a week, but Saturday was a half-day.

Usually an usher or praepositore met the students first and the day began with a prayer, in English, which students would have memorized and recited every day. In *Shakespeare's Education,* Pogue quotes what was a typical prayer and includes it as an example of the complex language students became familiar with in schools. It is one wonderfully long sentence leading to and followed by the Lord's Prayer:

> Most mighty and merciful father, we sinners by nature yet thy Children by grace, here prostrate before thy divine Majesty, do acknowledge our corruption in nature, by reason of our sin to be such, that we are not able as of ourselves to think one good thought much less able to profit in good learning and literature, and to come to the knowledge of thy son Christ our savior, except it shall please thee as thy great grace and goodness to illuminate our understanding, to strengthen our feeble memories, to instruct us by thy holy spirit, and so pour upon us thy good gifts of grace, so that we may learn to know to practice those things in these our studies, as may most tend to the glory of thy name, to the profit of thy Church, and to the performance of our Christian duty, hear us, O God, grant this our petition, and bless our studies, oh heavenly father, for thy son Jesus Christ's sake, in whose name we call upon thee, and say Our Father, who art in heaven, etc.

Next the usher checked hands and faces for cleanliness and took role. The first hour was devoted to the study of Lily's Grammar, the Latin accidence—the part of grammar concerned with changes in the form of words for the expression of tense, person, case, or number. They would spend that hour declining nouns and conjugating verbs. For the rest of the day it was all Latin. The headmaster arrived at 7:00, and study of literature began, the headmaster working with the older boys in the front of the room and the usher with the youngsters in the back. All the boys were in one room, and in some schools as many as fifty or more students might be reading, scratching away in their copy books or "tables" and reciting memorized lessons at the same time, so one would imagine they were very good at taking turns and using their indoor voices. Instruction was organized around a sort of tutorial system that involved everyone. Younger students would repeat their daily lessons to older students, which reinforced the learning at both levels, recalling Erasmus' recommendation in *De ratione studii*: "Lastly, I urge, as undeniably the surest method of acquisition, the practice of teaching what we know."

Discipline was strict and was enforced with the help of a switch made of a birch branch with several smaller branches at the tip, for striking students who misbehaved. Flogging was not uncommon. Various student recollections used euphemisms like "marrying the master's daughter," or "learning to sing a new song today." But many schoolmasters, Mulcaster and Queen Elizabeth's tutor Roger Ascham among them, disparaged its use and urged kindness over cruelty to gain the respect of students. Nevertheless, the switch was ever present as a warning and probably did much to encourage civility in the classroom. Schools were not required to keep unruly students, and incorrigible ones presumably did not stick around for long. Fridays were for rewarding and punishing. Student monitors recorded infractions, such as the use of English instead of Latin. Boys could avoid whipping by demonstrating rhetorical ability or declaiming extra credit memory work. Learning Latin well enough to give a witty response was a great way to escape the lash.

We must remember that the 16th century was still new to the printed word, and memorization still guided everything in school practice. Books were scarce and expensive, and from the very beginning students had to be trained, in composition and in argument, to "fish" for sources from memory. The memorized phrases increased in difficulty over the years, and in the upper forms typically they memorized a dozen lines of Ovid, Cicero, or another classical writer per week. They would copy into their tables, the phrases that they had to memorize every day and any others that they found particularly useful or illustrative. As an adult, Hamlet retained this habit (as I'm certain Shakespeare did) as he pulled out a notebook after encountering his ghost father and hearing the account of his murder, saying, "My tables—meet it is I set it down, / That one may smile, and smile, and be a villain." As Erasmus recommended, they would have columns or pages in their copybooks to sort the phrases into topics or examples of effective rhetorical devices.

They also constantly had to "turn," or translate, phrases from Latin to English and English back to Latin. As they advanced, this practice became more and more complex and required a great deal of skill in the careful use of language. A common practice recommended by Roger Ascham was to have students translate a passage from Latin to English, and then, after an hour or so, turn the same passage back to Latin, a process that was called "making Latins." This done, the student, with the instructor, would compare the re-translation to the original and highlight errors in grammar and style.

In the two first forms of the lower school, students had to demonstrate mastery of the accidence. For this and all their subsequent studies they would use Lily's Latin Grammar, *De Constructione*, which, as we will see, had been much revised and improved by Erasmus. Anyone studying Shakespeare's education should note the scene from *The Merry Wives of Windsor* in which Sir Hugh Evans interrogates the boy William. If Windsor stands in for Stratford and the Welshman Sir Hugh stands in for the Welshman Simon Hunt, it is impossible not to imagine that the boy, William, is the child Shakespeare himself, struggling with the accidence. Mistress Page and Mistress Quickly are taking young William Page to school and they meet the headmaster in the street. The hilarity of the scene stems from what any self-respecting 8-year-old would do—turn any opportunity into a dirty joke.

This is as vivid a picture of a street encounter in rural England in 1574 as you could find anywhere:

Mistress Page: I'll be with her by and by; I'll but bring my young man here to school. Look, where his master comes; 'tis a playing-day, I see.
Enter SIR HUGH EVANS
How now, Sir Hugh! No school today?
Sir Hugh Evans: No. Master Slender is let the boys leave to play.
Mistress Quickly: Blessing of his heart!
Mistress Page: Sir Hugh, my husband says my son profits nothing in the world at his book. I pray you, ask him some questions in his accidence.
Sir Hugh Evans: Come hither, William; hold up your head; come.
Mistress Page: Come on, sirrah; hold up your head; answer your master, be not afraid.
Sir Hugh Evans: William, how many numbers is in nouns?
William Page: Two.
Mistress Quickly: Truly, I thought there had been one number more, because they say, "Od's nouns."
Sir Hugh Evans: Peace your tattlings! What is 'fair,' William?
William Page: Pulcher.
Mistress Quickly: Polecats! There are fairer things than polecats, sure.
Sir Hugh Evans: You are a very simplicity 'oman: I pray you peace. What is 'lapis,' William?
William Page: A stone.
Sir Hugh Evans: And what is 'a stone,' William?
William Page: A pebble.
Sir Hugh Evans: No, it is 'lapis:' I pray you, remember in your prain.
William Page: Lapis.
Sir Hugh Evans: That is a good William. What is he, William, that does lend articles?
William Page: Articles are borrowed of the pronoun, and be thus declined, singulariter, nominativo, hic, haec, hoc.
Sir Hugh Evans: Nominativo, hig, hag, hog; pray you, mark: genitivo, hujus. Well, what is your accusative case?
William Page: Accusativo, hinc.
Sir Hugh Evans: I pray you, have your remembrance, child, accusative, hung, hang, hog.
Mistress Quickly: 'Hang-hog' is Latin for bacon, I warrant you.
Sir Hugh Evans: Leave your prabbles, 'oman. What is the focative case, William?
William Page: O—vocativo, O.
Sir Hugh Evans: Remember, William; focative is caret.
Mistress Quickly: And that's a good root.

Sir Hugh Evans:	'Oman, forbear.
Mistress Page:	Peace!
Sir Hugh Evans:	What is your genitive case plural, William?
William Page:	Genitive case!
Sir Hugh Evans:	Ay.
William Page:	Genitive—horum, harum, horum.
Mistress Quickly:	Vengeance of Jenny's case! fie on her! never name her, child, if she be a whore.
Sir Hugh Evans:	For shame, 'oman.
Mistress Quickly:	You do ill to teach the child such words: he teaches him to hick and to hack, which they'll do fast enough of themselves, and to call 'horum:' fie upon you!
Sir Hugh Evans:	'Oman, art thou lunatics? hast thou no understandings for thy cases and the numbers of the genders? Thou art as foolish Christian creature as I would desires.
Mistress Page:	Prithee, hold thy peace.
Sir Hugh Evans:	Show me now, William, some declensions of your pronouns.
William Page:	Forsooth, I have forgot.
Sir Hugh Evans:	It is qui, quae, quod: if you forget your 'quies,' your 'quaes,' and your 'quods,' you must be preeches. Go your ways, and play; go.
Mistress Page:	He is a better scholar than I thought he was.
Sir Hugh Evans:	He is a good sprag memory. Farewell, Mistress Page.
Mistress Page:	Adieu, good Sir Hugh.

—Act V, Scene i of *The Merry Wives of Windsor*

Master Slender would have been the usher who, in his leniency, let the boys off to play. The Welsh pronunciation of "vocative" sounding like "focative" would give an audience a rowdy laugh, as would the comment on Jenny's "case." The word horum speaks for itself, and hicking and hacking would also have sexual connotations. (At least in his colloquial scenes, Shakespeare seldom passed up a ripe opportunity for gutter humor.)

Once the accidence was fairly well memorized, students would begin their study of literature by memorizing and reciting simple phrases called sententiae, from Leonard Culman's *Sententiae pueriles* (sentences for children). These were short moral statements that remind one of Polonius' long list of do's and don'ts, covering cleanliness, piety, courtesy, fairness, thrift, obedience, diligence, and all the other virtues in which we still attempt to indoctrinate our young. Shakespeare's frequent use of short, Latin phrases in his plays include some memorized from the *Sententiae*, which would have been familiar to his audience. The earliest readings would then include Aesop's Fables in Latin translation. They would begin what was "making Latins" by translating simple sententiae into Latin without seeing them in a book, and then examining their work with the teacher and memorizing the grammatical rules that would apply. This daily exercise would gradually build their facility, but, as Erasmus insisted, the memorization always had to come out of the reading and reciting of actual literature, not simply of rules standing alone.

In the first and second form they would speak a mixture of English and Latin, responding in Latin to prompts from the teacher and increasing their fluency over time. They were taught to speak clearly and to project the voice appropriately for the content spoken. By the third form they were expected to speak Latin only, at all times, even on their way to and from school.

There are many statutes from schools similar to Stratford Grammar which detail what literature was read from one form to the next, but virtually all of them are variations on the curriculum designed early in the century for Saint Paul's School by Dean John Colet, based on the recommendations of Erasmus. In 1528 Cardinal Wolsey prescribed a curriculum for his school at Ipswich, which was based on that of Saint Paul's. His curriculum was in eight forms, but the first would have been very similar to the last year of petty school, and by the second half of the century it appears that most schools had six or seven. Since I've already described the activities of students in the first forms of the lower division, I will briefly sketch Wolsey's literary selections for the third through the eighth, understanding that this is only a rough outline to show progression that a school with fewer forms would still have followed:

Third form: Terence for purity of style; some carefully chosen Plautus; Aesop in Latin translation.
Forth form: Virgil's *Eclogues*.
Fifth form: Cicero's *Epistles*.
Sixth form: History, using Salust and Caesar's *Commentaries*.
Seventh form: Epistle's of Horace; Ovid's *Metamorphoses* and *Fasti*.
Eighth form: Cicero again, for oratory; Lorenzo Valla's *Elegantiae* for rhetorical figures and style.

These were not the only authors read, of course. It is clear that Shakespeare read Seneca and probably did so at school. Justin, Cato, Livy, Apuleius, Martial, and others are listed for the upper forms in many statutes, as are more contemporary moral poets such as Palingenius, Castiglione, and Mantuan, a 15th-century poet who wrote sweet, simple pastoral poetry quoted by Holofernes in *Love's Labor's Lost*. There were certainly others, but these writers constituted the starter set of Latin authors, the literary spine of the seven or eight years a boy spent at grammar school. Note again: there is not a single Christian religious text in this reading list.

If Greek were introduced, it would have been in the last two years of the upper division. Thomas Jenkins was a graduate of Saint John's College at Oxford, which excelled in its Greek curriculum. As we have seen, he began his study of Greek at Merchant Taylors' under Mulcaster, so it is highly likely that Shakespeare learned his "Lesse Greeke" (per Ben Jonson's quote in the First Folio) from Jenkins, reading selections from Aristotle, Lucian, and Demosthenes among others.

This formal curriculum was not universally loved by the church. Dean Colet wrote humorously to Erasmus that there were clerics who disdained the classical poets, and by the end of the century some puritanical schoolmasters were writing tirades against the "filth" and "corruption" of Ovid, Lucian, and others, but such was the weight of Erasmus and the humanists that the works listed earlier survived pretty well intact in schools for over one hundred years, and Shakespeare was a student when their popularity was at its zenith.

In writing, too, students closely followed the recommendations of Erasmus. They learned to "turn" poetry into prose and prose into poetry, employing all of the rules of versification and getting practice in literary flexibility. As we will see, they practiced daily recognizing and correctly applying the many rhetorical figures studied in their text by Johannes Susenbrotus. As outlined by Erasmus in his *De ratione studii*, they progressed from epistles to themes to orations, and all along the way they were scratching into their tables examples of verbal embellishment encountered in their readings that they could adapt to enliven their own writing.

In all writing exercises, students were urged to collaborate, and it seems that for Shakespeare and his peers, writing in school was not a solitary endeavor. It is generally assumed that Shakespeare began his career in theatre as an actor and a play fixer, collaborating with others in rewriting and filling in parts of older plays. He would have been comfortable with this practice, as it began in school.

Students usually began writing epistles in the third form, the way our primary scholars today learn to write letters in various voices: gratitude, curiosity, explanation, persuasion, narration, or congratulation. This, of course became more and more sophisticated so that when they encountered Cicero's *Epistles* they could analyze and critique the style. Eight styles were taught for epistles: suasory (persuasive), disuasory (unpersuasive), hortatory (encouraging), dehortatory (discouraging), narrative, gratulatory, expository (reasoning or remonstrating), commendatory, and consolatory. Examples of just about every one of these can be found in Shakespeare's plays.

For writing themes, students used the *Progymnasmata* of Aphthonius. Progymnasmatas (or "fore-exercises") were rhetorical models that dated back to ancient Greece, and Aphthonius' version, written in the 4th century, had long been the standard for students of rhetoric. It gave examples of themes based on fables, historical maxims, and anecdotes, demonstrating refutation, encomium, dramatic narration, confirmation, comparison, and invective. Here students learned to organize their themes according to the strict structure: the *exordium* (introduction), *narratio* (stating the facts), *divisio* (outlining the thesis), *confirmatio* (supporting arguments), *confutatio* (counter arguments), and a *peroratio* (conclusion). There are countless examples of this structure in Shakespeare, the most famous, perhaps, being the two contrasting speeches of Brutus and Antony in *Julius Caesar*.

Dramatic Oration

In the upper forms students advanced to orations. A choice bit in John Aubrey's brief life of Shakespeare was the comment, "When he was a boy he exercised his father's trade, but when he killed a calf he would do it in a high style, and make a speech." Clearly he learned the high style reading, writing, and performing orations in school, studying the Roman *Rhetorica ad Herennium* along with Cicero's *Topics* and the works of Quintilian.

Oratory often involved competition, and another tantalizing detail that Aubrey left us was that "there was at this time another butcher's son in this town that was held not at all inferior to him for a natural wit, his acquaintance and coetanean [contemporary], but died young." So Will had a clever buddy with whom to test his wits—a good friend who died: a Mercutio, if you will. Erasmus recommends competition as a classroom strategy, and there are many references to oratorical contests that were typically held toward the end of the final two forms and that would have been attended by families and community members. Perhaps Shakespeare and his ill-fated acquaintance, probably a schoolmate, both got to demonstrate their showmanship in a contest of this sort. If so, they were impressive enough to be remembered almost a century later.

When practicing oratory, students would be given a topic and argue it on one side, then the next day argue on the other. This activity was called "in utramque partem," which means arguing both sides. It might be the origin of today's high school debate clubs, and it had to be done with all the persuasiveness of an actor. As we shall see, some of the topics were those recommended by Erasmus in his *De ratione studii*, and in his *De copia* he suggests many more, such as whether or not one should marry, travel, or learn Greek; whether a boy owes more duty to his parents or to his master; or whether a woman should or should not nurse her own baby. He also pulls many examples from history. We see resonances of this training in every play that Shakespeare wrote because every play is an argument in utramque partem. Was Brutus or Antony the good guy in *Julius Caesar*? In *Richard II*, who was the better king, Richard the poet or Bolingbrook the warrior? Is *Henry V* the greatest war play ever written or the greatest anti-war play? Was Shakespeare's portrayal of Shylock anti-Semitic or profoundly empathic? Was Hamlet a hero or a misogynistic brat? There will be debates about every play of Shakespeare's for as long as they are performed. In utramque partem.

The goal of all of this reading and writing and performing in school was the formation of "gentle" men able to engage in civil society with eloquence. Eloquence was authority. Eloquence was power. And eloquence was attained through the rigorous study and practice of the art of rhetoric, in writing, in speaking, and in acting.

Training in Performance: A Good Man Speaking Well

Acting was not just for rehearsed public performance. It was woven into the school day, every day. It was also not just for recitation of lessons. Many statutes show that scenes by Terence and Plautus were scheduled for weekly classroom performance, and, as we've already seen, colloquies were performed for the practice of Latin conversation. What is more, students often presented plays to the public at Christmas and Shrovetide, and rehearsals would have taken place during the school day.

In fact the schoolroom was constantly a showplace for theatricality. The Alexander Nowell woodcuts shown at the beginning of this book are from a book published in 1573, when Nowell was the dean of Saint Paul's. Shakespeare was 9 years old at the time pictured, so it is as close as we can get to an imaginary schoolroom in which we could place him. Again, what you can see is that classrooms typically were not furnished with individual desks for students. There was a throne-like seat and writing desk for the headmaster, and usually a large table for drawing and calligraphy, but students sat along the sides of the room on benches, reading and writing with their copybooks on their laps. The center of the classroom was open space for students to be heard—an *audit*orium, or a theatre.

What happened every day in the academic theatre of the classroom, and its enduring impact on the culture of the Elizabethan Age, is ultimately a focus of this book. We know that grammar school students could project meaning and emotion with speech and with what was sometimes called rhetorical dance or physical rhetoric. We also know that schools provided the early training for most of the boys who went on to become actors in the famous boys' companies, and some of them, like Salathiel and Nathaniel Field, went on to become professional actors of note. More than a few, of course, also became playwrights. But these things don't happen by themselves. Great actors, great plays, and great productions don't materialize out of tea steam. How did they do it? We have to assemble the picture from glimpses.

The quote at the beginning of this chapter is from H.N. Hillebrand's book, *The Child Actors*, which we will refer to quite a bit in the chapter focusing on the famous boys' acting companies. He tells us that schoolboys learned speech and bearing, "Thalia's handmaidens," and we know that in many small towns they provided entertainments at holiday times; but we know little of the daily practice except through implication.

Ursula Potter, in an article from the journal *Tudor Drama before Shakespeare*, titled "Performing Arts in the Tutor Classroom," makes the following revealing statement:

> At any given year then, up to 100,000 boys across the nation of varying ages and varying abilities were receiving instruction in skills that we today would consider more suited to an actor than to a scholar.

Potter makes the assertion based on her calculation of the number of students passing through Latin grammar schools in any year during the reign of Elizabeth, and she backs up her assertion with considerable evidence. Academic acting, eloquence of the body, or rhetorical dancing were considered oratorical arts and were a part of the overarching focus on rhetoric as Quintilian defined it: "a good man speaking well." This was presentational acting rather than representational. In simple language, it was probably *over*acting, but it was also probably fun!

Potter bemoans, as I do, the scant amount of serious research done on this topic and does her best to remedy the situation by citing numerous references to classroom dramatics from primary sources. She also points out, rightly, that in addition to whatever other benefits dramatic training might bestow on future citizens participating in public life, grammar schools were nurturing a huge, enthusiastic, and highly sophisticated audience for the golden age of Elizabethan theatre.

Not one of the dozens of pedagogue-dramatists that we know of back then sat down and described in detail exactly how students were taught to perform, how to realistically embody a character, how to amplify their speech and gestures, what vocal exercises they did, how practices were scheduled, what tips they were given to protect their voices, how blocking was done, how props were used, costumes and sets designed, built, stored, etc. I wish Shakespeare had found a place in one of his plays to insert a scene that depicted schoolboys rehearsing a play. He came close. Imagine if the mechanicals in *A Midsummer Night's Dream*, Peter Quince, Bottom, Flute, Snout, and all, had been 12-year-old children. The comic possibilities are endless, and we would have had a firsthand look at the process.

As it is, my task has been a little like Hansel and Gretel's—following a trail of crumbs. Potter has followed the same trail, as has Lynn Enterline in *Shakespeare's Schoolroom*, each with a slightly different aim, and I am indebted to both. Baldwin, Hillebrand, and others have helpfully scattered tidbits here and there, and taking them all together there are enough to allow one to imagine what the training in the best of the schools would have looked like.

To begin with, as noted previously, the Tudor Age was still emerging from educational customs established before printing presses made textbooks readily available, and memory and recitation were built into every aspect of the curriculum. Again, what Erasmus called "this endless tedium of memorization" began on day one of schooling and continued every day throughout all the forms. Memorization is a mental skill that involves the ear, the imagination, and the cognitive ability to sequence ideas. It is a vital skill for the actor, and it is a skill every grammar school boy had acquired by the second form.

Another essential skill for an actor is the ability to project the voice with expression, both in speech and in song. We know that Richard Mulcaster was renowned for the training of boys' singing voices, and that training was probably very similar to what it is like today. Song schools attached to grammar schools, such as the one at Saint Paul's, would also have offered rigorous voice training, as would any of several schools whose students performed for the queen. They would have offered the highest-level training, but all schools prepared students for public performance and would have used similar strategies.

To envision the training, I consulted with my friend and colleague, Connie Covert, a trained opera singer and former music teacher in the Los Angeles Unified School District's Arts Branch. She explained how training would begin and progress. It starts with the ear, learning to listen and echo back to the teacher single tones and simple melodies. Eventually this leads to singing more complicated harmonies in polyphony and antiphonal singing. Children have vast quantities of youthful elastin that allows for the relaxation of the larynx and flexible vocal cords, and so with an open throat and laryngeal control they can release their voices and expand their range. Students must exercise the articulation of the larynx, jaws, lips, and tongue so that the sound they produce is pure and the words clear. All of this requires regular, sustained practice over time, and the exercise of the voice would have been built into daily instruction for all forms.

The training of the singing voice worked for the acting voice as well. Mulcaster describes having students take random sounds from the lower registers, up to the higher and back again, a simple daily exercise to clear the airways from the lungs. In a play by Richard Zouch titled *The Sophister*, there is a scene in which a schoolboy rehearses "pronouncing" with fingers gagging to improve voice production, reminiscent of Demosthenes speaking with his mouth full of stones. These are exercises not unlike what you would expect see in any actor's warm-up today.

The most illuminating glimpses that help us picture classroom training in delivery are those buried in the hundreds of pages of books written by educators of the day. Almost all of them at some point addressed it in some way, and it is clear that the teaching of *prosodia*—tone, accent, and timing—started in early years. The following are some of the choice passages.

In 1520 we have the following passage from Robert Whittington's *Vulgaria*. A vulgaria was a Latin primer, which provided instruction in teaching students to speak "vulgar" (e.g. common) phrases. In this one, Whittington reminds instructors to assure that students present themselves well in speech (spelling updated):

> It is a rude manner a child (have he never so syelde [sic] a tongue and pleasant pronunciation) to stand still like an ass; and on the other side (like a carter) to be wandering of eyes, picking or playing the fool with his hand and unstable of foot. Therefore take heed the countenance be made conformable to the purpose: now with gravity, now cheerful, now rough, now amenable, shaping meat unto the matter (as I may say) like a glove to the hand. Also see the gesture be comely, with seemly and sober moving, sometimes of the head, sometimes of the hand and foot, and, as the cause requires, with all the body.

There is an echo here of Erasmus' schoolmaster's admonishment from earlier: "don't stand titter, totter, first standing upon one foot, and then upon another, nor playing with your fingers, biting your lip, scratching your head, or picking your ears." We also hear Hamlet's voice here, speaking to his actors: "suit the action to the word, the word to the action."

Later in the 1520s, we find Cardinal Wolsey directing teachers of the first form, while teaching the Latin accidence (spelling updated):

> Let your particular attention be to form their tender articulation, so as in a full, elegant tone of voice they may pronounce the elements they are taught; for it is possible to mold their rude materials into any form.

Then in the fourth form, for Virgil, the Prince of Poets, he asks that students "pronounce his majestic lines in a deep, full articulation."

In our upcoming chapter about Richard Mulcaster and his books on education, *Positions* and *Elementarie*, we will see that he explored extensively the training and uses of the voice. The chapter in *Positions* that he himself counts as most important is *Of Loud Speaking. How Necessary, and How Proper an Exercise It Is for a Scholar*. "I have dwelt the longer in this exercise because it is both the first in rank, and the best means to make good pronouncing of anything, in any auditorie [audience] and therefore an exercise not impertinent to scholars." He further explains how great orators would "utter their beginnings . . . with a gentle and moderate voice, their narrations, and reasoning discourses with more straining, and louder: their perorations, and closings, with a descent and fall of the voice." Articulation, rhythm, emphasis, timing, pitch, volume, and tone were also examined. He also wrote chapters with the titles: *Of Loud Singing, and in What Degree It Cometh to be One of the Exercises*; *Of Loud and Soft Reading*; *Of Much Talking and Silence*; *Of Laughing and Weeping*; and *Of Holding the Breath*—all of which are focused on physical health and virtue, and certainly they also support dramatic training.

For gesture, Mulcaster calls upon his classical readings of Demosthenes (spelling updated):

> The eloquent Demosthenes, being demanded what was the chief point that did belong to an orator, answered, "to gesture well," and doubled the point.

(This, indeed, is yet another adaptation of the Greek, of Demosthenes' famous quote "actio, actio, and actio.")

And then:

> That Demosthenes' action was the soul of his orations, and assured the truth of his judicial answer, who is better witness than even Aeschines, his enemy? Who being banished his country by the only means of Demosthenes' tongue, did confess in his exile that he was more sorely wounded with the force of his action, which gave life to his words, than with the strength of his words, that found work for his action.

William Kempe, in *The Education of Children in Learning, Declared by the Dignitie, Utilitie, and Method Thereof*, emphasizes the importance of students being able to embody the meaning of "every trope, every figure, as well as words in a sentence" in a recitation and insists that a student of poetry be able to express "the rhetorical pronunciation and gesture fit for every word, sentence, and affection."

John Brinsley, schoolmaster at Bury Saint Edmunds, who in 1612 published in *Ludus Literarius, or the Grammar Schoole*, wrote,

> From the first entrance, boys should be taught to pronounce everything audibly, leisurely, distinctly and naturally, sounding out specially the last syllable that each word may be fully understood.

And more, boys are not to speak "as a boy who is saying his lesson," not like a recitation spoken "at random and without understanding like parrots, but are to pronounce with pleasing and apt modulation tempered with variety." He recommends Corderius, Aesop's Fables, Terence, Ovid's *Metamorphosis*, and Virgil's *Eclogues* as works that would best promote authentic sounding speech, to "express the affections and persons of Shepherds; or whose speech soever else, which they are to imitate."

Christopher Johnson, headmaster of Winchester School, speaking to his students about the value of performing plays:

> From these stage plays, which we have lately exhibited publicly to the view, I think you have derived this benefit besides others, that must be pronounced with what expression, with what gestures not only you yourselves learned, but were also able to teach (if need were). For there should be in the voice a certain amount of elevation, depression, and modulation, in the body decorous movement without prancing around, sometimes more quiet, others more vehement, with the supplosion [stamping] of the feet accommodated to the subject. These I remember I taught, all which you expressed dexterously enough.

Finally we have Charles Hoole, teacher and cleric who published *A New Discovery of the Old Art of Teaching Schoole* in 1660, long after the Tudor era was over, but who hearkened back favorably to the teaching of the previous century:

> When you meet with an Act or Scene that is full of affection and action, you may cause some of your Scholars, after they have learned it to act it, first in private amongst themselves, and afterwards in the open School before their fellows; and herein you must have a main care of their pronunciation, and acting every gesture to the very life. This acting of a piece of a Comedy, or a Colloquy sometimes will be excellent means to prepare them to pronounce Orations with a Grace, and I have found it

an especial remedy to expel that subrustic bashfulness, and unresistable timorousness, which some children are naturally possessed withal, and which is apt in riper years to drown many good parts in men of singular endowments.

Delivery is also mentioned frequently in school statutes. Just a few examples: The 1541 statutes of Worcester charge the master and usher to "teach their pupils to speak openly, finely, and distinctly, keeping due decorum both with their body and their mouth." Westminster School decreed that every year the master and usher together

> shall cause their pupils and the choristers to act, in private or public, a Latin comedy or tragedy in Hall, and the Chorister's Master an English one [in order that the boys] better become accustomed to proper action and pronunciation.

And many school statutes assigned days and hours for students to declaim memorized orations "without book." At the Ruthin School for instance, it is stated that "At ten of the clock in the Morning, two or three of the Boys, being thereunto appointed eight days before by the master, shall with great Silence be heard declaiming on some subject."

The schoolmaster was expected always to set a lively example of delivery for the students, and apparently many of them did so with gusto. The Italian poet, Palingenius, popular in protestant English schools, has this to say about one of them:

> The master sits with book before that open wide doth lie,
> And spitting oft, he well doth view, his great assembled crowd, And when he sees them bent to hear, with lofty voice and loud, He then expounds some dreadful ghost of doleful tragedy,
> Or else some harlot's tricks declares, in wonton comedy.

Many schoolmaster playmakers in the mold of Holofernes were hacks, of course, especially in the provinces; but several that we still know of were themselves accomplished dramatists. Nicholas Udall, Ralph Radcliffe, Christopher Johnson, and Mulcaster all were skilled enough for their students' productions to bring acclaim to their schools. They were well versed in dramatic conventions that went back centuries, and their students benefited from their knowledge.

Schoolmasters were also enjoined to set an example of moral authority for students, which protected them from the accusation that dramatic activities were somehow leading them down the path of sin. This view was an ever-present undercurrent of the time, voiced by such as the critic Stephen Gosson, who railed against the public theatres as "the invention of the devil" but grudgingly accepted academic theatre, provided that "that which is learned, must be learned of the best, lest the example of ungodly masters poison us rather than instruct us."

In *The Staple of News* Ben Jonson satirized the negative view of school theatricals that occasionally surfaced even among parents, when his character Censure, posing as a disaffected mother, says:

> I would have ne'er a cunning School-Master in England. I mean a Cunning-Man, a School-Master; that is a Conjuror, or a Poet, or that had any acquaintance with a Poet. They make all their scholars Play-boys! Is't not a fine sight, to see all our children made Interluders? Do we pay our money for this? We send them to learn their Grammar, and their Terence, and they learn their play-books!

This ambivalence about the value of school "rowdy" or "edgy" dramatics surfaces occasionally from parents and teachers still today. But again and again we find the Elizabethan state protecting academic theatre. In 1559 it was exempted from censorship because headmasters were trusted moral overseers, keeping the students' virtue intact. Occasionally school performances were censured, but usually Puritan prohibitions against theatre were not applied to schools. In 1584, a statute prohibiting plays during a time of plague signed by the theatre-loving Earl of Leicester, exempted "tragedies, comedies, and other shows of exercises of learning, as they are commendable and great furtherances of learning" (as long as decorum was maintained!).

A fine distinction was made between school performances and the work of "common players." There were dozens of troupes of traveling players who performed in the inn-yards of villages all over England; and Stratford, being a commercial hub, with its fine bridge over the Avon, was a likely place for many visits. During the plague years, London companies had to resort to the provinces because they were banned in the city, so the finest actors were frequently members of traveling companies. Students at Stratford Grammar probably had multiple opportunities to see professional expertise on the stage, so it is instructive to take a look at what they may have witnessed.

My best sources for learning about what the acting of "common players" looked and sounded like are threefold: B.L. Joseph's book *Elizabethan Acting*, commentators contemporary to the Elizabethan and Jacobean era, and Shakespeare himself. (I also have a bit of my own modest experience performing on the Globe stage to call upon, but will save that for a later chapter.) Let us start with the best source. Here is Shakespeare (in the voice of Hamlet) directing players on how to perform the play he has adapted for them to "catch the conscience of the king":

> Speak the speech, I pray you, as I pronounced it to you, trippingly on the tongue: but if you mouth it, as many of your players do, I had as lief the

town-crier spoke my lines. Nor do not saw the air too much with your hand, thus, but use all gently; for in the very torrent, tempest, and, as I may say, the whirlwind of passion, you must acquire and beget a temperance that may give it smoothness.

Act III, Scene ii

Mouthing the words and sawing the air with the hands were very likely habits picked up in grammar schools, where oratorical acting was valued and lively amplification was emphasized. Any theatre teacher today will agree that to release their beginning students from bashfulness or inwardness, they first have to learn to ham it up, and advanced students then have to refine their delivery to attain a more natural style. It would have been the same then.

In *Elizabethan* Acting, B.L. Joseph quotes dozens of contemporary witnesses who describe the acting of Richard Burbage, Edward Alleyn, and others of the time as *natural*. Burbage was described by a Richard Flecknoe as "a delightful Proteus, so wholly transforming himself into his part, and putting off himself with his clothes, as he never (not so much as in the tiring-house) assumed himself again until the play was done." The tiring-house (or *attiring*-house) was the dressing room. Burbage stayed in character on stage and off so long as he was in costume. Stanislavsky would have approved.

Joseph cites many other references to actors "doing it to the life," appearing "lively" and "naturally" and embodying the role they are playing so completely that the audience accepts them as the "very person" portrayed. Sir Richard Baker, who frequently saw both Alleyn and Burbage perform, praised their acting in these words: "We may well acknowledge that gracefulness of action is the greatest pleasure of a play; seeing that it is the greatest pleasure of (the art of pleasure) Rhetoric." Clearly the critical audiences of the day valued naturalness and grace in their favorite Thespians.

Thirty years after Shakespeare's death John Bulwer published his *Chirologia: or the natural language of the hand. Composed of the speaking motions, and discoursing gestures thereof. Whereunto is added Chironomia: or the art of manual rhetoric. Consisting of the natural expressions, digested by art in the hand, as the chiefest instrument of eloquence.* In this book he includes many drawings of gestures, particularly hand gestures, expressing every possible emotion or reaction. Many who just look at the pictures and do not read the text conclude that an actor paying close attention to chirologia did indeed "saw the air," and that acting was highly stylized and formulaic, with a lot of histrionic gesturing, but they would be entirely mistaken. Bulwer was not an actor and was not writing about acting. He was doctor and an observer of nature. He wrote in the genre of a naturalist, noting, closely and precisely, the way people typically use their gestures in speech. He would have paid particular attention to the gestures of the very *natural* actors that he saw on the stage.

Brinsley, in *Ludus Literarius*, as we have seen, urges his students to develop a natural and "lively" expression in their recitation, suggesting "what they cannot utter well in Latin, cause them first to do it lively in English." Mulcaster, too, valued gesture, voice, and pacing appropriate to the matter. It is probable that excessive affectation was frowned upon. The nuanced and modulated performance of the professional actor is acquired with time and maturity, and only the rare child can achieve it, but evidently that is what they were ultimately aiming for.

Connecting all the dots, I hope it is clear by now that hardly a day went by in the life of an Elizabethan schoolboy when he was not on his feet, at some point, in front a schoolmaster, an usher, an older student, a praepositore, or groups of his peers, declaiming, articulating, expostulating, projecting, emoting, and, as Potter says, "receiving instruction in skills that we today would consider more suited to an actor than to a scholar." One would think that all this acting and interaction would add up to a raucous environment, but in trying to imagine what a classroom would have looked like on a typical afternoon, it is possible to envision collaborative groups practicing in muted or muffled voices and saving their histrionics for the time when they would have the opportunity to show off and shine.

By now we have a pretty good idea of what would have been expected of any child in Shakespeare's classroom every time he stood up to perform, whether in the daily memorized passages from his reading, his classroom performances of Latin scenes from Plautus or Terence, his arguments in utramque partem, his oratorical competitions, his theatrical roles in Christmas plays, or his comical engagement with Erasmus' *Colloquies*. His classroom was a stage, and actio was ever present.

5

CONTEXT: THE HATCH AND BROOD OF TIME

A Brief History of the English Reformation

FIGURE 5.1   Queen Elizabeth I exhibits a timeline.

Context: The Hatch and Brood of Time

> *. . . which in their seeds*
> *And weak beginnings lie intreasured.*
> *Such things become the hatch and brood of time.*
>
> Act III, Scene i *of* Henry IV Part II

I am pretty well educated, as were most of my teacher colleagues, but until I started my research my mind drifted into a vague memory zone when I heard the name Desiderius Erasmus. When I started learning about him and talking about him to my friends, I recognized the glassy look I got back from them. We knew he was somebody important and we had covered him briefly in college, but it hadn't stuck. He was pre-modern history, somewhere in the mist between the dark ages and enlightenment. But teachers, maybe more than anyone today, owe him a huge debt, so I hope this book will burnish a bit his faded star. Before we get into the meat of my topic, I want to help you, my readers, by putting Erasmus and the student Shakespeare into context.

If you take the three decades between Erasmus' death in 1536 and Shakespeare's birth in 1564, it would look as though someone had taken a herculean sledgehammer and cut the century in two. During the English Reformation, wedged within the convulsions occurring on the continent, England went from the Middle Ages to the Elizabethan Renaissance. It was a bloody and chaotic transition, with head spinning swings away from the pope, back, and away again. Hundreds of heretics, recusants, and political conspirators on either side were burned at the stake, beheaded, hanged, drawn and quartered or banished. Of the most powerful and high ranking, those who had already died in miserable exile from the court included Cardinal Wolsey, and those executed included Sir Thomas More, Bishop John Fisher, Thomas Cromwell, Archbishop Cranmer, the poet Thomas Wyatt, more than a dozen dukes, viscounts, barons, and earls, and three queens: Anne Boleyn, Catherine Howard, and Jane Grey. No one of any influence came out entirely unscathed, and the battered survivors, for better or for worse, were the ones who gave birth to the modern era.

The 16th-century Reformation is a vast and complex subject and has been covered in many excellent books, the best of which, from my reading, is the Michael Massing's *Fatal Discord: Erasmus, Luther, and the Fight for the Western Mind*, which covers in granular detail the theological thicket that caused the upheaval and continues to haunt us in the modern world. My treatment of Erasmus' role in history needs context, but I've had to pare down an intense and electrifying novel into a short story. This book surfaces Erasmus' contributions to education above those to religion, and that is a simpler narrative, so to simplify it further, here is my "History of the English Reformation for Dummies" diagram of the most relevant changes (broad strokes describing highly complex developments. No apologies).

In Religion

Before 1534	After 1564
Catholic	Protestant
The pope the head of the church	The king the head of the church
The Latin Vulgate Bible	The Geneva Bible, in English, required in every church. 90% of it taken directly from Tyndale's translation
Tyndale's English Language Bible banned and Tyndale executed in exile, probably by agents of Henry VIII	
Powerful and wealthy monastic orders owning a sixth of the realm	Monasteries closed, their wealth confiscated by the state and redistributed.
People generally knew where they stood in regard to their religious instruction	Nobody quite sure whom to trust or what was coming next

In Society

Before	After
Platonic admonishment to "walk in thy calling" kept people in their place in the social order	New flexibility, the result of increased trade, continental travel and a growing middle class, allowed for increased social mobility
Agrarian peasantry limited in world view	Growing urban middle class developing taste for arts, literature, music, and theatre

In Theatre

Before	After
Biblical mystery plays	Secular comedies, tragedies, and histories
Court masques and pageantry	

In Language

Before	After
Latin the lingua franca of all religious and professional dialogue	An explosion of delight and fascination with the English language
French still used frequently in the Courts	English the language of the courts
English considered a base, street language	Increasing value of the vernacular in the professions of navigation, architecture, publishing, craftsmanship, and trade
English language free of rules of grammar and orthography	
Most serious literature written in Latin	Dictionaries written and a new interest in standardization of spelling and grammar

Before	After
Popular literature in the continental vernaculars, mostly French and Italian	A golden age of English poetry, drama, and criticism
	Hundreds of English translations of ancient texts and of contemporary literature from France, Italy, Spain, and Germany

In Education

Before	After
Purpose: theology and chivalry	Purpose: *The benefit of the commonwealth.* Humanizing and civilizing of responsible leadership
Schools centered around the church, the chantry, the monasteries, and cathedrals	Secular education, funded by guilds and municipalities
Educators mostly clerics	
Education choices the responsibility of the parents	Education a lay profession with teachers free of religious instruction, though still under oath to adhere to "the true religion"
Still strongly influenced by medieval education, mostly oral: the "listening" student	
Elementary education conducted in Latin	Growing awareness that the commonwealth must take responsibility for education
Education limited to the wealthy, the clergy, and the nobility	Education increasingly text-based due to the rapid increase in printed schoolbooks: emergence of the "reading" student
Many poor students attended choir schools, or "song schools," to train for church choirs	Latin still the language of education, but a new appreciation of English emerging, with students encouraged to apply their learning of rhetoric to English composition
Encyclopedia: the sense that universal knowledge was attainable in one's lifetime	
Elementary education: the trivium: grammar, logic, and rhetoric, with logic emphasized over rhetoric.	More and more students from the newly emerging middle class
	Poor students who showed ability allowed into free schools
University education: the quadrivium: arithmetic, geometry, music, and astronomy	Rapidly increasing complexity and formalization of narrow areas of study
	"The New Learning": focus on the Greek and Roman classics: the bonæ litteræ
	The trivium still core: grammar first, but rhetoric emphasized over logic
	"The New Learning:" Latin, Greek, and Hebrew literature
	Growth of the Inns of Court, providing training in law and commerce

Of course every one of these shifts was cataclysmic in itself, and the seeds for the change were decades, even centuries, in the growing.

With the Act of Succession in 1534, the king replaced the pope as the head of the English church. This made it possible for Henry VIII to annul his own marriage, which had not produced a son, and to marry a younger and more fertile woman. From the perspective of many reasonable people at the time (including Erasmus, by the way), this was an eminently practical solution to a grave threat to the stability of the kingdom. The king and his realm needed a male heir (or so it was thought!). England had been wracked for centuries by civil wars and struggles between the monarchy and the powerful earls. Henry, in his youth, was a popular and forward-thinking ruler; and if the Tudors were to continue their peaceful dominion, the beloved but aging and barren Queen Katherine would have to be sacrificed. If only she had understood this and stepped aside willingly, all might have been well; but, alas, she had the temerity to consider her marriage sacred and inviolable, and she had enough love among the people and enough powerful friends and relatives across Europe to make it rather difficult for the pope to approve a divorce. Henry's Act of Succession launched the English Reformation and had consequences that we still feel six hundred years later. It also prepared the ground for the changes in education spurred by the work of the humanists, led by Erasmus.

The hunger to make the word of God available to the barely literate masses was possibly the most democratizing force in history. At the same time, the dominance of the papacy, despite its splendor, had been tottering for more than century, and heresy was popping up in different forms up all across Europe. Keeping people in ignorance was a source of power for the church, and maintaining the mystery of the language of the Bible was key, so heretics had to be brutally opposed. But ultimately their message could not be suppressed. When William Tyndale was burned at the stake in 1536, he shouted out with fervor, "Oh Lord, open the King of England's eyes." Perhaps the Lord was listening, or perhaps when Henry VIII finally ordered that the English translation of *The Great Bible* be placed in every church in the realm, his eyes had been opened by the influence of humanism, which brought so many millions into the light.

The humanist movement replaced the medieval Christian teachings with the "New Learning" or the "bonæ litteræ," primarily the Greek and Latin classics. It started with the rediscovery of the works of Aristotle. In the 6th century, Boethius had translated some of Aristotle's *Organon*, which collected his works on logic, but he was killed for treason, and because very few people back then knew Greek, Aristotle was almost forgotten. But in the 12th century new translations of the larger body of his surviving works were made, and he was revived in a mini-precursor of the Renaissance. Then in the mid-14th century, Petrarch and his book-loving friends started rediscovering more and more ancient texts by other Greek philosophers hidden away in the scriptoria of monasteries all over Europe.

They were so enchanted by the knowledge and wisdom therein that (in a much simplified view of history) they launched the Renaissance.

The Ottoman conquest of Constantinople in 1453 resulted in the exodus of many Greek and Hebrew scholars, who made their way mostly to Italy, feeding this new love of the ancient languages. Over the following decades, European scholars in great numbers crossed the Alps to learn Greek in Milan or Venice, and their followers set about replacing medieval Christian education with the New Learning and trying to reconcile this with the teachings of the Bible.

Education was front and center of the aspirations of the early humanists. They adopted the Platonic ideal of a republic supported by an enlightened and literate population. Although it took more than two centuries to take root, they actually started the conversation about universal education, for boys and girls, rich and poor, paid for by the common treasury. Before the humanists, scholarship was deemed essential only for the clergy or for those headed for university degrees in religion, medicine, or law, and the private education of the nobility was mainly in the "manly" arts of chivalry. There were chantry schools taught by priests in most small towns, to which tradespeople could send their children for an elementary education in reading, writing, and the casting of accounts (basic marketplace math), but they suffered from a dearth of trained masters and were inconsistent in quality. There were also song schools attached to cathedrals for the training of choristers in the church. But overall, access to an adequate elementary education was spotty, and the rate of literacy was low. The humanists began to view greatly expanded, even universal, access to education the way we view it today, once again, *"for the benefit of the commonwealth."*

The impact of humanism on the church was profound. The grand old church, which had held together the fragile scraps of Europe during the dark ages, had become wealthy and powerful, and, in the process, had become immensely corrupt—so much so that in retrospect it is clear that reform was inevitable. The quiet monks who for centuries had patiently copied and recopied the classical texts in Greek, Latin, Hebrew, Arabic, and Sanskrit, heroically saving them for future civilizations, had sunk into a culture of venality and idleness. The secular clergy, too, was everywhere guilty of simony: the buying and selling of ecclesiastical privileges such as indulgences, pardons, and benefices. Nepotism was rampant.

The papacy, which headed up this mess, was no model for betterment. The Papal Schism, during which there were two popes at a time vying for power in France and Italy, ended in 1417, but it was followed by a secession of popes, many of whom were, themselves, manifestly cruel and corrupt. To site a few examples: Pope Sixtus IV authorized the Inquisition. Pope Innocent VIII authorized the burning of witches. Pope Alexander VI had concubines and children, of whom Lucrezia Borgia is the best remembered today. Pope Julius II was more of a military general than a religious leader. The popes had little need or will to disguise their egregious behavior because the church was a law unto itself, beyond the reach of the state and ultimately concerned with taking care of its own.

This was the theological landscape that lay before the early humanists. The 15th century saw Petrarch's followers, armed with the New Learning and the perspective of ancient writers, begin to tear at the fabric of Catholicism. Lorenzo Valla, Marcilio Ficino, Poggio Bracciolini and others, some outside of the church and some within, pried open the doors of ignorance and let in the light of curiosity, criticism, and even humor. Valla proved that the document that established the Orthodox Church in Constantinople and gave the Western Church to Rome was a forgery. Bracciolini, even while working as secretary to popes and enjoying their protection, wrote salacious satires about the established church. Some even expressed doubts about faith altogether and got away with it.

What must be recognized, however, is that in the beginning these chinks in the armor of the church were tolerated and even encouraged. The need for reform was so evident that even those whose power was most at risk appreciated the new perspective of the humanists. Martin Luther, Calvin, the Anabaptists, and all the convulsions they caused, all the hardening of doctrine, were still in the distant future.

From the start, education was a predominant concern of the humanists. A "liberal education" was deemed necessary for the bringing up of a "free man" with the leisure to contribute to civil society. In 1423 Vittorino da Feltre founded what was probably the first true humanist school, near Florence. It enrolled children of the aristocracy along with poor boys who showed intellectual ability. So delightful were da Feltre's methods that his school became known as La Giocosa, or, literally, the Joy House. Da Feltre's teachings were based on the educational writings of Plato and Aristotle and added the Latin classical writings of Cicero and others, but he expanded the classroom into the neighboring fields and forests, taking his classes on field trips to study nature. Music, the arts, and natural philosophy were included in the curriculum, and although he continued to emphasize the mediaeval trivium (grammar, rhetoric, and logic), rhetoric, or the embellishment of language, began to take precedence over the drier, and often tortured, logic of the medieval "scholastics," who had endeavored endlessly and argumentatively to reconcile Christianity with the pre-Christian philosophers. Rhetoric soared. Logic limped.

The young men who came out of this house of joy joined those impassioned with the enthusiasm for the New Learning and became emissaries of the bonæ litteræ. Many of them traveled across the Alps to the rest of Europe, and the rest of Europe traveled to Italy, and over the course of the 15th century the influence of humanism moved north, settling in the university centers of Holland, Belgium, France, and Germany and stirring the intellectual ferment that surrounded the youth of one who became the voice, face, mind, and body of humanism in Northern Europe: Desiderius Erasmus.

Erasmus's star was the brightest in the intellectual firmament in the first decades of the century; but, as we shall see, the ambivalence of his role in the Reformation, his determination to find a harmonious middle ground, his refusal to align himself with any faction, almost erased him from history. His impact on education, however, may be felt to this day. He was not a practitioner. He was never a schoolteacher himself, but he created the framework for the humanist curriculum that Richard Mulcaster and every headmaster in England implemented for more than one hundred years. It was at its height at the time Shakespeare attended school. I hope this book will help bring his refreshing intellect back to life.

6
ERASMUS' EGG

FIGURE 6.1 Will collects eggs.

Who Wrote the Works of Shakespeare?
Get in Line, Erasmus!

> *Without Erasmus, we might have had the John Milton of popular concept, but not William Shakespeare.*
>
> —*T.W. Baldwin*

Every good story needs a hero, and here we will introduce the hero of this one. The heading of this chapter is a joke, of course. I take it on faith that William Shakespeare went to the King Edward's Grammar School in Stratford and, with occasional collaborations, wrote the plays attributed to him. But there is no denying that Shakespeare, who may just possibly have possessed the most retentive brain in human history, pulled material out of everything he encountered. His influences were vast, and among them, T.W. Baldwin gives an outsized role to our friend Desiderius Erasmus.

But Shakespeare wrote in English! Erasmus didn't even *SPEAK* English! What could Baldwin possibly be talking about?

Well, it's a long story, but here we go.

Melvyn Bragg, in his hugely entertaining book, *The Adventure of English: The Biography of a Language*, identifies what is the span of Shakespeare's adult lifetime as the time when modern English literature came into its own:

> In the thirty of forty years that bridged 1600, the English language could lay fair claim to being reborn, yet again, but with a self-conscious luxuriance and a world reach quite new.

Think about this. It is just about impossible to name a single piece of literature written in modern English before 1580 that has made its way into the Western canon. There were plenty of comic plays and bawdy poems in English, but their popularity was fleeting. *Utopia* was in Latin. *Tottel's Miscellany* was a collection of love poems published in the 1550s, mostly targeted for law students at the Inns of Court who needed to brush up their rhetorical skills in the newly fashionable vernacular; but of the poets represented there, Thomas Wyatt is the most familiar to us today, and he is better remembered as a consort to Anne Boleyn than for the invention of the English sonnet! The eloquent Tyndale Bible would certainly qualify as great literature, and much of it, indeed, eventually made its way into the King James Bible; but for its first decade in publication the English navy was guarding the channel to keep it out of England, and what bits of it were smuggled in were so dangerously held as to have an impact only on a small, though brave, group of freethinkers.

And yet between 1580 and 1620, a mere forty years, works by dozens of playwrights, poets, critics, and essayists were written that are still read today and that make up the foundation of our literary heritage. Shakespeare had many contemporaries. Among his fellow playwrights were Lyly, Peele, Kyd, Nashe, Greene, Marlow, Jonson, Decker, Middleton, Webster, Chapman, Marston, Mundy, Ford, Fletcher, and Beaumont. Adding essayists and poets we have Bacon, Sydney, Spenser, Donne, Marvell, Drayton, and just about every gentleman of the realm and his sister, because educated women were writing too.

What happened? What was in the water?

To begin with, as we shall see, the long-time headmaster of the Merchant Taylors' School, Richard Mulcaster, in his books on pedagogy, gave voice to an emerging phenomenon: a new appreciation for literature written in the vernacular. He wrote in 1581: "I do not think that any language, be it whatsoever, is better able to utter all arguments, either with more pith or greater plainness, than our English tongue is . . . I honor the Latin, but I worship the English." The Reformation and its consciousness of England as a commonwealth, separate from the papal states of Europe, supported the unique expressiveness and elasticity of the English language. Along with the newly translated Bible, there was an explosion of English writing. Elizabeth's early favorite, Robert Dudley Earl of Leicester, commissioned several translations of classics so that they could be read in English. Edmund Spenser published the first truly great works of modern English verse and inspired others to follow suit. It was a time when an increasingly educated population was finding delight and entertainment in our language.

There are other theories, of course, which are sound. Fifty years of relative domestic peace and stability during Elizabeth's reign, after decades of civil and religious conflict, allowed a middle class to evolve out of rapidly growing commerce. This encouraged theatre and literature to flourish among those non-Latin speakers educated, outside of the universities, in more practical skills. It is no surprise that so much of the earliest English literature came out of the theatre, with works written for popular audiences.

Also, when Henry VIII took England out of the Catholic Church and shut down all of the monasteries, the church's wealth was pumped into the economy, mostly into the aristocracy, and the patronage system expanded. Today Gates, Annenberg, Broad, Geffen, Koch, Walton and the lot slap their names on public buildings or attach their wealth to social policies. In Shakespeare's day, if you wanted immortality you'd be smart to buy a poet. Case in point: Shakespeare made Henry Wriothesley Earl of Southampton, immortal and in return received enough money to become a share-holder in the Globe and buy his family a beautiful house in the country.

But I propose yet another causal factor: *schools*. Or, to be more precise: Latin grammar schools. And here we must start decades earlier, with Erasmus.

First of all, education enjoyed a huge expansion under Henry VIII and the brief reign of Edward VI, which was then continued by Elizabeth. Chantry schools and choir schools attached to the closed cathedrals and monasteries were replaced by secular schools supported by trade guilds or state grants. Teaching priests were replaced by lay headmasters who took an oath to teach the new religion but were able to marry and lead secular lives. This decoupling of pedagogy and theology during the English Reformation was perhaps the first step in the separation of church and state, and it was largely due to the influence of the English humanists, mainly Sir Thomas More and John Colet, both of whom were lifelong friends of Erasmus. By the end of the 16th century there were schools in nearly every town in England, and England enjoyed the highest rate of literacy in Europe. Latin grammar schools were still for boys only, but more and more girls were receiving an elementary education in English and were continuing their studies privately. Education was still mostly for the moneyed classes, but schools were all required to have places for the sons of tradesmen who showed capability and promise. Both Christopher Marlowe and Ben Jonson were examples.

Students went to Latin grammar schools to learn Latin. One had to become fluent in Latin if one wanted to go to the university or join any of the professions: religious, medical, or legal. All intellectual discourse across the continent was conducted in Latin. Latin was the lingua franca and, for many, still a living language. Thus students spent about seven years of their youth in daily exercise translating Latin to English and English back to Latin. From the second form on, only Latin was spoken in school. Discipline was strict, and this rule was rigorously enforced. In fact, students could be marked down for punishment if overheard speaking English, even on the playing field or on the way to or from school.

If on the surface it seems ironic that the genius of our English literary tradition should have sprouted from the study of Latin, we need to look more deeply into the wellspring of humanist educational theory. When we start to examine the sources of pedagogy in Elizabethan Latin grammar schools, literally all roads lead us back again and again and again to Erasmus. The extent of Erasmus' direct influence on Shakespeare's writing may be debated (and it will be very clear in this book which side of the debate I would be on), but his influence on his education and that of his entire generation was irrefutable and all-encompassing, both on the formal and the informal, or "colloquial," curriculum.

There is no evidence that Erasmus was fluent in any vernacular besides Dutch and German. He spent many years in England, France, and Italy but was always in the company of educated friends who were, like himself, entirely comfortable conversing in Latin. He had a poor regard for vernacular literatures in general. He would have been appalled that a mere two generations later, Richard Mulcaster and others would imagine a time when English would be the language of education in their own country. Erasmus even bemoaned the fact that Dante had chosen to write in Italian! One wonders what he thought of Chaucer, or if he ever encountered him at all. Certainly he never *wrote* a single word in English. This may account for the fact that his gargantuan influence on our literature has not received the recognition that it deserves. That said, I was delighted when I read the quote by T.W. Baldwin at the beginning of this chapter. In *The Origins of Shakespeare*, Emrys Jones makes a convincing argument that "without humanism . . . there could have been no Elizabethan literature: without Erasmus, no Shakespeare." Jones and Baldwin both agree with me that humanism is responsible for Elizabethan literature and that Erasmus is responsible for humanist education, and thus the works of Shakespeare.

Latin to English

So . . . Latin literature turns into English literature? Let's explain.

> *Logic, which was taught in the Middle Ages through disputation, was the formulation and the organization of ideas, while rhetoric was their packaging.*

In 1510, when John Colet founded the Saint Paul's School for Boys, he turned to his good friend Erasmus to help him devise the curriculum. Erasmus had already established his reputation in this area with the first publication of his *Adagia*, a collection, with commentary, of Greek and Latin phrases and aphorisms written for students of the languages. Of the hundreds of entries in the collection many are still familiar to us: "a dog in the manger," "to teach an old dog new tricks," "to be afraid of your shadow," "to leave no stone unturned," "to break the ice," "the tip of the tongue" all come to us from the ancients, via the *Adagia*. Always the over-achiever, when Colet asked for his help he responded by writing two seminal works on education: *De copia rerum et verborum* (On Copia of Words and Ideas) and *De ratione studii* (Upon the Right Method of Instruction). These two foundational works were the what-to-teach and how-to-teach of the classics. They were universally adopted and standardized throughout the realm for well over 100 years, and we still feel their resonance today.

Donald B. King, in his English translation of *De copia*, defines Erasmus' use of copia, as "variation, abundance or richness, eloquence, and the ability to vary and enrich language or thought." It is the key to elevated language in poetry and prose, and it relies on the ancient formulas of rhetoric, which, at the time that Shakespeare attended school, had been central to education for over two thousand years. The ancient trivium of the early years of schooling were grammar, logic, and rhetoric. Grammar came first, of course, because it provided the basics for reading and writing, but all three were taught as core. The subtle shift that occurred in humanist education was that rhetoric eclipsed logic as the most highly valued of the three. Logic, which was taught in the Middle Ages through disputation, was the formulation and the organization of ideas, while rhetoric was their packaging. Erasmus and the humanists truly believed that all wisdom and knowledge was to be found in classical literature, and that it was the artistry of their expression that made that wisdom and knowledge accessible, universal, and eternal.

I will devote a chapter to the creative art of rhetoric. For now, suffice it to say that when Shakespeare went to school, ideas mattered, but what mattered more was the language in which the ideas were adorned and decorated. Rhetoric was taught daily and relentlessly, and instruction was done in accordance with the precepts laid out by Erasmus.

At the same time, English was beginning its ascendance, and students were encouraged and *expected* to apply their rigorous training in rhetoric to English composition as well. It's that simple.

Erasmus' Life

I hope to highlight a huge historical injustice here. There is the Lutheran faith, but no sect named after Erasmus! But he was way more fun!

I have read several biographies of Erasmus, all of which focus primarily on the titanic clash between him and Martin Luther. Michael Massing's *Fatal Discord* is by far the most exhaustive and detailed in the telling of all aspects of his religious life and influence and that of Luther. It is a treasure and a must-read for anyone interested in the history of the Reformation. A hugely satisfying but much older work by Stefan Zweig, *Erasmus of Rotterdam* is a joy to read, as it waxes poetic in its evocative eloquence. But those two books tell the dark and bitter story of the last half of Erasmus' life: his contribution to the wrenching history of that blood-soaked era. This book focuses on the much sunnier, funnier, and more sociable Erasmus: that of the first half, when he basked in his fame as the greatest intellect of his time. It focuses not on his influence on religious history, but his profound, lasting, and (sadly) little remembered influence on education.

Nothing tells the story of his life quite as vividly as his own letters. He was a prolific letter writer, communicating with persons of power and prestige all over Europe, and hundreds of his letters remain for posterity. In some ways, at least today, they are more readable and entertaining than the most famous of the works on which he labored with such dedication and erudition during his lifetime. Their spontaneity and immediacy provide snapshots into his day-to-day amusements and struggles and the lives of his friends during an extraordinary period in history. He wrote colorfully about his views on religion and politics, sometimes contradicting himself, as one will do when living through rapidly changing times. They are often ironic and affectionate, full of petty grievances, profound concerns, and humorous anecdotes. They reveal his lively style without the rhetorical fastidiousness of the published works that he himself took seriously. We probably know as much about the personal quirks of Sir Thomas More, John Colet, Martin Luther, several popes, and dozens of influencers and theologians from his correspondence than from many of the troves of historical documentation of the time.

An aside: It makes you wonder, because Shakespeare too must have written hundreds of personal letters, with his family and many friends living days away in Stratford. As we have seen, the writing of epistles was a huge part of his education, and, in fact, there are one hundred and eleven letters extant, written by him—but they are all written for characters in his plays! Almost every play has a plot point that turns in some way upon a letter. But what of the letters he wrote for himself? What a treasure it would be if someone had taken the pains to save them! Erasmus did not leave that chore to others. He kept copies. He assured their immortality himself.

Erasmus was born near Rotterdam in either 1466 or 1469, depending on which resource you read. The contradictory dates may lie in a sensitive detail about his birth. His father, Gerard, was a priest, which meant, of course, that his parents were not, and could not be, married, and thus he was illegitimate. His real name was Gerard Gerardson, but from a young age he called himself Desiderius (greatly desired) Erasmus (Greek for Gerard, which means beloved). There is every reason to believe that he was, indeed, greatly desired and beloved of both his parents, and here follows a good reason for the confusion of the dates:

The 19th-century gothic novel, *The Cloister and the Hearth*, gives a wildly fantastical account of his parents' romance. It's an exhilarating read—full of suspense, hair's breadth escapes, and do or die heroism; but the broad outlines of it are actually based on Erasmus' own telling, and many domestic details are pulled from his writings, including his *Colloquia familiaria*. If we may believe his dramatically embellished account, his mother, Margaret, was the daughter of a physician. His parents were in love and may have been verbally contracted to one another when they "lay together"; however, his father's family was violently opposed to their marriage, as they had Gerard pegged for the priesthood. They arranged for him to be sent on a long trip to Rome on business, and while he was there they wrote to inform him, falsely, that Margaret was dead. In despair he resigned himself to his fate and embarked on a career in the church. When he returned and learned of the lie he had been told, he remained celibate, but he was a loving and caring father.

The author of this romantic fiction was Charles Reade, and one of the sources he used was a formal letter Erasmus wrote to Pope Leo X requesting to be released from his monastic obligations. Unfortunately, there are some problems with his story. For one thing, Erasmus had an older brother who is not mentioned and doesn't fit the picture, since one can easily see that Gerard "lay with" Margaret for at least a few years before Erasmus was born and before they were so romantically separated, practically at the alter. The explanation for this is lost in the fog of time, but there is a good hint in the discrepancy about the date of his birth. We know exactly what *day* he was born, October 27, but in his writings he is ambivalent about the year. Most of the comments he makes about his age point to the year 1469, but in this letter he gives the year 1466. A possible reason for his falsifying the year of his birth lies in a technicality: if his parents conceived him out of wedlock but before his father became a priest, it was less of a sin than if he was already ordained. As Erasmus does not mention an older brother in this important letter to the pope, but in other letters claimed a difference of three years, it appears that he may have pilfered his brother's year of birth to use in place of his own. Erasmus had suffered humiliation because of his illegitimacy, and he may have had some interest in altering his story. He was hypersensitive about his reputation, and although he prided himself on his honesty, we know from other instances that he was not above telling a white lie to protect it.

Whatever the truth may be, we do know that Gerard senior took great care of his sons' education and remained close to Erasmus' mother. Sadly, both parents died of the plague when their children were in their teens, so Erasmus ended up an orphan *and* a bastard. This was not an auspicious beginning for the light of the Northern Renaissance.

Erasmus was first sent to the choir school attached to Utrecht Cathedral, and then to a famous school in Deventer, under a schoolmaster of some note, Alexander Hegius. The Deventer school was run by a religious community called the Brotherhood of the Common Life, a group formed around the teachings of Thomas à Kempis, the author of the popular devotional work, *The Imitation of Christ*. It was sort of a semi-secular monastic order that flourished in the Netherlands in the 15th century, made up of clergymen who lived communally. It's hard to know how much impact the Brotherhood had on the young Erasmus. He had many complaints about his time there, but he was certainly influenced by the emphasis that à Kempis laid on the need for the individual to have a direct connection to God, apart from all the rites, rituals, and trappings of the church. Later in his life he regretted that he had not entered the community himself, but that was only because if he had, he would have been able to leave. The vows taken by them were not irrevocable.

We do know that the Brotherhood was famous for its teachers, but Erasmus did not have many good words to say about his own education, and much of his subsequent fascination with curriculum and instruction seems to derive from his learning from their mistakes. Nevertheless, he did become exceptionally well accomplished in Latin, and he imbibed an ardent passion for the Greek and Roman classics that defined his entire career. Apparently he memorized all of the comedies of Terence and could be counted upon to spout them at will, entertaining his friends after candles out, with all the comic timing of an actor.

A few stories that entered this legend lead us to believe that despite his brilliance he was not, in fact, merely a bookworm. Although not physically hearty as a child, he was spirited and even something of a ringleader. He was apparently the head of a gang that liked to steal pears from a neighbor's garden, and he complained of the excessive whippings at the school, which, apparently, he experienced himself a few times too often. He was a famously engaging companion as an adult, and most likely the same as a child: outgoing and jolly.

While still a child he attracted the attention of Rudolph Agricola, a friend of Hegius and one of the first scholars to bring the New Learning of the classics north from Italy. There is a story that this distinguished man came to inspect the school at Deventer, and while there, patted the clever boy's yellow curls and said, "This little man will do something by-and-by." Erasmus later eulogized him, claiming him as a mentor and calling him "the first to bring a breath of better literature from Italy."

When Gerard died he left in the hands of three trusted guardians an inheritance adequate to complete the education of his sons and launch them in careers. Sadly, either though malfeasance or neglect, the money was wasted well before Erasmus reached adulthood. He was a brilliant child and it was clear from his youth that he would be an ornament to any profession, but when he finished his studies at Deventer his guardians pressured him to join a monastery, presumably to save the expense of the university. According to his letters, this pressure was intense and unrelenting. He was first placed for three years with a group of "collationary fathers" to guide his religious education. Not much is known about them today, but from Erasmus' depiction of them they sound like Dickensian thieves of children, with nests all over Europe, established to grab up promising orphan boys with some wealth attached to them. The monasteries depended on them for bodies and funds, and the methods they used to persuade the young Erasmus to join the religious orders, by his own description, included lures, lies, threats, bribes, and bullying. His subsequent experience as a monk left him with a profound and lifelong distaste for the monastic orders. But more of that later.

Erasmus spent roughly eight years at the Augustinian monastery in Steyn, near Gouda, and eventually became a priest. According to his later memories, he entered the order reluctantly and endured his time there miserably. He hated the food; he hated the cold and the damp. He had a few intense friendships, but for the most part he was disgusted by the illiterate and coarse society of his fellow monks. To the extent possible he devoted himself to his love of literature and immersed himself in solitary study.

In his late twenties his luck turned. The Bishop of Cambray had heard of his intellectual gifts, and, needing a good Latinist as a secretary, petitioned the pope and received a dispensation for Erasmus to join him. This must have felt to him like a release from prison. The first dispensation was temporary, but Erasmus soon became famous and influential enough to be able to get it extended indefinitely. He never returned.

This was the launch of a peripatetic lifetime as a nomadic and often entertaining scholar. There is no need to track all of his travels here. In its most abbreviated telling, the forty years between his departure from Steyn and his death, in Basel, he spent time in almost every country in Europe. The lingua franca for scholars was Latin, and in that language Erasmus could communicate with friends, enemies, and admirers wherever he went. He undoubtedly knew Dutch and German and may have picked up smatterings of French, Italian, and English, but it can't be said that he ever really had a home base or a home language. His home language was Latin, and his home base was his intellectual passion for the classics and his efforts to reconcile that passion with Christianity.

There were, however, a few pivotal times in Erasmus' life that this chapter must address to illuminate his trajectory into his many works on pedagogy. First would be his years at the University of Paris where, after a brief time in Cambray with the Bishop, he was able to further his education. Paris was Europe's greatest center of learning, and the area around the university, with all its students and pedants, was known as the Latin Quarter, as it is to this day. It was during this heady interlude that he encountered, and was utterly exasperated by, the theological thicket influenced by a movement known as scholasticism.

Scholasticism grew out of the intellectual ferment occasioned by the 12th-century rediscovery and translation of the works of Aristotle, and it was still a dominant thread in the curricula of universities throughout Europe. Erasmus was exposed to the often-snarled arguments of theologians like Peter Abelard, Peter Lombard, Thomas Aquinas, William of Ockham, and Duns Scottus. Their attempts to apply Aristotelian logic to Christianity, their endless debates over fine technicalities such as what qualities angels share with humans or whether one angel can be at two places at once (without questioning whether, in fact, angels even exist), ultimately seemed silly to Erasmus, and his dismissal of their arguments gave him an enduring distaste for exotic interpretations and layers of error in the translations of the Bible and other ancient texts. This was the beginning of his desire to go back to the source materials, to search for the "pure spring" of ancient wisdom.

After finishing his degree, and facing poverty, he jumped at an invitation offered by a well-connected student to visit him in England. It was during his youthful sojourn there and the beginning of several new friendships, mainly with Thomas More and John Colet, that Erasmus developed his lifelong fascination with the topic of education. It was in England, at Oxford, that he first encountered scholars of ancient Greek and resolved to learn the language in order to read the original texts of Aristotle, the early philosophers, and earlier versions of Bible. For Erasmus, Learning Greek and being able to read the ancient texts in their original language was like having cataracts removed from his eyes, allowing him to see brighter and more vivid colors of meaning.

But we will return to this later. Here we must pause and put Erasmus into the religious and political context of his time.

His Influence on the Church and the Reformation

This is the dark part of Erasmus' history and the story that most colors the way he is viewed today. I need to get it over with quickly to refocus on the happy side of his character that made him so loved and, for a time, so very influential.

We already know that the Catholic Church at the turn of the 16th century was phenomenally powerful, wealthy, and corrupt. What surprised me when I started learning about Erasmus was how widely understood the need for reform was at time that he started publishing. Well before Luther, Zwingli, and Calvin, before the Diet of Worms in 1521, and especially before the Council of Trent in the 1530s, Catholic theology was much more fluid. Criticism and satire were allowed and even welcomed. Erasmus had been disillusioned by his monastic experience and by the muddled and tangled theology of scholasticism, and in Italy, especially in Rome, he had observed firsthand the profoundly troubling money grubbing that financed the lavish constructs of the Holy See. He was certainly critical. He was not silent. But his way of addressing it was nuanced and gentle, as was his nature. Intelligent humor and satirical mockery were appreciated—even at the highest levels—even by the popes themselves, several of whom, in succession, admired, liked, and protected Erasmus. Eventually the Reformation pushed the Church into a hardened orthodoxy that simply did not exist when Erasmus started his career. His views in many ways were more radical than those of the zealots he inspired, but they were popular. In the early years of the 16th century, he was an intellectual rock star, at the height of his fame, and hugely influential; but his writings might have had him burned at the stake as a heretic if he had published them a mere twenty years later than he did.

An important thing to remember here is the role of the printing presses. It has been said that if Petrarch was the father of humanism, Gutenberg was its midwife. When Erasmus began publishing, the printing trade was rapidly growing but still relatively new, and he himself was not unlike some of our early computer nerds who dabbled in the new technologies and envisioned early on the future of the Internet but could not begin to imagine the extraordinary reach of its influence. He was utterly fascinated by print. The famous printers Johann Froben in Basel and Aldus Manutius in Venice were practically family to Erasmus. He dedicated some of his educational writings to Froben's son, and in Venice he actually moved into the establishment of the Aldine press and set the type for much of his *Adagia* himself. But even he, to his later despair, vastly underestimated the power of the printed word to spread ideas far and wide, convulse the times, and change the course of history.

Erasmus knew intimately, from inside experience, the shamefulness of the dross and superstition created for profit by the monks and the secular clergy. He railed against simony, the abuse of dispensations and absolution and the avaricious selling of indulgences. He pointed out the corrupt heaping up of benefices, which created the wealth of cardinals and bishops. He mocked the worship of the saints, the shrines, the pilgrimages, and the selling of relics, pointing out that enough bits of the cross had been sold to build an armada. He thought that the celibacy of the clergy was a farce, that lechery and pederasty were rampant among the orders, and, surely with a thought to his own parents, that priests should be allowed to marry. He argued that the edicts against matrimony were founded in a mistaken reading of the writings of Saint Paul. Clearly, some of his views would be radical in the Catholic Church even today!

Above all, Erasmus despised the contorted arguments and tortured logic of a long line of theologians, scholasticists, Neo-Platonists and Sophists, from Augustine to Thomas Aquinas and Duns Scotus on, to try to explain the unexplainable in the Christian faith. He considered their views to be intellectual vanity. His rebellion manifested itself in an eagerness to re-translate from Greek the original texts of Christianity. The Latin Vulgate version of the Bible universally used at the time had been translated by Saint Jerome in the 4th century and was full of ambiguities that Erasmus felt had opened the door to layer upon layer of erroneous interpretation. He longed to show the gospels and the Creed of the Apostles purified and clarified. In his own opinion the greatest achievement of his life was his translation of the New Testament from the original Greek. It consumed years of his work and his passion, and was published to great acclaim in 1516.

The introduction to this translation, known as the Paraclesis, is one of the classic statements of Erasmian biblical humanism. It is significant that a full twenty years before Tyndale was burned at the stake for translating the Bible into English, Erasmus announced his strong support for translations in *all* the vernaculars (translated from the Latin original):

> I wish that the Scriptures might be translated into all languages, so that not only the Scots and the Irish, but also the Turk and the Saracen might read and understand them. I long that the farm-laborer might sing them as he follows his plough, the weaver hum them to the tune of his shuttle, the traveller beguile the weariness of his journey with their stories.

This view, which became so very dangerous so very soon, was not inconceivable when he first voiced it. Erasmus could not possibly have envisioned the shattering impact that this and many of the other commentaries he wrote attending his translation would have in the years to come.

Many in the clergy were threatened and angered by Erasmus' mockery, but what made his views palatable to his friends and protectors in high places was not just his erudition. He was witheringly critical of what he considered erroneous interpretations of the Gospels, but he wrote with honesty, eloquence, grace, and humor. He was incapable of rigidity in thinking, and he was, to the very end, unalterably opposed to schismatic factions. He believed, naively, that reform was possible and that good people in the right places could make it happen from within the church. In 1517 he wrote a remarkably optimistic letter to a celebrated preacher in Basel, parts of which I think are worth including here as an indication of his perspective in his still-productive middle age. The following passage is from *Life and Letters of Erasmus* by James Anthony Froude:

> I am now fifty-one years old and may be expected to feel that I have lasted long enough. I am not enamored of life, but it is worthwhile to continue a little longer with such a prospect of a golden age. We have a Leo X for Pope; a French king content to make peace for the sake of religion when he had means to continue the war; a Maximilian for Emperor, old and eager for peace; Henry VIII, King of England, also on the side of peace; the Archduke Charles "divinae cujustam indolis adolescens" [divinely gifted youth]. Learning is springing up all around out of the soil; languages, physics, mathematics, each department thriving. Even theology is showing

signs of improvement. All looks brighter now. Three languages are publicly taught in the schools. The most learned and least malicious of the theologians themselves lend their hand to the work. I myself, insignificant I, have contributed something. I have at least stirred the bile of those who would not have the world grow wiser, and only fools now snarl at me. One of them said in a sermon lately, in a lamentable voice, that all was now over with the Christian faith. There were persons who were talking of mending religion, and even mending the Lord's Prayer. An Englishman clamors that I profess to be wiser than Jerome, and have altered his text, when all I have done has been to restore his text.

But the clouds are passing away. . . . I do not want the popular theology to be abolished. I want it enriched and enlarged from earlier sources. When the theologians know more of Holy Scripture they will find their consequence undiminished, perhaps increased. All promises well, so far as I can see . . . I wish there could be an end of scholastic subtleties, or, if not an end, that they could be thrust into a second place, and Christ be taught plainly and simply. The reading of the Bible and the early Fathers will have this effect.

You can easily see here the hopefulness of man who believed that the labors of his life had contributed to a positive cultural change. His optimism was well founded. He had met the young Prince Henry and had returned to England for a time when he became king, believing him to be a true humanist monarch. He knew the Emperor and the French king as well, and was in a position to advise them. What is more, he trusted their intentions. Pope Leo had shown himself to be a reliable friend. The European power struggles between the nations and the empire were at a temporary resolution, and the leadership—the pope, the kings, and the emperor—were all leaning toward peace and reform. Erasmus himself was at the height of his fame: read and admired by the thousands. It was fair sailing ahead. In his ingenuousness, Erasmus truly believed that clarity of thinking was all it would take to cure all the ills of the church.

And then came Martin Luther. Here I will quote Froude again, because I cannot say it better:

> Suddenly, as a bolt out of the blue, there came a flash of lightening, which scattered these fair imaginings and set the world on fire. A figure now steps out upon the scene which has made a deeper mark on the history of mankind than any one individual man has ever left except Mahomet.

> ***There was no doubt in the minds of the religious hard-liners at the time: it was Erasmus who set fire to the world, not Luther.***

Erasmus' personal struggles after Luther's appearance are mostly beyond the scope of this book, but they are worth summarizing here for two reasons. The first is that they had the impact of eclipsing his reputation for centuries after his death, and that may be the reason its influence on Elizabethan literature has been undervalued. It is noteworthy that Mulcaster, writing years later, hardly makes mention of Erasmus. He cites all the same authorities that Erasmus cites, among them Aristotle, Plato, Cicero, Quintilian, and Plutarch; but despite the fact that *De copia* was the basis of the curriculum in his and every other school in England, he scarcely tips his hat to its author.

The second reason is that Erasmus' conflict with Luther reached a level of high drama worthy of a Shakespeare, and it permanently diminished his star.

There is an often cited quote attributed to papal nuncio, Jerome Aleander: "The monks said that Erasmus laid the egg and Luther hatched it. 'Yes,' said Erasmus, 'but the egg I laid was a hen, and Luther hatched a game-cock.'" There is no question that Erasmus' new translation of the gospels, with his commentaries, influenced Luther, and Luther was not the only heretic they influenced. Tyndale relied heavily on it when he translated the Bible into English, and he was burned at the stake in 1536. Giordano Bruno was known to keep a copy of it close by him at all times, and his pantheistic views, which bordered dangerously on atheism, had *him*, in turn, burned at the stake in Rome in 1600. There was no doubt in the minds of the religious hard-liners at the time: it was Erasmus who set fire to the world, not Luther.

But by his own repeated admission, Erasmus was not cut out for martyrdom. His was a peaceful disposition and a neutral temperament. He was not a joiner of factions. He always sought to harmonize conflicting ideas and see all sides. His contemporaries coined the term "Erasmism" to define the desire for conciliation and common ground. But whereas Erasmus was a seeker of harmony and the middle way, Luther, in stark contrast, was a pugilistic populist. Luther was thunderous, earthy, scatological, preaching in German, not Latin, and penetrating into the consciousness of the common people. Where Erasmus sought to change minds through education, Luther pummeled minds with his brute, raging force of persuasion. He made Erasmus' reasonable and humorous arguments seem pale by comparison.

And in the end, Luther won. For all of Erasmus' outsized reputation for intellect, his weapons for argument were humor and irony. These gentle spears had thus far served him well, but they were no match for Luther's virulence. For the last decades of his life Erasmus had to turn himself into an equivocating puppet to confront the cataclysm that was Luther. He was caught in a tightening noose. His was the classic dilemma of the cautious reformer overtaken by the firebrand and left in the dust. When Luther first nailed the Ninety-five Theses to the door of the Wittenberg Cathedral, Erasmus hoped that this defiant act would jump-start reform of the worst of the abuses. He admired Luther as a good and well-meaning monk. They never met, but they communicated in writing back and forth a few times in increasingly contentious letters. At first Luther respectfully sought his support, and Erasmus replied in a kind letter, offering his advice but admonishing him to tone down his rhetoric a bit so that his message could be heard more clearly. But as the world began to roil around him, Erasmus was under more and more pressure to take sides, to denounce Luther and all of his followers. He was the most famous and admired intellect in Europe, and everyone wanted his endorsement. Luther was pulling him in one direction while the popes and the cardinals were pulling him in the other. He was desperately trying to stay in the reasonable middle, but after the Council of Worms, after Luther's final "Here I Stand, I can no other," that was not possible.

In 1522 Pope Adrian VI wrote to Erasmus offering to bring him to Rome and give him a bishopric, or even the red hat of a cardinal, if only he would crush Luther. Erasmus had been offered benefices before but had never been tempted. He had always clung to his independence like a barnacle. Such an offer might have given him pause, but this one he turned down as well. Here is an excerpt from his response to the pope (translated from the Latin original):

> This is no ordinary storm. Earth and air are convulsed—arms, opinions, authorities, factions, hatreds, jarring one against the other. If your holiness would hear from me what I think you should do to make a real cure, I will tell you in a secret letter. If you approve my advice you can adopt it. If not, let it remain private between you and me. We common men see and hear things that escape the ears of the great. But above all, let no private animosities or private interests influence your judgment. We little dreamt when we jested together in our early years what times were coming. With the Faith itself in peril, we must beware of personal affections. I am sorry to be a prophet of evil, but I see worse perils approaching than I like to think of, or than anyone seems to look for.

The tone of this letter reveals the anxiety bordering on paranoia that Erasmus felt by then every time he put anything down in writing. Adrian repeated his request that Erasmus come to Rome, but Erasmus pleaded ill health. He wrote his suggestions for reform, but, in fact, since they included the termination of simony and extortion, they would have eliminated well more than half the revenues of the Holy See. Aging popes came and went at a rapid rate back then, and they did not actually have that much power. Even if Adrian had wanted to initiate the changes Erasmus suggested, he was unable to do so, and that was the end of that. Some things will never change. When it comes to challenging those hanging on to tremendous wealth, it takes a something akin to a revolution . . . or a bloody Reformation.

Eventually Erasmus buckled under the pressure. However, always the one searching for harmony, he did so by half measure. When he finally broke decisively with Luther it was over the subject of free will. Erasmus was the free will man and Luther was the predestination man. This had been a subject of intellectual debate all the way back to Pelagius of Britain (free will) and Augustine (predestination: man is born in sin, doomed, and only faith, the embrace of Christ and the grace of God can save him). In fact it goes further back to Aristotle's belief that man is defined by his works, good or bad. Aristotle always gave the scholastics a lot to chew on, and free will was a great subject for the kind of complex theological debate that Erasmus himself alternately relished and despised; but taking on Luther on such an arcane topic was hardly the denunciation that the pope and the cardinals were asking for. To both sides he seemed wishy-washy and irresolute. His aversion to conflict only hurt his reputation. Nobody was satisfied. Erasmus was still the towering intellect of his age; he continued to write, however cautiously, and he continued to publish. His books sold faster than ever, but his optimistic glory days were over. His former rock star renown gradually declined until his death, and it did not follow him into his afterlife.

One can only imagine what it must have been like for him to hear of the beheading of his dear friend, Sir Thomas More, by the order of Henry VIII, the king in whom he had had such exalted hopes. More was executed in 1535 for refusing on principle to sign on to the Act of Succession. He was one of many. Erasmus died of old age the following year.

During the final years of his life, in declining health and an embattled correspondence with both his enemies and his friends, Erasmus must have reflected with a poignant nostalgia on the years he spent during his two extended trips to England in his youth. He would have recalled it as a joyful time, full of lively intellectual conversation and laughter. Many of the hilarious colloquies he wrote in his old age echo back to the bantering, the jests, the comical stories, and the dry satirical humor of travels, dinner parties, and gatherings at the homes of Thomas More, John Colet, and others. Characters based on More, his wife, his father-in-law, and his daughter Meg show up in some of them, as do a host of others who will forever remain nameless but who light up the pages with their wit.

The only reference to More's execution that Erasmus made in the letters I have read was a hearty prayer that the news he had heard was not true. How his memories must have pained him. More's condemnation must have seemed unimaginable. More was one of Henry's oldest and most trusted friends and mentors. In fact, he was the one who first introduced Erasmus to Prince Henry when he was still a child. A character sketch Erasmus once wrote describes him with admiration and affection bordering on idolatry.

It was for More that Erasmus wrote what is today by far his most lastingly popular work, the satire *In Praise of Folly*. When Henry became King, in 1509, Erasmus was in Italy. More wrote to him full of enthusiasm, urging him to return to England and take part in the new age promised by this brilliant young monarch. He did, and he wrote the work while he was traveling and published it to an ecstatic reception. In fact, the title was a play upon More's name. The word for folly in Greek is morias, so the Greek title would be *Morias Enkomion*. The

Latin title was *Stultitiae laus*, but it was often translated as *In Praise of More*. It was a scathingly funny send-up of all the pretenses of the society of that day, especially the pious abuses and corrupt practices of the church and the foolishness of pedants. It was written in the style of the Greek satirist Lucian, whose writings More and Erasmus, in an early collaboration, had translated into Latin, and it is spoken in the voice of a delightfully free spirited goddess, Folly—or Morias. Folly praises herself and invents herself as the daughter of Plutus, the god of wealth, and a nymph. The satire represents the shared hilarity of its creator and the greatly loved man to whom it was dedicated.

His Writings on Education

> *Non scholae sed vitae discimus*
> *(We learn not for school but for life)*
> —Text depicted on a monument to Erasmus in Deventer

Erasmus first went to England in 1499. When he was at the University of Paris, he had taken on students as a tutor. One of them, a wealthy young Englishman named William Blunt, Lord Mountjoy, recognized his growing fame as a man of letters and invited him to Oxford, giving him a pension and becoming a lifelong friend and patron. That first trip lasted only a few months, but it was during those months that he became acquainted with the "learned" John Colet and the "sweet" Thomas More. It was also during this visit that More introduced him to a group of children at their games, which turned out to be the royal nursery. One of those children was the 9-year-old Prince Henry.

He returned to England first in 1505, staying for one year, and again in 1510 at the invitation from More related previously. The last visit lasted four years and included time spent lecturing at Cambridge. This time, when he left, it was forever. He had been disappointed in the young king, who seemed more interested in pursuing foreign wars than in advancing the goals of humanism, and his restless intellect shuttled him back to the continent. But his warm friendships with Colet (for whom he designed the curriculum at Saint Paul's) and for More continued through correspondence for the rest of their lives.

This was a jolly group. More was youngest, hardly more than twenty when Erasmus first met him and in his thirties during his longest stay. Colet was the eldest and most sober, well into his sixties, but was known for his ironical sense of humor. They shared an intellectual passion for all things classical, but above all they were devoted to the promise of the New Learning.

Remember that in the hopeful letter quoted earlier, which Erasmus wrote at the height of his fame, he takes specific pride in his contributions to education: "All looks brighter now. Three languages are publicly taught in the schools. The most learned and least malicious of the theologians themselves lend their hand to the work. I myself, insignificant I, have contributed something." The three languages were, of course, Latin, Greek, and Hebrew, and the fact that even the clergy were engaged in teaching gave Erasmus great satisfaction.

His pride was not misplaced. I have always considered that the definition of a genius is one who clearly expresses an idea which, when one hears it for the first time, seems like something one has always known. Suddenly perceptions that have been clouded by complexity or ignorance seem like common sense. My example for this has always been Darwin, who simply read the evidence for evolution in the geological formations he saw during his travels on the Beagle. Once *he* saw it, everyone could. By my definition alone, Erasmus qualifies. He was the genius who enshrined pedagogical practices we still honor, to best instill learning. We still honor them because they seem obvious. Common sense in many ways defines all of Erasmus' writings, on theology and on education.

Erasmus' preoccupation with education increased as he aged and as his theological writings put him in more and more peril. One of his evasive responses when he was being pressed on all sides to take a stand against Luther was to eschew theological arguments and retreat into his educational works, claiming, "My business is to further the cause of education." In fact this is evidenced by the sheer volume of his writings on the subject. He never stopped. The *Adagia*, the *Copia*, and *De ratione studii*, already mentioned, were the works most relevant to this study, but there were many others. William Lily's Grammar, *De Constructione*, which by law became the required text for the teaching of Latin, was so thoroughly revised by Erasmus that Lily himself wanted to remove his name from it. *Institutum Christiani* (1514) was his playful attempt to make the Catechism at Saint Paul's more palatable by putting it into verse. *De civilitate morum puerilium* (1526) was a handbook on teaching children good manners and reflects the view that morality and social skills were important goals of humanist instruction. *De pueris instituendis* (On Education for Children) (1529) was addressed to parents and set forth his own educational philosophy, emphasizing, among other things, the importance of play and pleasure in learning, the depreciation of rote-learning, and the rejection of corporal punishment. He also wrote a textbook on the writing of epistles, *De conscribendis epistolis*, that was used in schools for many decades, and he had a hand in translating into Latin the grammar school editions of Aesop and Lucian.

We must also include two works he wrote for the edification of adults that could fall into the category of education. *Enchiridion militis Christiani* (The Manual of a Christian Knight) was written to school the wayward husband of a pious woman who sought his counsel, and *Institutio principis Christian* (The Education of a Christian Prince) spells out his model for humanist leadership which stands as a stark contrast to Machiavelli's *Prince*, written at approximately the same time.

His humanist views pop up in his colloquies as well. He believed that mothers should nurse their own babies and not give them over to wet nurses as was the custom then, especially among wealthier women. He believed that women could be scholars. His fingerprints are all over every aspect of 16th-century curriculum, and his works on education were all concerned with the physical and emotional health of children, always as important as their intellectual growth. They are of a piece with the overarching belief of humanists that the comprehensive education of the whole child was crucial to the foundational underpinnings of a civil society.

De ratione studii

We will examine *De copia rerum et verborum* more closely in the upcoming chapter on rhetoric, but here I would like to focus on *De ratione studii* (Upon the Right Method of Instruction), because it reveals so much about the way Shakespeare and his peers experienced their schooling. What I like about it is that it shows how accessible, sensible, and wise Erasmus was. Of course, we teachers are no longer expected to teach Latin, Greek, and Hebrew; we no longer teach scores of rhetorical tropes, schemes, and devices; and we are no longer expected to teach the exordium, narration, partition, confirmation, refutation, and peroration of a composition with the same diligence and rigor of the past. The difference in the expectations for instruction in today's classroom may make *De ratione studii* seem irrelevant to some, but it is the *way* Erasmus suggested that content be taught that still captivates.

Erasmus had a profound understanding of what we now call child development. He echoed Plato in the belief that children should be exposed early to the best in literature and that they begin learning languages (in his case, both Latin and Greek) at the very beginning of their education, understanding that language patterns are most adaptable in the very young. He opposed rote learning, and I particularly like his quote, "I have no patience with the stupidity of the average teacher of grammar who wastes precious years in hammering rules into children's heads. For it is not by learning rules that we acquire the power of speaking a language, but by daily intercourse with those accustomed to express themselves with exactness and refinement, and by copious reading of the best authors." He addresses the art of composition with a colorful list of suggested topics, and he outlines "the true method of criticism," so that the student may "distinguish good literature from mediocrity." He also instructs the teacher, giving an exhaustive list of subjects both academic and practical about which even teachers of small children should be knowledgeable. No mere plodding pedant was Erasmus' ideal schoolmaster!

But What of the Arts?

I wish, for the purposes of this book, that Erasmus had written more specifically about instruction in the arts. He was and still is known as a defender of all the arts, not just literature. No less a man than Rabelais called him a champion of the arts. He himself was the subject of portraits by Hans Holbein, Albrecht Durer, and Lucas Cranach the Elder. But it is strange to think of him spending many months in Florence and Rome at the very time that Raphael, Leonardo da Vinci, Michelangelo, Correggio, and so many others were producing great works, and that in all his thousands of letters he scarcely mentions the visual arts, except to point out the vanity of their use in decorating the lavish and costly trappings of the church. He does list architecture and music as essential subjects to be included in instruction, and he mentions that students showing giftedness in music or drawing should be encouraged to further their learning—the clear assumption being that a teacher would have the opportunity to observe those gifts during regular instruction. He himself certainly received instruction in music at the choir school in Utrecht, and I quote one passage here from *De copia* that shows that he must have been deeply knowledgeable. Here he is giving an example of embellishment from Lucian, in the *Harmonides*:

> For although he could summarily have said "I have learned the art of flute playing," he preferred to display copia by developing the details in this manner. "You have taught me how to play the flute correctly, and to blow on the mouthpiece lightly, as it were, and with harmony, then, with skilled and facile touch to use my fingers in frequent raising and lowering of the tone; moreover, you have taught me to keep time, and, furthermore, to note what is proper to any type of harmony, the divine impetus of the Phrygian, the Bacchic fury of the Lydian, the sobriety and restraint of the Doric, the cheerfulness of the Ionic, so that the modes harmonize with the dance."
>
> *(Translated from the Latin original)*

I love this passage. For one thing, I myself, though somewhat educated in music, somehow missed learning the difference between the Bacchic fury of the Lydian and the sobriety of the Doric! But I also appreciate the implication that, at the time this was cited, instruction in music was hand in hand with instruction in dance, as well it should be. He clearly was drawn to the arts, but for all he says about arts instruction, he left much for Mulcaster to say seventy years later.

But looking ahead to Mulcaster in our narrative, there is an important point to be made here. In all of his many works on education, Erasmus was always writing from a theoretical perspective. He was not in the day-to-day, hands-on business of educating hundreds of children. Richard Mulcaster, teaching only a few decades after Erasmus's death, put his views into practice. As we shall see, music (combined with dance), visual arts, and physical rhetoric were core in the daily exercise at the Merchant Taylors' School under Mulcaster, and dramatic presentations by students were the norm all across England. The performing arts flourished in those schools, and if the sophistication of audiences at the time is any indication of cultivated, conscientious citizens, humanist education was demonstrably doing its job. Erasmus may have simply assumed the presence of the arts in educational programs and saw no need for change. We can't know. Sadly, music, dance, painting, and drawing just don't come up much in his works.

But what of theatre? Well that we shall see when we get to the colloquies!

7
THE DELIGHTFUL MULCASTER

FIGURE 7.1 Mulcaster instructs his students in music.

> The soul and body being co-partners in good and ill, in sweet and sour, in mirth and mourning, and having generally a common sympathy and mutual feeling in all passions: how can they, or rather why should they, be severed in training?
> —*from* Positions, *by Richard Mulcaster*

76 The Delightful Mulcaster

> *. . . from what imaginable retreat may the delightful Mulcaster be enticed?*
> —*Janus Dousa, from an ode to Alexander Nowell,*
> *Dean of Saint Paul's*

Fast forward now to Richard Mulcaster, headmaster of the Merchant Taylors' School, who was famous in his time for his daily instruction in music and his use of playacting in instruction. He is also known for training two of the headmasters who presided over Stratford's Latin grammar school while Shakespeare was a student.

> **Mulcaster trained two of the headmasters who presided over Stratford's Latin grammar school while Shakespeare was a student.**

The humanist movement made education a hot topic of much study, and there were many books written about pedagogy in the 16th and 17th centuries, among them those of Juan Vives, Roger Ascham (tutor to the young Elizabeth), Sir Thomas Elyot, William Kempe, Edmund Coote, John Brinsley, and Charles Hoole. But Mulcaster was by far the most forward thinking of them all, and he was the only one to call out the importance of teaching in and through the arts. In fact, according to Richard deMolen, who wrote the best biography of him I have found, the two books that he wrote about education were supposed to be followed by three more: he intended to write a book about the teaching of singing, one about instrumental music, and one about drawing. My personal regret that he never completed those additional books is up there with the regret over the lost works of Aristotle and the burning of the libraries of Alexandria! These books would have been the only detailed descriptions from that time of instruction in the arts by a practitioner, a teacher actually engaged in the day-to-day work of the classroom. It would have been pay dirt: exactly what I am looking for now. But what he *did* write is still a treasure for one like myself, searching for historical clues about arts in education.

If you live in Los Angeles and have ever had the good fortune to attend one of the performances of the Hobart Shakespeareans under the tutelage Rafe Esquith, you will have seen a teacher in action who is, in my imagination, a direct descendent of Richard Mulcaster. Esquith taught fifth grade at Hobart, one of the largest elementary schools in the Los Angeles Unified School District, right in the middle of Korea Town. Every year his students performed, exquisitely, a play by Shakespeare, and accompanied it with instrumental and vocal rock music. Among his enthusiastic followers were the British actors Sir Ian McKellen and Michael York. If you haven't observed this phenomenon, you can rent the documentary film "The Hobart Shakespeareans" or read one of his books, *There Are No Shortcuts*, *Teach Like Your Hair Is on Fire*, or *Real Talk for Real Teachers*.

If you ever visited Esquith's classroom after school, during a rehearsal, a student would approach you and bring you a seat, offer you water, and explain whatever scene was being rehearsed. If asked, any child in the room would be able to recite any scene in the play or step into the role of any character.

If you visited during the school day you would be treated to the same courtesies, and you would see children reading *Huckleberry Finn*, *The Catcher in the Rye*, *Lord of the Flies*, or another classic novel. They might be studying math through logical reasoning exercises or doing rigorous study in science or social studies. In addition, each of his students learned to sing and to play an instrument: guitar, keyboard, drums, or one of the brass or string instruments.

If you visited his classroom on a Saturday, you would see him tutoring returning students, preparing them for their SATs or helping them with their college essays, and you might meet former students, now adults and graduates of top rated colleges, who are there to assist.

But if you ever said to Rafe, "Your students are amazing!," he would scoff and say: "They're not amazing, they just work hard." Esquith's only rule in his classroom, indeed his mantra, was "be nice; work hard" (in that order), and this was evidenced in everything he did and everything his students did.

"Be nice; work hard." I would equate that with Richard Mulcaster's two stated purposes for education: learning "knowledge to increase understanding" and "behavior to enlarge virtue." He was solidly in the humanist tradition that advocated for education in support of a civil society, as a "benefit to the commonwealth."

I have no idea if his classroom demeanor was anything like Esquith's but I like finding parallels over the centuries. Rafe earned the right to be proud, and to some this came with a whiff of arrogance. He was disdainful of the ever-changing adopted curriculum of a huge public school district, and this didn't win him any medals for compliance. What little we know of Mr. Mulcaster, he shared these exact same characteristics. But most of all, seeing what Rafe's students, many of them from impoverished homes, accomplished in one year of fifth grade, it is easy to imagine Mulcaster's students becoming fluent in Latin, proficient in Greek and Hebrew, *and* learning to draw, to play musical instruments, to sing beautifully, and to perform entire plays for the queen.

Sadly, another characteristic Rafe may have shared with Mulcaster was a testing of the limits of what was deemed appropriate and professional in familiarity when joking with students, and he was discharged from his position for reasons that stemmed from his off-color humor. He was eventually exonerated but never returned to the District. Mulcaster, too, was relieved of his duties at the Merchant Taylors' School after many distinguished years, and the reasons are lost in time. They may have been at least partly financial, as he frequently expressed unhappiness about the poor salary that a headmaster received, but there is some evidence that his "dramatic" teaching style got him into difficulties. There is an amusing story about him stopping for a moment before whipping the naked hind side of a boy, and, quoting the request by a minister at a wedding, intoning, "I ask the bans of matrimony between this boy his buttocks, of such a parish, on the one side, and Lady Birch of this parish on the other." ("Lady Birch" was the switch the schoolmaster always had at the ready.) One boy stood up and made a witty case, claiming that "all parties are not agreed," and Mulcaster let the victim off with a slap on the wrist. To be fair, paddling boys was not an uncommon practice back then, but perhaps making a salacious joke of it was. And then there were the plays. Rafe Esquith's students were always exceedingly polite and his audiences small by design, but Mulcaster's rowdy audiences at Merchant Taylors' were probably responding to a lot of satirical wit and high spirits in his young actors, which may not have endeared him to his employers.

Clearly Mulcaster, known for his ego, felt secure enough in his own prestige, despite the idiosyncrasies of his practice, to think he could get away with stretching the rules. It didn't always work out that way. If he was released from his duties at Merchant Taylors' for reasons of perceived misconduct, he was not alone. One of the most famous head masters of the 16th century, Nicholas Udall, was actually suspected of pederasty as a young man. He was fired from Eton but managed to talk himself out of the penalty of hanging demanded of the Buggery Law of 1533, and he went on to be the famous headmaster of the Westminster Grammar School for many years and serve as Master of the Revels for Queen Mary. There was no whiff of that kind of behavior around Mulcaster, but his departure was not amicable. He was famously temperamental and tangled often with his employers, and when he quit the stodgy Merchant Taylors' he did so with the exit line, "Fidelis Servus, perpetuus asinus" (Faithful slave, perpetual ass).

There is one other similarity. From his writings it is clear that Richard Mulcaster, like Rafe Esquith, loved teaching and did it well. He was a headmaster for almost fifty years, teaching at two of the most prestigious grammar schools in London. He was at the Merchant Taylors' from 1561 to 1586 and at Saint Paul's from 1596 to 1608. Both of them also felt a need to share their love of and expertise in teaching with others, and both wrote books about pedagogy.

Unfortunately, I cannot recommend Mulcaster's two books for casual reading. *Positions Concerning the Training Up of Children*, written in 1581, and *The Elementarie*, written the following year, have been described as excessively "discursive and euphuistic" (flowery and all over the place) even for the style of the time. This is an understatement! He is solidly in the school of "never say anything in one sentence that you can say in forty" and "never make a point until you have circled around it for at least five pages." I have attempted to redact some of his more pertinent chapters for the modern reader and have found it to be an exhausting and unrewarding process. His sentences are endless, repetitive, and brain tangling. Just imagine the following paragraph, chosen at random from the first chapter of *The Elementarie*, submitted for a comprehension assessment on a modern Common Core test: (The spelling has been modernized. It's even worse in the original.) And if you give up after the first sentence, I will have made my point!

> That this five branched Elementary, which I seek to persuade, is very profitable and good, there be many private presumptions in our common experience, besides the general proofs, which shall follow hereafter. First,

because the most of these principles be in use with us already, though not with all persons, yet sure of all places where the liking of these things and the ability to bear charge do occur in parents. Secondly because even those which have them not, yet do wish they had them when they fall in thinking of them, upon some either pleasant or profitable object which they find wrought by them: though upon so private either too sparing or too precise, some kind of people either care not, forgetting them at first, or for wishing them at last, least they might seem to condemn their own selves, if they did wish for that which they would not once, as condemning that of passion, which they allow of in judgment.

If you got the gist of this passage in one reading, you're a far better reader than I. I'm still bewildered by it. As Holofernes (a character who may have been partly based on Mulcaster) would say in *Love's Labour's Lost*, "He draweth out the thread of his verbosity finer than the staple of his argument." In his introduction he felt that he had to defend his decision to write his books in the vernacular instead of Latin, but clearly he was not comfortable writing in our language (although, like Holofernes, he considered himself quite the ultimate literary stylist!). In 1582 English was not the language of academics, and his books pre-date Strunk and White's *Elements of Style* by three hundred and fifty years. He could have used some help, but none existed.

On the other hand, to give him credit, there may have been reasons for his obfuscations. When he requested permission to publish his first book, *Positions*, the Stationer's Registry specifically indicated that permission would be denied "if this book contain any thing prejudicial or hurtful to the book of Master Ascham." Roger Ascham, who was, among other things, Elizabeth's tutor and author of the most highly regarded book on education, *The Schoolmaster*, apparently had a monopoly on educational theory and enough clout to censor any views that contradicted his own, which Mulcaster's most definitely did. Ascham believed that education was to be limited to the elite, and Mulcaster thought it was for everyone. In order to retain his position at Merchant Taylors' and continue to publish, he had to walk a very fine line, sometimes circling cautiously around controversial subjects and seeming to praise where he condemned.

> **(Mulcaster) was one of the most prescient and original thinkers in the early modern history of education.**

But Mulcaster didn't do posterity any favors by writing in such a tortured style. This is regrettable, because if you take the time to decipher what he was saying you realize that he was one of the most prescient and original thinkers in the early modern history of education. Ascham and Elyot, writing primarily about the education of the nobility, wrote in more lucid prose, but had far less to say to us today. The Moravian Amos Comenius is considered by many to be the father of public education, but many of Mulcaster's views pre-date those of Comenius by many years.

Ironically, although he was best known at the time as a grammar school headmaster, famed for his scholarship and his instruction in the three classical languages (Latin, Greek, and Hebrew), the two books cited, *Positions* and *Elementarie*, are devoted to the education of the very young child learning to read and write in English. Called "the petties" because traditionally they learned their elementary skills in "petty schools," or what would today be preschool through first grade, they were roughly the ages of 4 to 7. Petty schools were also called "dame schools" because they were often taught, for a small fee, by an educated woman in her home. Another name for the person offering this elementary instruction was an "abecedarian," skilled, one would hope, in the teaching of early literacy. The founding statutes of many of the best grammar schools specifically state that students could not be admitted until they were proficient in reading and writing, so they had to spend one to three years in petty school first. This begs the question: what was Richard Mulcaster doing concerning himself with the little ones?

The reality of the times, it appears, was a bit more complicated. Not every small town had a petty school, and it was not uncommon for a grammar school to assign the task of early teaching to an assistant teacher or an "usher" in the first form. In many cases even older students acted as tutors. It is also apparent that many towns and cities had elementary schools that were distinct from Latin grammar schools for boys *and girls* up to the age of 10, training for the trades rather than the professions. They were frequently taught in the church by the local pastor.

Mulcaster himself, at least occasionally, filled the position of abecedarian or elementary teacher in addition to his role with the upper school forms. He took young students into his own home to augment his income, a custom that more than a few times got him into trouble with the authorities, and they were presumably educated there according to the precepts that he sets out in his writings. The chapters in *Positions* that he devoted to the education of girls leads one to believe that they may have been among the scholars who received instruction in his home. Merchant Taylors' was the largest school in London, with over two hundred and fifty students, so he would have had at least three ushers beneath him to share in the instructional duties, but he clearly states in his books his view that the teacher of the first years is the most important. If he did not teach the young ones himself, he clearly took close oversight of their instruction very seriously.

This fascination of his in early learning is evidenced in one of his most radical views—one that would be radical even today. He actually believed that the first teacher a child has is the most important and should be the best trained and the highest paid. A child's earliest exposure to formal education shapes his learning habits for a lifetime. There is plenty of research today that would affirm Mulcaster's opinion, but it is highly unlikely that in the 21st century we will see the instructors of preschool children getting salaries topping those of college professors. The one year that I taught first grade was the hardest work I've ever done. Only a hefty financial bribe would have lured me to try it again. Mulcaster and I see eye to eye on a great many issues, but, sadly, on that one we might be a minority of two.

Many of Mulcaster's recommendations for the reform of education were not realized for well over two hundred years, but they were rooted solidly in the humanist debate of the time. He was born in the north, near the Scottish boarder, and being the son of a gentleman, was educated at Eton. There the curriculum mirrored the most rigorous designed by early 16th-century humanists, and he may have encountered the famous headmaster, Nicholas Udall. He may even have performed in plays written by that eminent educator. Students in the highest level at Eton were often used to instruct the younger students, and that was probably where he got his earliest experience as a teacher. From there he went to Kings College, Oxford, and then on to get his complete his degree at Cambridge. The professors he had at those two institutions included some of the most noted Greek and Hebrew scholars and the most famous of the early English humanists: among them John Cheke, William Buckley, and John Caius. Through them he had a direct connection back to the scholars who, as we shall see, were the architects of the humanist vision for education: John Colet, Sir Thomas More, Leonard Cox, William Grocyn, Juan Vives, and, especially, Desiderius Erasmus.

Even in that august company, Mulcaster was remarkably forward thinking. Note the following:

- He was not the first to suggest universal elementary education—that credit probably goes to the Spanish humanist, Vives—but he was the first to seriously argue for it, with the suggestion that it be paid for out of the public treasury.
- He spent several chapters on what we today would call "readiness," stating essentially that a child's physical, emotional, and cognitive development is more important than age in determining the timing and pace of their education.
- He believed that the physical training of the body was equal in importance to the training of the mind: in other words, what we today might call the education of the whole child. He insisted that the same teacher should be responsible for both.
- He believed that education was a natural, not an artificial process as "It is hard to haul against the stream, as it is wondrous easy to row down with it."
- He valued the development of judgment over memory and critical thinking over rote learning.

- He wrote chapters defending the education of poor children and girls, supporting opportunities for higher education offered to those who showed ability.
- He believed that a teacher should conference regularly with his students' parents, and even neighbors and community members or colleagues who shared in a child's well-being.
- He disapproved of private education for the aristocracy, noting that it was important that privileged young men test their wits against a larger population of students.
- He advocated for the construction of schools in the countryside, in healthy outdoor spaces away from the city pollution.
- He proposed the establishment of teacher preparation programs in the universities to standardize practice and assure a uniformity of quality throughout the realm.
- He foreshadowed the first stirrings of interest in vocational education to prepare students not heading for university with practical knowledge to be used in apprenticeships for the various trades.
- All of his views were based on patriotism. He was a passionate supporter of the concept of a British commonwealth. It was for the benefit of the commonwealth to turn "seven year old apes" into civilized gentlemen, and it would be for the benefit of the commonwealth to have a common language that would unite all tongues of the British Isles—the Celtic, Gaelic, Erse, Welsh, and Irish languages—and a common body of learning that every citizen of the commonwealth would share. We hear echoes of Mulcaster's view even today in the embrace of the Common Core curriculum being adopted throughout our commonwealth of the United States.
- Perhaps most astonishing, he foresaw a time when education would be conducted entirely in English! He even encouraged his students to apply their learning in classical structures to writing in English. This was a radical idea then. The entire purpose of a Latin grammar school, or Ludus Literarius, was to teach the lingua franca. One could not enter any of the professions without Latin. Doctors, lawyers, clergymen, scholars, merchants, and secretaries across all of Europe communicated in spoken and written Latin, and anyone hoping to distinguish himself as a scholar had to know Greek and Hebrew as well. But Mulcaster, himself a noted linguist, believed fervently that the English tongue had a vitality all of its own and that it was capable of expressing great ideas. Indeed, he believed, correctly, that English literature was approaching a Golden Age. He predicted a time when all of education could be in English, when it would be seen as waste of seven years for students to have to know Latin in order to access learning. It's almost comical to think of the originality of that view in 1581, but this was well before Shakespeare, Marlowe, Jonson, Donne, Bacon, and the lot. Back then English was only just emerging as a literary language, still struggling to take its place among the other vernaculars of Europe.

- But for the purposes of this study, the most significant of his views was the importance of the arts in instruction. He insisted that as a child's first experiences with learning are the most important, learning should begin with pleasure, and out of pleasure, beauty. Teach a child to use his natural abilities to make beauty, he said. A child has a voice: teach him to sing with beauty, to speak with beauty. He is active: teach him to move, to dance, with grace and beauty. He scribbles: teach him to draw and write with beauty. Again and again he refers to the five essential things that a young child should learn to "prepare the mind for learning": reading, writing, drawing, singing, and playing a musical instrument. He was famous for his daily instruction in both vocal and instrumental music, and, indeed, music has two of the five essentials. With drawing, the arts have three of the five, and if you include writing and speaking prose and poetry with elegance, grace, and beauty—four of the five. He calls upon Plato as his source, as Plato "setteth down all five principles by name and allegeth great reasons why the mind is to be fashioned by them for learning, as the body is by gymnastics for exercise."

> *Again and again he refers to the five essential things that a young child should learn to "prepare the mind for learning": reading, writing, drawing, singing, and playing a musical instrument.*

This articulation of the need to "prepare" or "fashion" the mind for learning and the body for exercise profoundly resonates with me as I have searched for years to find the exact words or the convincing formula to show the link between engagement in the arts and the development of cognition. Those of us who have spent our lives as educators know it's there. We say that the arts foster lifelong learning, but how do we prove it? Mulcaster was on to something. He was cogitating on the same conundrum.

What is missing from Mulcaster's early scope of study? Well, arithmetic for one thing. In petty schools children learned the "casting of accounts," which was a system rather like the abacus, of sorting numbers in columns using casters or stones. It would have differed in one significant way from the abacus: it was based on the British currency and the calculation of pounds, shillings, and pence, which up until the late 20th century was not based on the decimal system, whereas the abacus, of course, is. The casting of accounts was primarily devised to teach a child the simple calculations one would need in exchanging money, measuring lengths, handling weights, etc., either at home assisting parents in a trade or in the marketplace. Apparently mathematical instruction ended there and was not taken up again until the university.

But Mulcaster does address mathematics. He asks (and I admit I am paraphrasing, but only slightly) why anyone would even try to teach mathematics before a

84 The Delightful Mulcaster

child can read music? What nonsense! If a child can read music he already knows arithmetic. He knows fractions, he knows value, and he knows measurement. This thinking goes back to the Greek philosophers, starting with Pythagoras, who defined the relationship between numbers and musical tones. They derived from that the idea that the order and beauty of the universe could all be boiled down to mathematics. This became the inspiration for Plato's idealized "forms" and the groundwork for the philosophical harmony of the spheres that was still very much an element of the Elizabethan world order.

Also, in drawing, when you see the old woodcuts of classrooms, you see that the tools of drawing included compasses and rulers. Much of it was what today we might call mechanical drawing, so children were learning arithmetic there too. Would you call that "math integration"? I suppose you could if it made you happy. When any teacher or principal tries to convince me that arts integration can be a substantive arts curriculum I always want to suggest that perhaps we should teach math through "math integration" like they did in the old days. (That, actually, was the way I learned math myself, in my Dewey-based education; and I learned it well!)

> When any teacher or principal tries to convince me that arts integration can be a substantive arts curriculum I always want to suggest that perhaps we should teach math through "math integration" like they did in the old days.

FIGURE 7.2 A drawing class in a 17th-century classroom, courtesy of the Mary Evans Picture Library.

History? Social Studies? Sciences? These were embedded in the classical readings. Students would have learned history from Livy and from Caesar's *Commentaries*, philosophy from Apuleius, politics from Cato and Sallust, civic duty from Cicero, geography from Ptolemy, natural history and cosmography from Pliny and Aristotle. As for science, which in those days was called natural philosophy, Mulcaster reflected a long held credo shared by artist/scientists back to Leonardo da Vinci and beyond that what is not drawn is not truly seen. The first step into the study of the natural world is observation, and how does one best teach observation? By teaching drawing!

What else was missing? Dance? Well, remember that Mulcaster was a huge advocate of physical exercise, "as quiet sitting helps ill humors to breed, and burden the body." His students needed to be active. He is noted even today as the first to describe the rules of football (our soccer), and he wrote chapter after chapter on a broad variety of outdoor and indoor exercises, including archery, running, and fencing. He also wrote an entire chapter on dancing. Back then he had to defend dance because of the influence of the Puritans who feared that it would lead to inappropriate behaviors between boys and girls, and he did so, vigorously. He pointed out the rigorous physicality of dancing in armor, which I would have loved to see! My favorite of his defenses was that "there is no better cure for kidney stones" than warming up the body through dance. It is also quite safe to say that dance was integral to his instruction in music, as well it should be.

But what about theatre? At first I was a little disappointed because in the entirety of the two books he never mentions the *art* of theatre. Gradually I realized that theatre in that day was not seen as a discipline separate from the components that make it up: music, dance, spectacle, and *actio*—or what Quintilian called "the bodily incarnation of the inward mind." In fact, as I now know after a great deal more reading, and as will be shown in subsequent chapters, theatre, or actio (acting) was absolutely core to humanist education. In fact, Mulcaster was one of the most famous of a great number of dramatizing schoolmasters, stretching back at least to 1525, when it is well documented that schoolboys at Eton and Saint Paul's School were regularly performing complete Latin comedies as a part of their study of the classics and were sometimes called upon to perform plays in English for visiting dignitaries.

In fact, there are enough recorded mentions of student performances even further back in history to convince one that dramatic performance by grammar school boys was deeply embedded in custom for several centuries. In 1119, Geoffrey of Maine recorded a grammar school performance and indicated that it was a custom of long standing, and in 1487, at birth of Prince Arthur, almonry boys of Saint Swithin's performed a miracle play of Christ's descent into hell. This custom was certainly far more widespread than we have recognized.

Mulcaster was not the only one noted for using theatre to cultivate "good behavior and audacity." Ease and confidence of conduct was valued in scholars, and in 1538 Ralph Radcliffe, the headmaster of the grammar school at Hitchin, was said yearly to present "merry and honest plays for the edification of the public, both to practice his charges in ease of bearing and to teach them to speak clearly and elegantly." John Heywood, a Master of the Revels serving Henry VIII, lectured school masters that student performance be "held necessary for the emboldening of their junior scholars, to arm them with audacity, against they come to be employed in any public exercise as in the reading of the dialectic." He further argued that performance trained a student in presentation and rhetoric and made him "a bold Sophister, to argue pro et contra, to compose his syllogisms . . . to reason and frame a sufficient argument to prove his questions."

Dozens of school statutes stipulated that plays were to be performed by students, particularly at Christmas, Twelfth Night, Shrovetide, or Whitsuntide. A frequently cited statute from Shrewsbury stipulating that every Thursday, highest form scholars "shall declaim and play one act of a comedy" was probably an example of a common practice. Students usually acted plays in Latin by Terence or Plautus, but many schoolmasters, Nicholas Udall and Mulcaster among them, also wrote their own material—in Latin for academic performances and in English for public performances. Indeed, as we have already noted, boy actors and the playwrights who provided them with material carved out their own niche in theatre history.

> *The master's switch was always there to remind one not to mumble through the declamations of Caesar or blush at the language of Ovid. When you spoke in class, you spoke like an actor.*

Humanists often had to defend the idea that education was not a pursuit only for the effeminate—that "manly" subjects were covered as well. This reminds me a bit of the conflict I saw year after year in some of my teenage, male students—especially students of color and those from communities marginalized by poverty or circumstance. Sadly, many of them feared that speaking like an English teacher was the surest way to being labeled and mocked as "gay," and that is an example of how little things change over the centuries. This is probably why Mulcaster clothed his dancers in armor, and it is certainly why he treated performance skills as robust physical exercise. In Whitlocke's quote which precedes this chapter, "audacity" should be read not as rudeness but as boldness, and boldness was seen as a masculine virtue, so it is not surprising that Mulcaster wrote chapters on speaking loudly, laughing, singing, speaking softly, crying, and gesturing all under the category of health and exercise. These also just happened to be the skills they would need to do their daily recitation of the classical passages they had to memorize. Remember that the 16th century was still new to the age of print, and pedagogical practice changes slowly, so "reading," in the Elizabethan classroom, meant memorization and recitation or oratory—speaking out loud. The master's switch was always there to remind one not to mumble through the declamations of Caesar or blush at the language of Ovid. When you spoke in class, you spoke like an actor.

One by one my presuppositions about Elizabethan education were being shattered. I had been taught again and again that school started at 6:00 AM and ended at 5:00 PM, six days a week, forty-four weeks a year, and that students spoke, read, and wrote Latin all day long. Now I began to envision music and dance lessons, drawing lessons, athletics, and boys on their feet, every day, vigorously reciting and performing. In addition, if they were not residential students but lived near the school in a rural town, students went home every day for lunch. Their lunch break was two hours, from 11:00 AM to 1:00 PM. Will Shakespeare lived a few minutes from school, and if you've ever watched a 10-year-old devour lunch, you would know that gave him at least one hour and forty-five minutes every midday to haunt the streets and fields of Stratford. In addition, most of the statutes of schools in the area that we still have show an hour of physical exercise scheduled every day at 3:00 PM. Not such a bad life for a boy after all. From that point on, the more I learned, the more the lens widened.

I mentioned earlier Holofernes, the pedagogue satirized by Shakespeare in *Love's Labour's Lost*. Richard deMolen in his biography argues that Mulcaster, with his florid, meandering verbosity, was in fact himself a likely candidate for that comical character. He also suggests that it may have been written on commission for one of the boys' acting companies because of the large number of female and boy parts. There is much circumstantial evidence to support this view, as it was probably written during plague years, when public theatres were closed but popular boys' companies were available for private audiences. In fact, the entire play, from start to finish, is a parody of rhetorical education. A boys' company would have found gleeful pleasure in the hilarious portrayal of their Latin curriculum and the most famous headmaster in London. If this was the case and deMolen is correct, Shakespeare did for poor Mulcaster what he did for that other Richard, King Richard III—he sullied forever the reputation of someone who was probably a far better man than the caricature portrayed.

Other schoolmasters have been suggested as models, and Holofernes was probably an amalgam of many, but aside from the endless Latinizing and the penchant for playmaking, which could have applied to any number of pedagogues of the time, four clues in the play point to Mulcaster. First is Holofernes' obsession with spelling, which was a controversial topic back then to which Mulcaster devoted many chapters in *The Elementarie*. Then there is his mention of the hornbook, because of Mulcaster's expressed belief that the first teacher of the ABCs was the most important. Also, Holofernes admonishes the young page Moth to "go whip thy gig," an indoor physical activity recommended by Mulcaster in *Positions* which involved a spinning top accelerated with a small whip. There is also a possible reference to the fact that Mulcaster occasionally taught girls, as we have stated, in petty school. Sir Nathaniel says: "Sir, I praise the Lord for you; and so may my parishioners; for their sons are well tutored by you, and their daughters profit very greatly under you: you are a good member of the commonwealth." (Shakespeare, of course, being Shakespeare, intended more than one meaning when he wrote that the daughters "profit very greatly under you," but let us not speculate further here about what that might tell us about this particular schoolmaster.) Finally, Mulcaster was known to be temperamental, vain, and overly dramatic, quite like Holofernes.

It may be futile to speculate, but there is always the temptation to imagine. In fact, there was almost a decade when he was missing in action, between his departure from Merchant Taylors' in 1586 and his employment at Saint Paul's. During that time there is speculation that he taught students somewhere in the country. Two of those years happen to coincide with the years from early 1593 through 1594, when theatre companies in London were out of work because of the plague. If, as several biographers have speculated, the popular young out-of-work poet, Will Shakespeare, was employed as a secretary by his patron, the Earl of Southampton, and lived with him at his estate at Titchfield Abbey, in Kent, is it not possible that the country schoolmaster caricatured in a play he wrote while there was, indeed, our friend?

John Dover Wilson makes an entirely persuasive argument that Shakespeare had three specific young men in mind when he wrote his early comedies. In play after play there are three spirited boy-men who careen through the action, sparring, tussling, joking, and taunting each other with thinly veiled erotic humor: Petruchio, Tranio, and Lucentio in *The Taming of the Shrew*; Bassanio, Gratiano, and Lorenzo in *The Merchant of Venice*; and, of course, Romeo, Mercutio, and Benvolio. I would add that there is occasionally, too, an older and slightly wiser companion like Antonio in *The Merchant of Venice*. *Love's Labour's Lost* has its trying-to-be-studious triad of Berowne, Longaville, and Dumain, with their older and wiser leader, Ferdinand, King of Navarre.

If Dover Wilson is correct, the three adolescents are based on the Earls of Essex, Southampton, and Rutland, and their more mature companion, Ferdinand, is Ferdinando Stanley, Lord Strange, Earl of Darby. There is plenty of evidence to support this. The acting company that Shakespeare was most likely attached to at the beginning of the decade, before the plague closed the theatres, was Lord Strange's Men. Ferdinando Stanley, Lord Strange, was a charismatic and dashing courtier known to be of "exalted genius as well as birth," a lover of the arts, who was in the line of succession to the throne through his mother, per Henry VIII's will. Sadly, this designation spelled doom for him. The Stanleys had dangerous Catholic leanings, and Lord Strange was implicated in a conspiracy known as the Hesketh Plot, by Catholics on the continent, to place him on the throne and return England to Rome. He vigorously denied any involvement in the plot but died under mysterious circumstances in 1594, poisoned, likely by someone on behalf of Elizabeth's protector, Lord Cecil. *Love's Labour's Lost* was written before his death, and the character of the studious Ferdinand, King of Navarre, was certainly based on Ferdinando Stanley. One of his closest companions in the years before his death was Robert Devereaux, the Earl of Essex, who was the favorite of the Queen Elizabeth. It is perfectly plausible that it was through Lord Strange and Essex that Shakespeare met his future patron, the 19-year-old Southampton, and his 17-year-old brother, Rutland.

By all accounts, all four of these young noblemen were dazzling personalities, and it would have been heady company for the young actor/poet/playwright. Any or all of them might have been the "diverse of worship" who, according to the printer Chettle, came to Shakespeare's defense in 1592 when the dying, dissolute playwright Robert Greene attacked him, calling him an "upstart crow" and "in his own conceit, the only shake-scene in a country." This charge is well known because it is the very first reference to William Shakespeare in London. It was made in a literary testament to the "university wits"—playwrights Greene, John Lyly, Christopher Marlowe, George Peele, and Thomas Nash—who up to that point had more or less ruled the Elizabethan stage. It told them, basically, to give up trying to write plays and find some more profitable employment because a mere actor was getting all the work. In other words, the silence of the "missing years" in Shakespeare's biography was over, and he appeared quite suddenly in the records as a fully established and successful playwright. Chettle's defense tells us that he was not only successful, he was "excellent in the quality he professes" and a person of "honesty" and "facetious grace," much loved by "diverse of worship," clearly meaning that he had powerful friends at court.

There is evidence that *Love's Labour's Lost* was written as a Christmas entertainment in 1593 while the London theatres were closed. If so, it would have been performed in a private home, probably in the country, either by actors from Lord Strange's Men or by one of the boys' companies that were popular at the time. It is chock full of obscure references and volumes have been written trying to identify what contemporary characters were being comically portrayed. Some think that Don Armado, the bloviating Spaniard, was Sir Walter Raleigh, and the study group was a send up of his atheist "School of Night." This theory would have been the height of irony because Raleigh despised the Spanish. John Florio, the distinguished linguist and Italian intellectual who later translated Montaigne, has been suggested as a model for Holofernes because he was, indeed, at the time, a tutor to Southampton and Rutland, but the sophistication of his educational offerings precludes that identity in my mind. Personally I am not persuaded by that argument. I am happy to think that, somehow, Shakespeare was spending some of the plague months in the company of some skylarking noblemen, and that Richard Mulcaster, a famously histrionic rival dramatist, was, at least in part, a model for the hilariously inept country schoolmaster.

If you've seen *Love's Labour's Lost* you may remember that Holofernes is asked, and enthusiastically agrees, to present an "entertainment" for the guests. He puts on a play called "The Nine Worthies," which he writes himself and in which he himself plays several of the nine. It is a comic disaster. This is clearly a reference to a playmaking schoolmaster, and Mulcaster himself was quite the impresario. As a young man in his early years of teaching, he was involved in producing pageant processions, sometimes of great magnificence. In 1559 he wrote the summary, or précis, of the pageant that introduced the young Elizabeth to her subjects, and he went out of his way to use his theatrical expertise to convince his fellow Englishmen that she was worthy of the role of Queen. Boy singers, players, and orators featured significantly in that and in most pageantry of the time. At prominent intersections in London, stages were erected for pageant wagons to pass, and boys would sing, play instruments, orate, or otherwise ornament these spaces; and Mulcaster's scholars were among them.

Subsequently, in 1561, when he took the position of headmaster at the Merchant Taylors' school, as stated by Whitelocke, his students were regularly invited to perform at court and for official occasions in London. Mulcaster's students performed at least eight times for Elizabeth, in plays he wrote in English. We don't know much about the content of the plays, but we can get the gist by some of the surviving titles. Plays for the court were either heroic fare like *Timoclia at the Siege of Thebes by Alexander* or romantic stories like *A History of Ariodante and Geneuora*, which Mulcaster borrowed from the same source Shakespeare later used for *Much Ado About Nothing*. Either way, they were probably overdrawn, histrionic, and unsubtle, like "The Nine Worthies."

Again, in *Hamlet*, Shakespeare may have been goading Mulcaster or his ilk when he mockingly referred to the "aerie of little eyases" (eaglets). Both Merchant Taylors' and Saint Paul's School for Boys were among the grammar schools often noted for nurturing the boy players selected for the popular professional boys' companies, especially the Children of the Revels, who were then performing at Blackfriars. By the time *Hamlet* was written, Mulcaster, then headmaster at Saint Paul's, would have been quite old, and the duties of the school dramatists, one might think, would have passed onto younger hands, and yet there is a mention of him in the accounts of the festivities around the coronation of King James I. First nine boy choristers performed ditties presenting the nine muses, followed by a Latin oration given by "One of Master Mulcaster's Scholars, at the door of the free school founded by the Mercers," evidence that the old man still had it in him. Of course, *Hamlet* and the coronation of King James came a full ten years after the writing of *Love's Labor's Lost*, but it is impossible not to grin at the mention of the nine muses after the comic sendup of Holofernes' nine worthies. It's certainly possible that Shakespeare satirized Mulcaster because he saw him as something of a professional rival.

Of course none of this speculation, however interesting, tells us how Shakespeare might have known Richard Mulcaster in person. The theatre world of London was a small one, and at least until the 1580s boys' acting companies and schoolboy performances were a significant part of that world, but Shakespeare and the adult acting companies had surpassed them in popularity by the 1590s. They were dominant both in public theatres and at the court. Shakespeare would certainly have been aware of Mulcaster, but there is no reason to assume that they were well acquainted.

That's where my imagination continues to weave on its merry way. When Whitlocke referred to Merchant Taylors' as a "famous" school, one must note that its fame was due to its headmaster, and indeed, among Mulcaster's friends there were many of great prestige. The Earl of Leicester, for whom he wrote text for some of the pageantry associated with Queen Elizabeth's Royal Progress to his estate at Kenilworth, was one of his patrons. He wrote Latin verses used by Thomas Tallis and William Byrd. Among the many of his students who went on to distinguish themselves were several of the translators of the King James Bible. His most famous student was Edmund Spenser, the first of the great modern English poets, and, indeed, Spenser credited him with his choice to write his verse in English. Two future playwrights numbered among his graduates: Thomas Lodge and Thomas Kyd, the writer of the early blockbuster, *The Spanish Tragedy*. There were many others who became renowned in the sciences, politics, and the church. In fact, one problem with associating him with the foolish pedant Holofernes is how often he was remembered as a witty and charismatic companion. A dedication to an ode written in 1586, shortly after he left Merchant Taylors', the question is asked, "From what imaginable retreat may the delightful Mulcaster be enticed?" Like many temperamental but charismatic persons, he had the ability to delight and offend in equal measure. He was a clearly a personage of note and stature in the world of London theatre, and there were many acquaintances and former students who could have connected the two dramatists. But there are two in particular that stand out irresistibly.

For the purposes of this book, the most tantalizing among those who studied with Mulcaster were Thomas Jenkins and John Cotham, who were to become headmasters, one after the other, of the Stratford Latin Grammar School and the teachers of a child who would become greatest master of the English language ever born. Nothing could be more feasible but that when the young Will Shakespeare made his way to London, he would have come into direct contact with the greatly revered and "famous" master of his own teachers.

Just how much influence Mulcaster's example had in grammar schools throughout the realm we will never know. His two books on pedagogy were not republished and may not have been popular. The typical rural school was probably far less progressive than the Merchant Taylors' under his guidance, and he himself says in his introduction to *The Elementarie* that he was swimming against the current and that his proposals for education reform might land on deaf ears, or at least be slow to take hold: "Good things grow on very hardly at their first planting." He even compares his peers' resistance to change to that of a drunkard unable to give up his bad habit:

> Which prejudice in opinion being grounded upon contentment with the acquainted evil, and loath to enter danger for a change of some trouble, so

bewitches the reason of the parties seduced, as drink doth that fellow which will rather lie in a ditch all night and call for more clothes when he feels more cold, and bid put out the candle when he sees the moon shine, than he will either be persuaded, that he is drunk at all, or else be entreated to get up and go home.

(Again, one cannot help but think of *The Taming of the Shrew*'s Christopher Slye in Mulcaster's description of a drunk calling for the blowing out of the light of the moon.)

Apparently he didn't think much of the receptivity of others in his profession.

That said, his influence would certainly have been felt by his own students, Thomas Jenkins and John Cotham. Both of them would have been under his influence during his early years at the Merchant Taylors', when we might imagine him at his most energetic and charismatic. Certainly they carried Mulcaster's inspiration with them when they took up their duties at Stratford.

Jenkins became headmaster in 1575 when Shakespeare was 11 years old and would have been his teacher at a crucial time in his development. Cotham took over five years later and would certainly been acquainted with the young Will. He would have had younger siblings from the family, and Shakespeare may have served as an older student praepositor under him. If they trained their students in the oratorical skills as they themselves were trained, and if their students performed regularly for audiences made up of the citizens of Stratford, they would have been following in the steps of their own master and, indeed, would have been in the company of many rural schoolmasters doing the same. There is no question but that Will Shakespeare would have been one of their principal performers.

It is recorded that Jenkins took a leave from Oxford for two years, to work as a teacher, and perhaps it is not entirely beyond the bounds of imagination that he may have spent that time as an usher at nearby Stratford under the previous headmaster, Simon Hunt. I fully admit that's a stretch, but it would not be the first time that a talented and capable usher took over the role of headmaster. If that were the case, he would have been the instructor closest to the young Will Shakespeare at an even younger age. Even if that were not true, it is tempting to observe the mind of Shakespeare and reflect upon Mulcaster's belief, going back again to Plato, that correct and careful teaching in the early years can influence a child's lifelong intellectual growth. This insight and the collation of the arts with developing cognition, the "fashioning" or "preparing" of the mind, is central to his belief system and is the reason I hold him in such high regard.

8
PER QUAM FIGURAM?

FIGURE 8.1 Will juggles with rhetoric.

Grumio: I pray you, sir, let him go while the humor lasts. O' my word, an she knew him as well as I do, she would think scolding would do little good upon him: she may perhaps call him a half a score of knaves or so; why, that's nothing; an he begin once, he'll rail in his rope tricks. I'll tell you what sir, an she stand him but a little, he will

> *throw a figure in her face and so disfigure her with it that she shall have no more eyes to see withal than a cat.*
>
> Act I, Scene ii Taming of the Shrew

Grumio, you may remember, is Petruchio's much-abused servant in *The Taming of the Shrew*, and here he is warning others not to mess with his boss. He is referring to Petruchio's dangerous facility with rhetoric, which, in his dialect, he calls "rope tricks." By a *figure*, he means a rhetorical figure of speech. Grumio is illiterate and probably doesn't know exactly what rhetoric is, but he knows it involves language and is powerful stuff: powerful enough to wound—or dis*figure*. This is just one of many examples of Shakespeare making fun of the study of rhetoric, with its dozens of rhetorical *figures*. In fact, one of his earliest plays, *Love's Labor's Lost*, was, from beginning to end, a send-up of his education in elevated language. But satirize it as he may, no one ever made better use of his rhetorical education.

Today in our literate world, we see rhetorical devices applied in both writing and speech, but the ancient meaning was from the rhetor: the orator. Rhetoric referred to the oral arts. It was all about the power of the *spoken* word. There were actually ancient rhetors who were themselves unable to read and write. Even Homer may have been illiterate, reciting his poetry only through memory. This emphasis on the spoken over the written word was true for two thousand years before Shakespeare studied rhetoric, and it was still true in his classroom not long after the printing press changed everything. As a child, Shakespeare was trained every day in the *delivery*, the *speaking*, of crafted language.

By the end of the 15th century, when Desiderius Erasmus took on the task of designing the curriculum for Saint Paul's School, rhetoric had been foundational in education for centuries. It was one of the three pillars of the trivium, along with grammar and logic, and was introduced to students in their earliest years of instruction. In practical application, grammar was dominant in the first years, because it included basic literacy, but logic and rhetoric followed close on its heels.

> *Logic demands ideas grounded in reason. Rhetoric involves the packaging, or the selling, of ideas. It involves elevated, persuasive, and occasionally deceitful language.*

As we have seen, Erasmus' profound impact on education was, in a subtle and nuanced manner, to shift the emphasis of the last two pillars. Throughout the Middle Ages, logic had prevailed, as philosophers used tortured versions of it to explain Christianity and faith. Over the course of the 16th century, Erasmus' passion for the rhetorical traditions embodied in classical literature elevated it above logic. *This is an important concept to keep in mind.* Logic demands ideas grounded, however weakly, in reason. Rhetoric involves the *packaging* or the *selling* of ideas. It involves elevated, persuasive, and occasionally deceitful language.

In the Elizabethan Age, the study of rhetoric morphed into a new passion for a new vernacular. Shakespeare's generation was in love with English. Both the literate reader and the illiterate speaker reveled in it. It was their pastime, their play, their identity, their disguise, and their power. It was a youthful passion featuring all the pleasures and delights of a young romance.

Because English was still unstandardized and adolescent, it unabashedly embraced foreign and newly crafted words. A heated debate raged between the linguistic purists and the exuberant poets over neologisms, or what were called "inkhorn" terms—alien invaders or words invented, sometimes pretentiously, by inky-fingered writers seeking ever new ways to express their ideas. The famous pedagogue, Richard Mulcaster, was on the side of the neologists, appreciating the need for a writer "to invent new [words] upon evident note, which will bear witness, that fitteth well, where to be used." Those opposed to inkhorn terms lost the battle resoundingly, as our language continued to absorb and discard words at lightning speed. Shakespeare is famous for coining hundreds of words, and he was far from alone. As much as he was a gift to our language, our language was a gift to him. English was a linguistic sponge, a fungible material, the "airy nothing" with no rules to break, with which a genius poet could work magic.

Happily, our language welcomes innovation to this day. When I was teaching in the inner city I used to have to have my students create a new-words-and-phrases glossary at the start of every year, because so much would change over the summer. Call it ghetto speech if you will, but it was some of the most creative and expressive language I've ever heard. Also, although they are far less colorful, no one can have failed to notice the dozens of new terms that have entered our language with the digital revolution.

As it is today, language was also evidence of status. Much comment and some mockery has been made of Shakespeare's successful application for a coat of arms, but nothing signaled his ability to climb the social ladder better than his overwhelming command of words and his genius in the use of rhetoric. He studied it first at school, where he must have been a voracious student, and he continued to build upon his mastery all of his life, challenging his audience to grow with him.

By the time of Elizabeth, a generation after Erasmus' death, books on rhetoric were immensely popular, devoured by men and women alike as they strove to advance in a newly flexible society. The best of these were Richard Sherry's *A Treatise of Schemes and Tropes*, published in 1550, and *The Art of English Poesy*, published in 1588 by George Puttenham. Puttenham fancied that his book could "pull" one "from the cart to the school, and from thence to the court." A cart was associated with agriculture. Polonius is referring to this in *Hamlet* when he says to Claudius, of Hamlet's feelings for Ophelia, "If he love her not/ Let me be no assistant for the state, / But keep a farm and carters." From the farm to school, and thus to court: indeed, the term "holding court" applies to one who is able to hold the attention of an audience because of his skill in rhetoric. The idea that even a farmer carting his goods to market could imagine himself a courtier by educating himself in the poetic arts was a fresh new concept in the history of social mobility, and nobody took better advantage of it than Shakespeare.

But in his day, Shakespeare was just one of hundreds. By the time he died, after retiring to Stratford, he was already a musty memory. When Ben Jonson died there was something like a national holiday, with parades in the streets! He had entirely eclipsed his friend, and there were plenty of other playwrights dazzling the audiences. It's hard to believe, but it was almost a century before anyone took notice and elevated the Shakespeare we know today to the stratosphere of literary fame. Back then rhetoric was in the cultural DNA. Everyone with any education was good at it, and it was an absolute necessity for anyone who wanted to have any impact in the world.

There are more than two hundred identified rhetorical figures, the number depending on which reference you use. You might go back to an ancient Greek source or the Roman *Rhetorica ad Herennium* or Quintilian or *De copia* or one of the later treatises. The terms overlap in meaning and sometimes duplicate themselves, which can make things confusing for the modern reader, but the basic list is essentially the same as it was more than two thousand years ago. The textbook on rhetorical terms that Shakespeare most likely studied in school was *Grammaticae artis institution* by the German humanist, Johannes Susenbrotus, published in 1539. In his *Epitome troporum* he defines one hundred and thirty-two figures and gives examples of their use in ancient and contemporary literature. Baldwin sites dozens of examples in Shakespeare's poetry that come directly from that text, evidence that Shakespeare was exceedingly familiar with it, so we can make a good guess at which figures he studied as a boy.

Today a well-educated person might be able to list about twenty-five figures that are still commonly used. Examples would be alliteration, allusion, amplification, analogy, antithesis, apostrophe, assonance, climax, dilemma, epithet, hyperbole, irony, metaphor, metonymy, onomatopoeia, paradox, parenthesis, personification, simile, and synecdoche. But there were dozens more that Shakespeare had to learn. How about:

Epizeuxis:
        Lear: Howl, howl, howl, howl, howl!
        or
        Never, never, never, never, never
        or
        Cecilia: O wonderful, wonderful, wonderful, and yet again wonderful

Anthimeria:
        Hamlet: I will speak daggers to her

Chiasmus:
    Richard III: I wasted time and now doth time waste me
    or
    Witches: Fair is foul and foul is fair

Anadiplosis:
    Richard III: My conscience hath a thousand several tongues,
    And every tongue brings in a several tale,
    And every tale condemns me for a villain

Hyperbaton:
    Escalus: Some rise by sin, and some by virtue fall

Hendiadys:
    Shylock: to have the due and forfeit of my bond

Or apophasis, or zeugma, or ekphrasia, or anthypophora, or anaphora, epistrophe, epanalepsis, or a whole lot of others that I'm not sure how to pronounce and that nowadays don't even pass spell check on my computer. In the 1940s Sister Miriam Joseph wrote a book called *Shakespeare's Use of the Arts of Language* that gives hundreds of examples of Shakespeare's use of figures. They can make you giddy. Learning them all is high on my bucket list but I fear it's beyond my aging memory. There is a huge jingle jangle of tropes, devices, and schemes that sound like flowers, constellations, rare animals, or exotic dishes. There are figures for the alterations of words, for changes in sentence structure, for the expression of moods, for the application of puns and ciphers, the coloring of nuance, and a variety of what we now simply call metaphor.

Shakespeare had to know them all. He had to identify them in passages from the classics, copy them into his copybook, invent his own examples, practice them in Latin and English, and recite them in daily lessons. This was rigorously enforced. All students did it. "Per quam figuram?" was a constant request from teachers. "What figure are you using?" And students had to be prepared to answer with definitions and examples. In fact, the more you learn about the study of rhetoric, the more it seems that the great speeches and quotable lines in the plays of Shakespeare and his contemporaries were simply vessels into which words were poured and shifted about to fit whatever figure the writer was using at the moment.

Thus when Brutus or Macbeth meditates on the murderous crime he is anticipating, he is exhibiting examples of *aporia*: doubting or questioning one's motives.

When Antony repeats again and again "Brutus is an honorable man," or Othello keeps interrupting Desdemona with his demand for "the handkerchief," or Hotspur repeatedly squawks "Mortimer" like a parrot, they are all using the figure *epimone*: the repetition of the same point in the same words.

Whereas when Othello is about to suffocate Desdemona with a pillow and says, "Put out the light, and then put out the light," he is using *diacope*: using the same phrase twice, but with two *different* meanings.

When Brutus asks the Roman mob, "Whom have I offended?" he is using *anacoenosis*: calling upon the counsel of an audience.

When the grave digger in *Hamlet* argues that if a man goes to water and drowns it is suicide, but if the water comes to him and drowns him he is "not guilty of his own death," he is using *cacosistation*: an argument that serves both sides.

When Cesario asks Feste if he lives by his tabor (e.g. is he a drummer) and Feste responds, "No, sir, I live by the church," we call that *antanaclasis*: two contrasting meanings for the same word, causing ambiguity.

When Macbeth contemplates the assassination of Duncan and considers that it will "catch/With his surcease, success," he is using *paranomasia*: the intentional use of two words with similar sounds but different meanings, to exploit confusion.

When Mercutio has been fatally stabbed and he responds to his friends' questions about his wound, "Ay, ay, a scratch, a scratch," the figure he is using is *meiosis*: a deliberate understatement.

When Prince Hal distracts the sheriff from his attempt to arrest Falstaff, he his using *apoplanesis*: evasion by digression to a different matter. Then again, when Falstaff pretends to be deaf when the Justice of the Peace wants to question him about a robbery, and babbles on, consoling the Justice about his own maladies, he is using *concessio*: where a speaker grants a point which hurts the adversary to whom it is granted. When he debates with himself about the virtues of honor and concludes that it is a "mere scutcheon, therefore I'll have none of it," he is using *hypophora*: reasoning with one's self by asking questions and answering them.

The examples are endless. All the folded language, all the layering and amplifying of extended metaphors, all the colorful and unexpected uses of words, all have their source in rhetorical figures. Once you start to learn them you see them everywhere, and as you get better at it, reading a passage in one of the plays can be enormous fun, like deciphering an intricately clever puzzle. But, oh, there are so many!

Actio

> *"The bodily incarnation of the inward mind:"* Actio, actio, actio:
> ACTING

Cicero, in his treatise *De inventione*, organized rhetorical oration around five canons. They were inventio (invention), dispositio (arrangement), elocutio (style), memoria (memory), and actio (delivery). Inventio and dispositio may relate either to writing or to oratory, but elocutio, memoria, and actio all relate directly to presentation, or performance. Most of the rhetorical figures we are familiar with today we identify with copia, or elevated language. Inventio covers the application of rhetoric to original verse and prose. But *actio* just has to do with *performance*!

Quintilian, in *Institutio Oratoria*, explored Cicero's five canons in greater depth. He defined actio as "the bodily incarnation of the inward mind." He notes that so important was actio to Demosthenes that he was known for this maxim: "the principal part of an oration is actio, the second the same, the third no other." Actio, actio, actio: ACTING.

Here are just a few examples of rhetorical figures that fall squarely under the category of actio:

> *Enargia*: liveliness of expression Orthopoeia: Correct expression
> *Imitatio*: imitation
> *Ethopoeia*: impersonation of a historical or mythological character.
> *Prosopopoeia*: impersonation of an abstract idea.
> *Idolopoeia*: impersonation of a dead person.
> *Pathopopoeia*: speech leading to an emotional response.
> *Mimesis*: mimicry.
> *Ekphrasia*: verbal painting or descriptive speech.
> *Tasis*: sustaining a word because of the beauty of its sound.
> *Mycterismus*: a mocking or nasty comment, tone, look or gesture.
> *Ominatio*: a prognostication of evil.
> *Stichomythia*: rapid dialogue in which two characters speak alternate or broken lines of verse.
> *Aposiopesis*: silence, or a loss for words mid-phrase.

The first inkling I had that rhetoric would become a fascination for me was a workshop I took years ago with Milan Dragicevich. He was a professor at UCLA at the time, but shortly after I first met him he moved to Amherst, to teach at the University of Massachusetts. He wrote a fantastic book, *The Persuasive Actor*. Despite its name, it is not just for actors! The book uses the metaphor of a magic carpet ride through the ancient, lost art of rhetorical speech. The comparison is apt. It is a tour that swoops and soars, pauses and accelerates as it surveys a breathtaking landscape, and it leaves us yearning for more. When I finished it I longed to start my entire education over from scratch. I wanted to be as adept as Shakespeare and tens of thousands of his peers were with the use of propulsive language that can electrify, enchant, seduce, and persuade.

> **Just as the intensive study of rhetorical copia accounts for the protean quality of Shakespeare's poetry, rhetorical actio was training for his life in the theatre.**

When a schoolboy recited a daily lesson, either for the schoolmaster, an usher, or one of the older student praepositores, actio was as rigorously enforced as accuracy. The Elizabethan humanists understood students well, and the passages recommended for them to memorize and perform were full of passion. Schoolboys had to perform women's parts as well as men's. Popular passages included Niobe weeping over her children, Medea raving in her jealousy, Lucrece bewailing the loss of her chastity, or Achilles threatening revenge for the death of Patroclus. When Hamlet asks one of the players to perform "a passionate speech," and chooses Aeneas's tale to Dido describing the slaughter of Priam and the fall of Troy, he is struck by the actor's emotion over the grief of the mythic Hecuba: "What's Hecuba to him or he to Hecuba that he should weep for her?" Shakespeare is almost certainly recalling a schoolroom performance of a version of that very speech, and if it were performed to the satisfaction of the headmaster, it would have been performed with all of the passion of a stage actor. Just like today's drama students, Shakespeare and his classmates had to practice voice, tonal modulations, gestures, and facial expressions to convey emotional authenticity. They would recite tongue twisters to better their orthopoeia. They studied dance for strength and grace, singing for vocal agility, and fencing for physical alertness and timing. Just as the intensive study of rhetorical copia accounts for the protean quality of Shakespeare's poetry, rhetorical actio was fantastic training for his life in the theatre.

A Brief History of the Triangular Relationship of Rhetoric, Theatre, and Law

Many of Shakespeare's most devoted fans were lawyers and law students, the members of the Inns of Court. This was to be expected, because rhetoric, law, and theatre have always been companions in both admiring and suspicious minds. After all, a trait that, for better or for worse, links thespians, lawyers, and politicians is the ability to use language to persuasively influence or deceive an audience.

This history starts with the sophists. From the time of Homer, and presumably much earlier, the art of speaking well was greatly valued. In pre-literate societies—the many centuries when literacy belonged to a tiny few—song, poetry, and the spoken word were the basis of education. The skillful use of rhetoric put enormous power in hands of orators, and this created a demand. The earliest teachers of rhetoric that we know of were the sophists, who first emerged in the 6th century BC. They entered the history of philosophy in the incipient stages of Athenian democracy, when an emerging mercantile class was less interested in the universal truths of the pre-Socratic wisdom lovers (e.g. "philosophers") and more interested in power. Indeed, it was democracy that *created* sophistry. Democracy meant that there were rights and property to defend. Athens had become rich and litigious, and since justice and rights were accorded to all male, propertied individuals, it was the ones who made the best use of language and argument who prevailed in any power struggle.

> **Sophists are now known as the original relativists, who held that truth was in the mind of the believer.**

This was before anything existed that could be compared to a modern system of education. There were academies, like that of Plato and like Aristotle's Lyceum, but there were no universities. Most of the few, elite, male children who were educated got a few years of reading, writing, music, athletics, and perhaps a little arithmetic, but beyond the approximate age of 14 they were on their own. If they needed help learning how to navigate the system and they could pay, they might seek out a sophist. Anthony Gottlieb, in *The Dream of Reason*, describes the sophist as "ambassador, tutor, public-relations consultant, lecturer, stage entertainer, speech-writer, philosopher, after-dinner speaker, psychotherapist," in other words, a jack of all intellectual trades—and a performer.

Plato, in his *Dialogues*, has Socrates ask the sophist Protagoras what he teaches a student, and the answer comes in following exchange:

> The proper care of his personal affairs, so that he may best manage his own household, and also of the state's affairs, so as to become a real power in the city, both as speaker and as man of action.
>
> Do I follow you? Said I. I take you to be describing the art of politics, and promising to make good citizens.
>
> That, said he, is exactly what I profess to do.

The art of politics, the art of argument, is the art of rhetoric; and in a good world it does indeed make good citizens. But of course it can go both ways. In the courts, even as it is today, the decision of the jury goes to the best argument, and the best argument is not always the most honest one. There was a huge thirst and a need for citizens engaging in the public realm to acquire the skills of rhetoric, and sophists flocked to Athens to fill the demand and make a buck.

The most famous of the sophists are now known as the original relativists, who held that truth was in the mind of the believer. They differentiated between the immutable laws of nature and the changeable laws of man, and pointed out that they are often in conflict. They put man, instead of the natural world, at the center of philosophy. They are known today for such quotes as Protagoras' "Homo mensura," or "man is the measure of all things," Thrasymachus' "Justice is in the interest of the stronger," and Gorgias' "Speech is a powerful lord that with the smallest and most invisible body accomplishes most godlike works."

The sophists traveled around Greece teaching that access to power came not through truth and ethical behavior but through oratory: the art of swaying public opinion. Many of the sophists were perfectly decent fellows, but to the less *sophistic*ated, they were all talk and much deceit. In addition, they charged high fees and became quite rich, so they were viewed with the same mixture of admiration and distrust that today we tend to reserve for lawyers, and, historically, at times, for actors. For the sophists and their descendants, manipulation of political thought through language became a fine art. Today's politicians and political strategists may be very good at it, but they couldn't hold a candle to the sophists.

For Socrates, Plato, and Aristotle, our best-remembered, ancient philosophers, the subject of rhetoric was a contentious one. The reasons for the trial of Socrates were actually pretty complicated and political, but Plato blamed the sophists. It wasn't that the sophists were out to get him; it was because the five hundred citizen jurors at the trial actually thought *he* was a sophist himself. In that sense, it was sophism that was on trial, not Socrates. All that questioning and arguing and persuading and examining was getting out of control among the youth and was undermining the authority of the gods. Socrates tried to distance himself from the sophists. He pointed out that, unlike them, he charged no fees for his services, and he consistently claimed to have no wisdom of his own to impart. He thought the art of rhetoric was shallow and manipulative, unworthy of study. He also believed, like his student Plato and *unlike* the relativist sophists, that there are universal, immutable truths that apply to the laws of humanity. Nevertheless, he was accused of corrupting the youth of Athens by opening their minds, and for that he had to die.

Reading Plato's *Dialogues*, we also learn that Socrates had a scolding wife, Xanthippe, from whom Erasmus borrowed the name for his shrew in the colloquy earlier in this book, and it is easy to see what annoyed her. He seldom bathed, had no interest in making money, and went around Athens bothering people with endless roundabout questions and tying them into mental knots. From one perspective, one might easily draw the conclusion that the man who steered the focus of philosophy away from the natural world toward ethics and human behavior, where it has remained ever since, ended up being tried, condemned, and martyred for being a pain in the ass. At his sentencing, more of the jurors voted to put him to death than had voted to convict him in the first place! It sounds like they just wanted to shut him up.

Even aside from the scorn he had for their role in the death of Socrates, Plato was no friend of the sophists. Their relativist arguments conflicted with his ideal and eternal "forms." Underlying these forms, in Plato's thinking, going back to Pythagoras and Parmenides, were divine patterns and numbers, not language and words. As he aged, however, he moderated his view somewhat, and in *Phaedrus* he acknowledged that in the hands of a true philosopher, rhetoric could be used for "winning the soul through discourse."

Plato's student and successor, Aristotle, however, saw that there was no resisting the persuasive power of elevated language, and instead of dismissing rhetoric out of hand, he sought to tame it through structure. One of his greatest and most enduring achievements was the foundation of the study of logic. He is responsible for the inclusion of the art of persuasion and dialectic as two handmaidens to logic in supporting philosophic debate. His *Rhetoric*, assembled from the notes of his students, covers every aspect of its use, its purpose, its various audiences, and its ethical bearings. Every work on rhetoric since has in some ways reflected upon the thinking of Aristotle.

In Book I of *Rhetoric* we find the five most common types of deliberative rhetoric: finance, war and peace, national defense, imports and exports, and the framing of laws. But it is in Book II that we can best connect Aristotle to our theatre/law/rhetoric triangle. He does not delve as deeply as later writers did into delivery, only mentioning casually the necessity for pacing and tone, but in Book II he delineates the three means of persuasion that an orator must master: argument based on "ethos" (wisdom and credibility), argument based on "pathos" (emotion and psychology), and argument based on "logos" (reason). Of these, of course, pathos brings us closest to the dramatic skills that persuasive speaker must acquire in order to be effective.

The greatest of the Greek orators, Demosthenes, was enamored of the performative components of rhetoric, or "actio." He was not a sophist, he was essentially a lawyer pleading cases and persuading politicians. He was also an exact contemporary of Aristotle, and their paths must have crossed, but Aristotle was a philosopher and teacher and Demosthenes was a statesman, so they may have traveled in different worlds.

Plutarch, writing in his *Lives*, relates that after Demosthenes' first disastrous attempt at public speaking, an actor named Satyrus befriended him and taught him oratorical skills. Coached by Satyrus, he would go down to the ocean in a storm and shout over the clashing of the waves to strengthen his lungs. He would rehearse his speeches while running, to condition his breath control. He would practice them with his mouth full of stones to improve his articulation. If you watched an actor in training today you would see plenty of voice exercises that are not at all dissimilar to these.

Fast forward to Rome in the 1st century BC, where we find the *Rhetorica ad Herennium*, which was the first Latin text on rhetoric. This is also where we first get the five parts of an argument or essay: the *exordium* or introduction, followed by a *narratio* stating the facts of the case, a *divisio* (sometimes called *partitio*) outlining the thesis, a *confirmatio* laying out supporting evidence and arguments, a *confutatio* responding to counter arguments, and a *peroratio*, or conclusion. *Ad Herennium* was viewed at first with suspicion because rhetoric and oratory were seen as elitist political tools to be kept in the hands of the upper classes. Indeed, the publication of *ad Herennium* and the opening of the first school of rhetoric in Rome were part of a liberal, populist movement in education.

Cicero was by far the most famous of the Latin orators, and he lived and wrote during the tumultuous era of Roman history that Shakespeare addresses in *Antony and Cleopatra* and *Julius Caesar*. He spent a long life maneuvering the political minefield, wrote volumes, and was hugely influential; but he was eventually beheaded by agents of Mark Antony and Octavian. Among his writings are several on oratory and rhetoric. Most of what he had to say came from the Greeks and was not original, but he said it well, and because the study of Greek languished in medieval Europe, the earliest humanists got their grounding in rhetoric in Latin, from Cicero. His most famous work on rhetoric was *De inventione*, and he also wrote *Topics*, which dealt with the choice and structure of subject matter.

Like the Greek Demosthenes, Cicero modeled his style on that of an actor: his friend, Quintus Roscius Gallus. Roscius, in return, studied the delivery and gestures of the greatest advocates in the Forum. In *De copia*, Erasmus tells us that Roscius and Cicero engaged in a friendly rivalry, arguing whether the actor or the orator was better able to move an audience, and Roscius wrote a treatise comparing acting and oratory. Indeed, the differences between the two, having to do with storytelling and the audience's suspension of disbelief, are minor compared to the similarities. Any lawyer would do well to study acting, and any actor could learn from Clarence Darrow and other great orators of the law.

It was the works of Quintilian, however, that made the art of rhetoric accessible to students after the Renaissance. He was a 1st-century teacher of rhetoric who became hugely popular among the humanists. Much of his textbook on rhetoric, *Institutio Oratoria*, had been lost during the Middle Ages but was found in a monastery, in a dungeon, buried in rubbish and dust, by the humanist book collector Poggio Bracciolini, and was brought back to life. This twelve-chapter book was really a comprehensive treatise on education seeking to train the orator in rhetoric and character: "I should like the orator I am training to be a sort of Roman wise man." He was a great lover of Cicero and was critical of the imperial style used by Seneca, which he considered corrupt and dangerous because it "abounds in attractive faults." This was a quaint way of saying that rhetorical style can be used to disguise the truth as well as to reveal it. Quintilian agreed with Plato, who in *Phaedrus* wrote that a true rhetorician must be just. He quoted Cato the Elder, who defined rhetoric as "vir bonus, dicendi peritus," or "a good man speaking well." In other words, he was polishing up the tarnished image of rhetoric given to it by the sophists, who used it as a manipulative language capable of dissembling.

As we have already stated, Quintilian goes into great lengths in describing the proper training of the orator in the fifth canon. Actio—gesture, pacing, voice, tone, and empathic delivery—delineated the dramatic skills needed for a variety of orations and audiences.

As a student, Shakespeare would have studied the *Progymnasmata* by Aphthonius, a series of rhetorical writing exercises. The exercises were of ascending difficulty, starting with fables and followed by narrative, anecdote, maxim, refutation, confirmation, commonplace, encomium, invective, comparison, personification, description, thesis, and introduction to law, which concluded with an oratorical performance. Shakespeare would definitely have studied the *Progymnasmata* in school while learning to write and would have participated in his school's annual, dramatic oratorical competitions.

Despite Quintilian's defense of rhetoric as a skill to be used only by the just, by the time that George Puttenham published *The Art of English Poesy*, in 1589, its inherent tendency toward duplicity was pretty well accepted. Puttenham was blunt about it. So was Shakespeare. In *As You Like It*, when the country wench, Audrey, says to the ironical clown Touchstone, "I do not know what 'poetical' is: is it honest in deed and word?" Touchstone answers: "No, truly; for the truest poetry is the most feigning." Here Shakespeare is voicing a view also expressed repeatedly by Puttenham that poets are "makers" and "counterfeiters." Puttenham points out that figurative speech was often outlawed in Athenian courts of law because of its ability to distort the truth and that a courtier poet could be suspect because of the "subtleties of his art." In the chapter titled "Of Ornament," he says:

> As figures be the instruments of ornament in every language, so be they also, in a sort, abuses, or rather trespasses, in speech, because they pass the ordinary limits of utterance, and be occupied of purpose to deceive the ear and also the mind, drawing it from plainness and simplicity to a certain doubleness, whereby our talk is the more guileful and abusing.
>
> *(spelling updated)*

He also sees a courtier as a kind of actor, dissembling by playing different roles in different circumstances. He even fancifully personifies many of the figures he defines, giving them English names like characters in a play. Thus *etiologia* becomes "the Tell-cause"; *prozeugma* "the Ringleader"; *epizeuxis* "the Cuckoo-spell"; *meiosis* "the Disabler"; *paradoxon* "the Wonderer"; *hyperbole* "the Loud Liar, otherwise the Over-reacher; and *climax* "the Climber."

In the mind of Puttenham, the voice of truth would be simple, unadorned language—not poetry. But Puttenham also exalts the poet. In his opening chapters he calls poets "the first priests, the first prophets, the first legislators and politicians in the world" and goes on to claim that they were also "the first philosophers, the first astronomers, and historiographers, and orators, and musicians." Here he is in complete agreement with Erasmus. As we have seen, again and again, Erasmus tells us that in seeking the source of all knowledge and wisdom we need go no further than the ancient Greek, Latin, and Hebrew poets. In his eternal good heartedness, Erasmus tended to downplay the pitfalls that are endemic to rhetoric.

What should be noted here is that the study of rhetoric teaches the skills of persuasion, which sometimes involves deceit, *but it also teaches one to decipher the deceit in others*, which involves what we today would call critical thinking.

Let us take a contemporary example of the figure *enthymeme*. An enthymeme is a syllogism in logic that is supported by two premises, with a third, weaker premise that is assumed but unstated. Donald Trump used enthymeme masterfully, although, I suspect, unwittingly. He pointed out repeatedly that our borders are porous and that some who cross them illegally commit heinous crimes, like rape or murder. These two premises are true. The unstated assumption would be that undocumented immigrants commit these crimes at a much higher rate than native-born citizens. But that is *not* true. In fact the very opposite is true, but an audience not trained in rhetoric might not take the mental steps necessary to question the weakness of the third, unstated, premise. If everyone were trained in rhetoric, everyone would be more capable of critical thinking, and the power of politicians would be greatly diminished. Humanist curriculum was designed with exactly that goal in mind: to further the movement toward a just and equitable civilization.

In *A Midsummer Night's Dream*, Theseus warns us that "The lunatic, the lover, and the poet/Are of imagination all compact," and that their words are "More strange than true." To these three we must add the lawyer and the actor. Like poets, they use captivating phrases but cannot always be trusted.

Erasmus and His *De copia*

No one did more to focus attention on the elegant language of the ancients than Erasmus, but along with his profound regard for artistry in language, he frequently warned of the dangers of its misuse. In his colloquy *Pseudocheus and Philetymus: The Dedicated Liar and the Man of Honor*, between a dishonest book salesman and an upright client we find the following exchange:

Philetymus: Then why are liars commonly cursed, thieves even crucified?
Pseudocheus: Not because they lie or thieve but because they bungle the job or lack sufficient experience in the art.
Philetymus: Is there any writer who treats the *art* of lying?
Pseudocheus: Your rhetoricians have explained a good deal of it.
Philetymus: Their subject is eloquence.
Pseudocheus: True, but clever lying is a large part of eloquence.
Philetymus: What's clever lying?
Pseudocheus: You want a definition?
Philetymus: Yes!
Pseudocheus: Lying in such a way that you gain by it but can't be found out.
(Translated from the Latin original)

As a writer who treats the art of lying, Erasmus is here taking an amusing shot at himself. Let us now take a look at his foundational document of humanist education, written to give students the finest examples of rhetoric: *De copia rerum et verborum* (On Copia of Words and Ideas). There were well over one hundred and fifty editions of *De copia* published in the 16th century alone, and its influence pervades everything about the curriculum of the time, but it is hard to know which edition Shakespeare might have studied. Erasmus was continually editing and revising all of his works, and every time they were published they were a little different. He often seems to have dashed out changes, mostly additions, on a whim, citing examples that amused him at the moment, and the result is disorganized but highly engaging. Much of it is not original. He relied heavily on Quintilian and others, not always crediting them appropriately. He wanted students to be familiar with a vast array of writers, citing, among others, Apuleius, Aristophanes, Aulus Gillius, Cicero, Euripedes, Homer, Horace, Livy, Lucian, Macrobius, Martial, Ovid, Persius, Plautus, Quintilian, Sallust, Saint Jerome, Seneca, Terence, Varro, and Virgil. Whew! What *is* original is the tone of the book. Like everything by Erasmus, it is user-friendly—and fun.

De copia is divided into two books: one on copia of words and one on that of ideas. The first chapter of Book I opens with a familiar refrain: "That the aspiration to copia is dangerous." He quotes Socrates' warning, "The ability to lie and tell the truth cleverly are the talents of the same man," but he is not just referring to deceitfulness here. He is also concerned with amorphous loquacity, inanity, and pretention. Among his suggestions to avoid the latter is his recommended reading of Homer, "who is equally admirable at both—now copia, now brevity." This reminds me of the way that many of Shakespeare's most complex, rhetorical, and copious speeches begin and end with brief phrases of piercing clarity.

After a few chapters dealing with the intelligent use of copia and who should use it and when, he follows with twenty chapters on different methods of varying in writing, using figures that would have been familiar to Shakespeare and some that are familiar to us still today. He closes with a chapter on *Practice*, which includes what are probably the most famous four pages in the book: one hundred and fifty variations on the sentence, "I liked your letter." Here, in translation, are a few examples chosen at random:

> On reading your most loving letter I was seized with an unusual pleasure.
> What clover is to bees, what willow boughs are to goats, what honey is to the bear, your letter is to me.
> As soon as your letter came you would have seen me drunk with excessive joy.
> No dainty so caresses the palate as your letter charms my spirit.
> He carried a sea of joys who brought me your letter.
> *(Translated from the Latin original)*

There is playfulness here, a joy—a creative exuberance

Etc. etc. etc. for pages. What is wonderful about this is imagining the little Will Shakespeare endlessly inventing new ways to say simple things. There is an activity done in Shakespeare workshops and used by many English teachers where students are given long lists of Shakespearean curses and endearments, and they stand in lines across from each other, and call them out in different voices. This abundance of expression came from his training via Erasmus. There is playfulness here, a joy—a creative exuberance.

Book II deals with the copia of ideas, in which he details eleven methods of embellishing or expanding upon a simple phrase: "The first way to embellish thought is to relate at length and treat in detail something that could be expressed summarily and in general." He follows this with numerous examples showing amplification or enlarging upon a concept using allegories, fables, digressions, comparisons, examples from nature, and examples from law.

Some of his examples clearly reflect his own point of view. He was a great lover of Cicero, so he was *not* fond of Mark Antony, Cicero's political enemy and assassin. He manages to excoriate him twice, once filling a page with Caelius' description of Antony's drunken stupor, which is full of loathing and disgust, and then again from Cicero's second *Phillipic*, a long and vivid passage about his vomiting. Here Erasmus is cleverly teaching well-constructed Latin and at the same time greatly entertaining his adolescent readers. This view of Antony doesn't really show up in Shakespeare's *Julius Caesar*, but there are plenty of glimpses of it in *Antony and Cleopatra*.

One other example that Shakespeare clearly copied into his tables and remembered was from "The Fourth Method of Amplification": "enumerating the concomitant or resultant circumstances." He gives the example of the phrase: "We will charge the war to your account," and amplifies it as follows:

> You will be able to expand it in this way: A treasury exhausted against barbarian soldiers, a youth broken by hardships, crops trampled underfoot, herds driven off, burned villages and farms everywhere, fields lying waste, overturned walls, looted homes, pillaged shrines, so many childless old people, so many orphaned children, so many widowed matrons, so many virgins shamefully outraged, the character of so many young people ruined by license, such great sorrow, such great grief, so many tears, and moreover, the extinction of the arts, oppressive laws, the obliteration of religion, the chaos of all things human and divine, the government of the state corrupted, this whole array of evils that arises from war, I say, we shall lay to your charge alone, since indeed you were the author of the war.
>
> *(Translated from the Latin original)*

It is impossible to read this without reflecting on two speeches from Henry V. One is in the voice of William, a soldier who is speaking to the disguised king, not knowing the grave danger in which he is putting himself with such frank speech. Henry has defended their actions in war as being in the service of a just cause, and William responds:

> But if the cause be not good, the king himself hath a heavy reckoning to make, when all those legs and arms and heads, chopped off in battle, shall join together at the latter day and cry all 'We died at such a place;' some swearing, some crying for a surgeon, some upon their wives left poor behind them, some upon the debts they owe, some upon their children rawly left. I am afeard there are few die well that die in a battle; for how can they charitably dispose of any thing, when blood is their argument? Now, if these men do not die well, it will be a black matter for the king that led them to it; whom to disobey were against all proportion of subjection.
>
> Act IV, Scene i

Again, in Act V, during the peace negotiations between France and England, the Duke of Burgundy speaks:

> ... let it not disgrace me,
> If I demand, before this royal view,
> What rub or what impediment there is,
> Why that the naked, poor and mangled Peace,
> Dear nurse of arts and joyful births,
> Should not in this best garden of the world
> Our fertile France, put up her lovely visage?
> Alas, she hath from France too long been chased,
> And all her husbandry doth lie on heaps,
> Corrupting in its own fertility.
> Her vine, the merry cheerer of the heart,
> Unpruned dies; her hedges even-pleach'd,
> Like prisoners wildly overgrown with hair,
> Put forth disorder'd twigs; her fallow leas
> The darnel, hemlock and rank fumitory
> Doth root upon, while that the coulter rusts
> That should deracinate such savagery;
> The even mead, that erst brought sweetly forth
> The freckled cowslip, burnet and green clover,
> Wanting the scythe, all uncorrected, rank,
> Conceives by idleness and nothing teems
> But hateful docks, rough thistles, kecksies, burs,
> Losing both beauty and utility.
> And as our vineyards, fallows, meads and hedges,
> Defective in their natures, grow to wildness,
> Even so our houses and ourselves and children

> Have lost, or do not learn for want of time,
> The sciences that should become our country;
> But grow like savages—as soldiers will
> That nothing do but meditate on blood—
> To swearing and stern looks, diffused attire
> And every thing that seems unnatural.
> Which to reduce into our former favour
> You are assembled: and my speech entreats
> That I may know the let, why gentle Peace
> Should not expel these inconveniences
> And bless us with her former qualities.
>
> Act V, Scene ii

Ben Jonson once recalled that the players at the Globe often commented on the fact that Shakespeare wrote with such fluidity that he "never blotted out a line." His answer was "Would he had blotted a thousand." He then justifies this view, saying

> I loved the man, and do honor his memory on this side idolatry as much as any. He was, indeed, honest, and of an open and free nature; had an excellent fancy, brave notions, and gentle expressions, wherein he flowed with that facility that sometime it was necessary he should be stopped.... As Augustus said of Haterius. His wit was in his own power; would the rule of it had been so too.

> **Let us consider what was happening to Shakespeare's brain when he indulged and over-indulged and endlessly indulged in wordsmithing.**

The majority of my high school students would agree with Jonson, and very often I would agree with him myself, but how often do we get to see a play by Ben Jonson anymore? I love the passage because it gives a glimpse of Shakespeare at work. Once he got started he couldn't stop himself. It seems as though writing was a kind of play for him, a game he started at school collaborating with other classroom wits, and then just kept going. Perhaps he was having too much fun. And he learned it from *De copia*.

But let us consider what was happening to Shakespeare's brain when he indulged and over-indulged and endlessly indulged in wordsmithing. From the age of 7 on, Shakespeare was trained to craft language around dozens of rhetorical models. His entire education was in one way or another connected to figurative language. He was taught to speak it and to hear it, to react to it and to argue with it. He was ever rewarded for his nimbleness with language and the fluency of his thought. He was held to the highest standard, in school competitions and, professionally, in the critical reception of his audience. He excelled, but he was one among equals in an entire generation. There were those who wrote, those who spoke, those who observed those who listened, and all of them knew the linguistic, aesthetic, and ideological structures within which he was working. It was so deeply a part of the culture that even those who did not benefit from a formal education, even (like Grumio) those who were illiterate, recognized the structures, and as a result they were better thinkers.

What Happened?

What happened to the teaching of rhetoric? It is still used, of course, for better or for worse. Language still persuades in Machiavellian ways, and we encourage students to be alert to it under the umbrella of critical thinking, but why, after two thousand years of uninterrupted status in the core of education did its formal study get marginalized to college political science courses and law schools? Why did it fall away with the study of the ancient languages? The answer to that is complex and mostly beyond the scope of this book—a mixture of its perception as an elitist skill, of a loss of its perceived relevance, and of an increased standardization of English, which allows for less flexibility. But it also may have been partly because the age-old suspect nature of rhetoric finally caught up with it. Just for fun I actually typed the question into Google and had to laugh out loud at some of the answers. So little has changed. Distrust of rhetoric and rhetoricians (e.g. lawyers and politicians) is the same as it has always been, but in modern jargon. Here are a few comments, directly from the Internet:

> "Liberal teacher's [sic] unions don't want people to think critically. That [sic] way, gullible people can be convinced that a campaign commercial caused a shooting."
>
> "Same reason that Latin is no longer taught. We are becoming stupider. People just want a celebrity politician who can repeat a few phrases like a parrot."
>
> "Point being, if everyone learned at least a little bit about formal rhetoric, politicians wouldn't be able to get away with quite so much shit."
>
> "I find the art of rhetoric incredibly pointless and stupid. Rhetoric does not teach you proper grammar or spelling (those two are covered in normal English classes) but it teaches you how to speak handsomely. Why does one need to speak handsomely when one could use simple words and get the idea across in a modest way? More difficult words could be used in order to make your concepts more specific but not just for the sake of speaking 'handsomely'."

Of course many of the other comments were thoughtful and intelligent, and many lamented the demise of universal instruction in rhetoric. I have to agree with them. Call me a stuffy pedagogue, call me out of date, call me a liberal teacher, call me whatever you like, but please, at a time when we cannot expect civil language even from our president, *please* speak handsomely!

The artistry of speaking handsomely, of thoughtfully clarifying, formulating, and expressing ideas, elevates them and empowers them. It also preserves them for memory. Here lies the powerful impact of classroom theatrics. One remembers what one performs. Public performance of thoughts, arguments, and knowledge plays a vital role in locking in knowledge.

Even beyond the civilizing power of well-crafted speech and the effect on long-lasting memory there are the cognitive consequences of an education in rhetoric: the daily practice in mental flexibility, the loss of which I confess that I mourn. That is a regret Erasmus would certainly have shared with me. He would have been devastated to know that four hundred years after his death, the sustained study of rhetoric would have disappeared entirely from the classroom.

But young people will forever love novelty, and we need to take another look at the creativity and eloquence found in the jargons of some of our alienated teenagers, realizing, of course, that to some extent, *all* teenagers are alienated. We noted at the beginning of this chapter the inventiveness of the language of marginalized communities. My students were utterly mesmerized by the plays of August Wilson, who elevated Black English to the level of high literature, and in the writings of Zora Neale Hurston, Sapphire, Langston Hughes, and others there is a rich history of linguistic innovation. The seeds of this highly expressive language are the same as those of rhetoric: the need to find ever more novel ways of telling our stories.

> **Valuing the ever-changing slang of our youth would be a way of directly connecting our inventive students to the genius of Shakespeare, Erasmus, and the ancients.**

The use of rhetorical speech in Shakespeare's education was applied to the formal, classical curriculum in the classroom, but let us take another look at actio. Physical rhetoric, or acting skill, was not just evident in the oratorical declamations of Cicero, Seneca, and Ovid. A less eloquent, more commonplace use of it was regularly applied to the teaching of *conversational* language and an entirely different kind of playacting: the performance of the simple colloquies.

9
ERASMUS WRITES COLLOQUIES

FIGURE 9.1 Will performs a colloquy.

> Kings make war, priests are zealous to increase their wealth, theologians invent syllogisms, monks roam through the world, the commons riot, Erasmus writes colloquies.
> —*from Erasmus' colloquy:* The Cyclops

To quote Eric Booth once again: "Engagement before information"! First try performing this in Latin. The characters are **Antronius** and **Magdalia**.

Antronius: Quam hic ego supellectilum video?
Magdalia: Nonne elagantem?
Antronius: Nescio an elegantem; certe perum decorum matronae.
Magdalia: Quam ob rem?
Antronius: Quia librorum plena sunt omnia.
Magdalia: Tu, tantus natu, tum Abbas, nunquam vidisti libros in aedibus matronarum?
Antronius: Vidi, sed Gallice scriptos; hic video Graecos et Latinos.
Magdalia: An soli Gallice scripti libri docent sapientiam?
Antronius: Sed decet hoc matronas, ut habeant quo delectent otium.
Magdalia: An solis iis licet sapere et suaviter vivere?
Antronius: Male conectis sapere et suaviter vivere; non est muliebre sapere.
Magdalia: Nonne omnium est bene vivere?
Antronius: Opinor.
Magdalia: Quomodo potest autem suaviter vivere, qui non vivit bene?
Antronius: Immo quomodo potest suaviter vivere, qui vivit bene?
Magdalia: Ergo tu probas eos qui vivunt male, modo suaviter?
Antronius: Arbitror illos bene vivere qui vivunt suaviter.

This is the beginning of one of my favorite colloquies by Erasmus: *Abattis et eruditae*. It is between an ignorant and venal clergyman and a clever woman who was based on Sir Thomas More's eldest daughter, the brilliant Meg. Now read my adapted translation. If you have a partner, read the Latin and English side by side. It opens with words a bit like the opening words of Edward Albee's *Who's Afraid of Virginia Wolfe*:

Antronius: What a dump! What is this mess?
Magdalena: Isn't my room neat enough for you?
Antronius: I don't know how neat it is, but I'm sure it is not very becoming, either for a maid or a matron.
Magdalena: Why?
Antronius: Because there are *books* lying about everywhere.
Magdalena: What, have you lived this long as an abbot and a courtier and never seen books in a lady's apartment?
Antronius: Yes, I've seen books, but they were in French. Here I see Greek and Latin ones.

Magdalena:	Are French books the only ones that teach wisdom?
Antronius:	What do you want with wisdom? Ladies should want diversion, something to pass away their leisure hours.
Magdalena:	Must ladies not be wise and enjoy life?
Antronius:	Don't connect wisdom with enjoying life. Women have no need of wisdom. Girls just want to have fun.
Magdalena:	Shouldn't everyone live well?
Antronius:	Of course.
Magdalena:	Who can have fun without living well?
Antronius:	What fun is it to live well?!
Magdalena:	So you approve of those who live badly as long as they're enjoying themselves?
Antronius:	I think those who have fun are living well!

That wasn't so hard, was it? Did you learn any Latin? I did. In fact, if I ever take seven years off to learn Latin, I will start with colloquies.

Shakespeare is often noted for all of his spirited women and his mocking wenches who show up in just about every one of his comedies (think Kate, Bianca, Adriana, Luciana, Rosaline, Maria, Katherine, Rosalind, Viola, Beatrice for starters), but we shall see that Erasmus' witty and opinionated women were mocking their male counterparts decades before Shakespeare was even born. This particular wench continues to bait her vacuous clergyman until she can't contain her laughter. At the very end of the conversation there is this exchange:

Antronius:	I have often heard it said that a wise woman is twice a fool.
Magdalena:	That indeed has been often said; but it was by fools. A woman that is truly wise does not think herself so. On the contrary, one that knows nothing thinks herself to be wise, and that is being twice a fool.

For good measure, here it is in Latin. This is how young Will would have performed it:

Antronius:	Audivi vulgo dici feminam sapientum bis stultam esse.
Magdalena:	Hoc quidem dici solet, sed a stultis. Femina quae vere sapit non videtur sibi sapere; contra quae, cum nihil sapit, sibi sapere, ea demum bis stulta est.

He must have remembered it when he wrote *As You Like It*. Erasmus was paraphrasing a passage from Socrates' futile search for a wise man here, and I appreciate that he put it into the voice of a woman. It appears again in the voice of Shakespeare's sardonic fool Touchstone, who says, "The fool does think himself to be wise, but the wise man knows himself to be a fool." I like to think

Shakespeare first encountered that sentiment in the classroom, not from Socrates but from Erasmus.

It is obvious that by the time Shakespeare left school, no matter what his tenacity may have been as a student, he knew enough classical Latin to intimidate most graduate students today. But along the way he also had to become fluent in casual, conversational Latin. As Quintilian advised, "The more common phrases suitable for play, for social life, for mealtimes, must be early learned and be apt and ready to hand." It wasn't enough to recite with authentic emotion passages memorized from Ovid, with all their passionate and sexy undertones: he had to be able to *chat* in Latin—to banter and joke around—and a common practice for the mastery of Latin conversation was the performance of colloquies.

We now have a pretty good idea of what the formal curriculum in humanist schools was, but when we come to the colloquies, we begin to explore what I will call the *informal* curriculum. While Shakespeare's great dramatic poetry may have been inspired by Ovid, Plutarch, Horace, Seneca, and the lot, the writing in his colloquial scenes came from another source. We might roughly compare the performance of colloquies to today's after-school activities, clubs, field trips, games, and other enrichment opportunities designed for students to extend their school learning. Brinsley himself recommended the standard long reading list of classical works, and then: "to all these may be added for them who have leisure enough, the reading of Erasmus' *Colloquia*," noting that these gave great delight. Shakespeare was certainly an example of a student who would have had leisure enough, and much delight they must have given him!

Extra-curricular activities are often are the most engaging and even the most life-changing experiences of the school years, but—perhaps because they give pleasure and don't feel like work—they are marginalized. Not many Shakespeare scholars have scrutinized closely the use of colloquies in the classroom. Foster Watson gives the best description of them that I've found, but he published his book in 1908. Since then, not much attention has been paid to them. Baldwin did not take them seriously enough to spend more than a few pages on them, and it seems nobody else has since. Maybe this is because they were not noted for their rhetorical eloquence, or because they were strictly classroom practice activities and were never performed in public. We forget that they, too, demanded performance skills.

Erasmus certainly did *not* invent colloquies! Their pedagogical use has a long history. No one knows exactly how Plato's *Dialogues* were used, whether they were read aloud by students or *for* students. Some believe they may have been performed by slaves for dinner entertainment. Either way, they were clearly used in Plato's Academy to instruct students in philosophy. He, in turn, was using a convention already established by Xenophon, Saphron, and probably many others.

Lucian, one of Erasmus' favorites, composed many of his satirical works as dialogues. He was not a schoolmaster or the head of an academy, but he was noted, among other things, for traveling about giving amusing and, presumably, instructive lectures, so we may include his dialogues as instructional material. They were listed in many grammar school statutes for the upper forms, and students may have encountered them when they embarked on the study of Greek or in Erasmus' Latin translation. I have excerpted passages from one that I found to be topical. It is a defense of dance, pantomime, and theatre by one Lycinus, who is arguing with his too-sober friend Crato:

Lycinus: Here are heavy charges, Crato; I suppose you have been fretting about this subject for some time. You are not content with attacking the whole pantomimic art, practical and theoretical. We too, the happy spectators thereof, come in for our share. We have been lavishing our admiration, it seems, on effeminate triflers. Let me prove to you how completely you have been mistaken. You will find that the art you have been maligning is the greatest boon of our existence. I will allow that there is some excuse for your strictures: how would you know any better, confirmed ascetic that you are, believing that virtue consists in being bored?

Crato: Now, my dear sir, can anyone who calls himself a man, and an *educated* man, and in some sort a student of philosophy, leave those higher pursuits, leave communing with the sages of old, to sit still and listen to the sound of a flute, and watch the antics of an effeminate creature got up in soft raiment to sing lascivious songs and mimic the passions of strumpets . . . to the accompaniment of twanging string and shrilling pipe and clattering heel? It is too absurd! These are not amusements for a gentleman; not amusements for Lycinus. When I first heard of your spending your time in this way, I was divided betwixt shame and indignation, to think that you could so far forget Plato and Chrysippus and Aristotle, as to sit thus having your ears tickled with a feather. If you want amusements, are there not a thousand things *worth* seeing and hearing? . . . Things that have been deemed worthy of state recognition? My friend, you have a long reckoning to settle with men of learning, if you would not be repudiated altogether, and expelled from the congregation of the wise. I think your best course will be a point-blank denial: declare flatly that you never did anything of the kind. Anyhow, you must watch your conduct for the future: we do not want to find that our Lycinus has changed his sex, and become a Bacchante or a Lydian damsel. Yours is a captivity of ear and eye, of body and soul.

Lycinus: Goodness gracious! All the cynic in you is loose, and snarls at me. But I think your Lotus-and-Siren simile is rather off the point: you see, the people who ate the Lotus and listened to the Sirens paid for the gratification of ear and palate with their lives: whereas I not only have a great deal more enjoyment than they had, but am all the better for it. I have experienced no oblivion of my domestic affairs, nor blindness to my own interests; in fact—if I may venture to say so—you *will find my penetration and practical wisdom considerably increased by my theatrical experiences.* Homer has it exactly: the spectator returns a *gladder and a wiser man.*

(*Translated from the Greek original*)

It is immediately apparent why Erasmus had such and affinity with Lucian. They both scorned the notion that pleasure could not be accompanied by wisdom. The one who delights in experience is a gladder and wiser man. And any drama teacher today would agree with Lycinus about how the penetration of thought and practical wisdom are increased by experience with theatre.

The use of colloquies to teach conversational Latin also goes far back in time. Long before printed material was ubiquitous, education was almost entirely oral, and colloquies would have used extensively in teaching conversation. Late in the 10th century Abbot Ælfric at Cerne Abbey in Devon wrote colloquies for his students to describe the functions of various trades. A student would take one of the following roles: ploughman, shepherd, oxherd, hunter, fisherman, birdcatcher, merchant, tanner, baker, cook, or lawyer—a nifty panoply of 10th-century

FIGURE 9.2 Students prepare to recite their lessons in a 15th-century classroom.
Source: William Caxton's "Mirror of the World."

occupations. He would then perform a dialogue about the role with the teacher. They're fun to read. Here, for instance, is a translation of the dialogue with the bird catcher:

Teacher: What have you to say, birdman? Tell us how you catch birds?
Bird catcher: I have many ways of catching birds. Sometimes I use nets, sometimes snares, sometimes lime, sometimes by using a decoy, sometimes with hawks and sometimes traps.
Teacher: Do you have any hawks?
Bird catcher: Oh, yes, I do.
Teacher: Do you know how to tame them?
Bird catcher: Indeed I do. What use would they be to me if I did not know how to tame them?
Teacher: Give me one of your hawks.
Bird catcher: I would give you one with pleasure if you gave me one of your fast hounds in exchange. Which hawk would you prefer, the bigger or the smaller one?
Teacher: Give me the bigger one. How do you feed your hawks?
Bird catcher: In winter they feed both themselves and me, but in the spring I set them free to fly away to the woods, and in the autumn, I catch young birds and tame them.
Teacher: But why do you let your birds fly away from you?
Bird catcher: Because I do not want to feed them in summer. They eat too much.
Teacher: But many men feed their tame hawks in summer in order to have them ready.
Bird catcher: Indeed, they do, but I do not want to have the task of looking after them.

(Translated from the Latin original)

These early conversation would probably have been between a teacher and one student at a time, but once printed texts were available there could be dialogues with two or more student players. In the humanist curriculum of the 16th century, colloquies came to resemble short plays. By far the three most common collections of colloquies to be shared in that way were those of Maturinus Corderius, Juan Luis Vives, and Erasmus.

Part of the fun of reading these educational colloquies is that they give you a glimpse into the schoolboy worlds of the time. Corderius and Vives are fascinating reading for those who would like to see idealized examples of what pious, studious, and well-mannered schoolboys might have been saying to each other back then: conversations about the purchase of penknives, for instance, or the travels of parents, or various routes to school through various neighborhoods.

Corderius had been Calvin's teacher, and his colloquies are the most theological and morally upright. They also used the most simplified language, so they would have been introduced to the little ones in the first or second forms along with the paternoster and the sententiae. Here is an example of a dialogue between two students, A and B, in Latin and in translation:

In Latin

A: Quid repetis?
B: Pensum qued praeceptor preserepsit nobis hodie.
A: Tenesne memoria?
B: Sic opinor.
A: Repetamus uni, sic uterque nostrum pronuncavit rectius coram praeceptore.
B: Incipe tu igitur, que provacasti me.
A: Age, esto attendtus, ne sinas me aberiare.
B: Sum promptior ad audiendum, quam tu ad pronunciandum.

Translated

A: What are you doing?
B: I am repeating myself.
A: What are you repeating?
B: The speech that our master set us today.
A: Do you retain it in memory?
B: I think so.
A: Let us repeat it together, thus each of us will say it the better before the master.
B: Begin you then, you who have challenged me.
A: Come on, be attentive that you do not suffer me to go wrong.
B: I am readier to hear than you are to speak.

They gradually grow in difficulty, but remain fairly proper and humdrum. It is not likely they engaged the imagination of a student like little Will.

The colloquies of Vives come next. Vives was one of the greatest of the humanists, much admired by Erasmus, who believed he would be remembered far longer than he himself would be. His colloquies are a bit more amusing. Here, for example, is an excerpt from the beginning of a conversation in translation, involving boys with Roman names: Tulliolus and Corneliola. It is titled *Reditus domum et lusus puerilis*, or The Return Home and Children's Play, and the entire colloquy gives an account of different kinds of childhood diversions:

Corneliola: Welcome home Tulliolus, shall we play some games?
Tulliolus: Not just now.
Corneliola: What is there to prevent us playing?
Tulliolus: We must go over again what the master set, and commit it to memory, as he bade us.

Corneliola:	What then?
Tulliolus:	You just look at this.
Corneliola:	I say, what are these pictures? I believe they are pictures of ants. Mother, Tulliolus is bringing home a lot of ants and gnats painted on a writing tablet.
Tulliolus:	Be quiet you silly thing. They are letters.
Corneliola:	What do you call this first one?
Tulliolus:	A.
Corneliola:	Why is this first one rather than the next one called "A"?
Mother:	Why art thou Corneliola and not Tulliolus?
Corneliola:	Because I am so called.
Mother:	And it is just the same way with those letters. But go and play now, my boy.
Tulliolus:	I am putting my tablet and stylus down. If anyone disturbs them, he will be beaten by mother. Won't he, mommy.
Mother:	Yes, my boy.
Tulliolus:	Let's go play!

This is followed by dialogues about the game of nuts, the game of odd and even, and the games of dice, draughts, and cards. All fun activities, certainly, but performing conversations about them would hardly have excited the restless imagination of a young Shakespeare.

But then came Erasmus! In the third or fourth form, when he was 8 or 9, Shakespeare would have encountered the *Colloquia familiaria*, or the "Familiar Colloquies," by our old friend. They are not listed in *De copia* and, in fact, initially, Erasmus may have been mildly embarrassed by them. They were like an illegitimate child who did well and was a credit to his parents, but not at all the way the parents intended! They might well have been literary companions to the earthy paintings of villagers and peasants by Bruegel. Up until Erasmus, colloquies were primarily schoolboy conversations. Erasmus turned them into spicy comic dramas.

Colloquia familiaria consisted of conversations Erasmus himself engaged in or overheard in his wide travels, with common people, many of whom would *not*, in fact, have conversed in Latin but in the vernacular of whatever country he was in at the time. It is commonly believed that Erasmus spoke only Latin when he traveled outside of Holland and Germany, but I suspect he picked up quite a bit of the vernacular in France, Italy, and England, all of which nations provide settings for his colloquies. They covered a wide range of topics contemporary to the time and place. They scandalized some in the clergy, who found them to be pernicious and heretical. It didn't help that they found in them thinly veiled caricatures of themselves in scathing parodies of corrupt monks, friars, and abbots. Erasmus had to defend his comic scenes against censure by the clerics at the Sorbonne, which he did in a delightful letter titled *The Usefulness of the Colloquies*, wherein we find this defense:

> Socrates brought philosophy down from heaven to earth; I have brought it even into games, informal conversations, and drinking parties.
>
> *(Translated from the Latin original)*

The scorn of the conservative clerics is understandable considering some of the content: Erasmus certainly intended them to be moral lessons, but his route to the moral was not always a direct one. Even Baldwin questions his choices: "We may have our doubts about the edification of such passages for boys of eight or so, but evidently Erasmus and the sixteenth century had not." How then did they become classroom staples?

The short answer to that question is that they were fun! Even a quick look at the *Colloquia* reveals the reason why they were so popular. Many of them are raunchy, ironical, witty, and off-color (Erasmus knew his audience, and the occasional fart joke surely delighted his youthful Latin scholars and guaranteed that his dialogues would migrate onto the schoolyard and beyond). In fact, although they were written half a century before Shakespeare was born, they now seem more than a bit "Shakespearean." Young Will certainly had a quick and retentive mind but it is quite possible that he was not an overly bookish child; in *Soul of the Age*, for instance, Jonathan Bate notes that he pulled most of his early literary influences, from Ovid and others, from the beginnings of the readings, as though he were too impatient to finish them. Performing the *Colloquia* with his schoolmates, however, would definitely have engaged him and his spirited classmates.

Erasmus, like all great minds (in my humble opinion), had a terrific sense of humor. As a young man studying in Paris in the 1490s, he took on some work as a tutor, and he had the novel idea that students should have some fun along with their studies. He started writing colloquies to amuse them. He didn't take them seriously at the time, and there is no evidence that he even saved them. Some of his students, however, kept them, and in 1518 they were published in Basel, without his permission and much to his annoyance. He eventually got over his pique, probably because they were so immensely popular and sold so well. So in the 1520s, perhaps as a distraction from the cataclysm that was Luther, he began to employ the genre as a way to informally expound upon his humanist views on society and religion. Think of them as "A Young Person's Guide to Humanism."

Here we must remind ourselves again that early on, Erasmus and Luther were seen as on a parallel trajectory, both highly critical of the corrupt clergy and the religious hierarchy. In their early careers they corresponded and even appeared to admire each other's views. Luther was excommunicated, but Erasmus remained as an internal reformer, and the split did not come until the mid-1520s. The final rupture between them was over the issue of free will: Erasmus was the free will man, and Luther the predestination man. Erasmus remained a

Catholic, but he did not bend to the power structure that had a firm hold on the orthodoxy of most of Europe. His colloquies are full contempt for the trappings of organized religion. He was an Augustinian monk himself, although not attached to a monastery, but some of the most fiercely satirical exchanges in the colloquies involve foolish and corrupt men of the cloth. This, of course, made them particularly popular in Protestant England, where the Tridentine Index held no threat.

Between 1520 and 1533 several authorized and expanded versions of the *Colloquia familiaria* appeared, and the collection grew to include more than fifty. They were republished eighty-nine times before Erasmus died and continued to sell in huge numbers thereafter. They entered the curriculum of grammar schools throughout all of Britain, where a lion's share of the editions were sold.

As we saw in the chapter devoted to him, Erasmus advocated learning through experience and practice. In *De ratione studii* he quotes Cicero: "The best teacher of style is the pen." Learn to write by writing, he says, and learn to speak by speaking. And so, using his colloquies, a young child might begin speaking Latin with simple greetings: "Salve pater," "Salve mi frater" ("greetings father," "greetings brother"), and quickly graduate to "Salve vini pernicies," "Salve et tu, gurges helluoque placentarum" ("greetings consumer of quart-sized pots of wine," "greetings back to you, glutton who devours cakes into the bottomless pit of your stomach"—think Falstaff!). From thence he would advance to fanciful conversations involving shipwrecks, new mothers, tall-tale storytellers, horse cheats, corrupt clerics, deceitful lawyers, prostitutes, entertaining dinner guests, and all manner of common and particular folk.

Because of their informal nature, the *Colloquia* were not always listed with the other Latin readings, but according to the school statutes that still exist, where they were listed, they were most commonly introduced in the third or fourth form. Baldwin points out that they are listed in four out of five of the statutes that he examined, and when they were not listed it does not mean that they were not included, only that they were not as highly valued. Some statutes even list the time of day and the days of the week that they would have been performed. To give one example: a 1568 copy of Westminster School's statutes, which would have been typical, indicate that they were performed for one hour, every Wednesday and Thursday, at 10:00 AM.

Listed or not, the books were purchased in huge numbers and they were evidently a staple commodity in every grammar school in the realm. There is no reason to doubt that they were used at the Stratford Grammar School when Shakespeare was a student; and, for that matter, if the oft-quoted comment from Aubrey, that Shakespeare was "in his younger years, a schoolmaster in the country" is true, he would have used them to teach his own students. Those who have taught school, know that what we teach adheres to the memory more closely than what we study. To quote *De ratione studii* again: "I urge, as undeniably the surest method of acquisition, the practice of teaching what we know."

William Shakespeare would have studied Lily's *Latin Grammar* and would have performed the colloquies of Corderius, Vives, and some of the simpler *Colloquia Erasmi* under the instruction of Simon Hunt or an usher, but from the ages of 10 to 16, in the fourth to final forms of schooling, he would have been under the guidance of the schoolmaster Thomas Jenkins. If he remained for another year at Stratford Grammar, he would have studied under John Cotham.

Certainly some schoolmasters were more attentive to performance than others, and we do not know what kind of teacher Hunt was; but Richard Mulcaster's students, Jenkins and Cotham among them, we may fairly assume, were expertly trained at Merchant Taylors'. They would have insisted, in turn, that *their* students, to quote Hamlet, "suit the action to the word, the word to the action." If so, with students like young Will, we may envision a lively classroom indeed. There is no reason to think that the same training in physical rhetoric required for the dramatic interpretation of classical oratory would not have been applied to the lowly colloquies.

Because we do not have the statutes from Stratford Grammar, we do not have conclusive evidence that Erasmus' *Colloquia* were used there, but the proof is in the textual pudding. Remember that only a very few of them were published in translation in Shakespeare's lifetime, so if he did encounter them it would have been in Latin, in school, and he would have performed them. He probably had to translate them himself because of the common practice of translating the same material back and forth, so he may have performed his translations in Latin *and* in English. Either way, they clearly stayed in his mind. When I read them, knowing Shakespeare's plays as I do, the resonances, or what I will call "echoes," leap out at me.

Let us start with more examples of Erasmus' many witty women. We've already looked at Erasmus' three-legged-stool-brandishing shrew and his clever learned woman, Magdalia, but they are not the only ones who appear in his colloquies. In fact, like Shakespeare, every female character he creates has a jousting spirit. His admiration for their ability to match wits with men is expressed in this exchange from a colloquy we will look at more closely later:

Eutrapelus: I see you are bent on single combat. For that reason, I think I'd better yield for the present . . . for where wars are fought with words, not even seven men are a match for one woman.
Fabulla: Yes, nature armed us with this weapon.

(Translated from the Latin original)

Erasmus was a priest, whether he liked it or not, so he was not married, and he seldom mentions women in his letters. He had a patron and close friend who was a woman, married to a dissolute man. It was she who requested that he write *Enchiridion militis Christiani*, the "Handbook of the Christian Soldier," for her husband. He was also well acquainted with Thomas More's daughters. But we don't know much else about his relations with the opposite sex. What is clear is that he liked and appreciated women who had some gumption. He certainly advocated for their education, and he must have enjoyed their conversations because so many have been enshrined in his colloquies.

The following excerpt is from the beginning of *Proci et puellae* (A Lover and a Maiden). Here the proci is named Pamphilus and the puellae is Maria. Again, imagine two children performing this scene. I will interrupt the colloquy occasionally to insert what I will call a resonance or "echo" from one of Shakespeare's plays. Remember that Will would have performed all the following colloquies in Latin, not English.

Pamphilus: Good morrow, Madam, cruel, hard heart, inflexible.
Maria: Good morrow to you, Mr. Pamphilus, as often and as much, and by what names you please: But you seem to have forgotten my name. It's Maria.
Pamphilus: It should rather have been Martia.
Maria: Why so? What is Mars to me?
Pamphilus: Because just as Mars makes a sport of killing men, so do you; saving that you do it the more cruelly of the two, because you kill one that loves you.
Maria: Say you so! Pray where's the great slaughter of men that I have made? Where's the blood of the slain?
Pamphilus: You may see one dead corpse before your face if you look upon me.
Maria: What strange story is this? Does a dead man talk and walk? I wish I may never meet with a more frightful ghost than you are.
Pamphilus: Ay, indeed, you make a jest of it; but for all that, you kill poor me, and more cruelly too than if you stuck a dagger in my breast. For now, I, poor wretch as I am, die a lingering death.
Maria: Prithee tell me, how many women with child have miscarried at the sight of you?

(Echo) *As You Like It*

Silvius: Sweet Phebe, do not scorn me; do not, Phebe;
Say that you love me not, but say not so
In bitterness. The common executioner,
Whose heart the accustom'd sight of death makes hard,
Falls not the axe upon the humbled neck
But first begs pardon: will you sterner be
Than he that dies and lives by bloody drops?
Phebe: I would not be thy executioner:
I fly thee, for I would not injure thee.
Thou tell'st me there is murder in mine eye:
'Tis pretty, sure, and very probable,

> That eyes, that are the frail'st and softest things,
> Who shut their coward gates on atomies,
> Should be call'd tyrants, butchers, murderers!
> Now I do frown on thee with all my heart;
> And if mine eyes can wound, now let them kill thee:
> Now counterfeit to swoon; why now fall down;
> Or if thou canst not, O, for shame, for shame,
> Lie not, to say mine eyes are murderers!
> Now show the wound mine eye hath made in thee:
> Scratch thee but with a pin, and there remains
> Some scar of it; lean but upon a rush,
> The cicatrice and capable impressure
> Thy palm some moment keeps; but now mine eyes,
> Which I have darted at thee, hurt thee not,
> Nor, I am sure, there is no force in eyes
> That can do hurt.
>
> Act III, Scene ii

or, also from *As You Like It*

Orlando: Then, in mine own person, I die.
Rosalind: No, faith, die by attorney. The poor world is almost six thousand years old and in all this time there was not any man died in his own person, in a love-cause. . . .. Men have died from time to time, and worms have eaten them, but not for love.

Act IV, Scene i

Pamphilus: My paleness shows I have no more blood in my body than a ghost.
Maria: Indeed, you are as pale as a violet; you are as pale as a ripe cherry, or a purple grape.
Pamphilus: You coquet it with my misery!

(Echo)

Rosalind: There are none of my uncle's marks upon you: he taught me how to know a man in love; in which cage of rushes I am sure you are not prisoner.
Orlando: What were his marks?
Rosalind: A lean cheek, which you have not, a blue eye and sunken, which you have not, an unquestionable spirit, which you have not, a beard neglected, which you have not.

Maria: If you can't believe me, look in the glass.

Pamphilus:		I would never desire a better glass, nor do I believe there is a better in the world than I am looking in already.
Maria:		What looking glass do you mean?
Pamphilus:		Your eyes.

(Echo) *The Taming of the Shrew*

Petruchio:	Nay, come good Kate, come, you must look not so sour.
Kate:	It is my fashion when I see a crab.
Petruchio:	Why here is no crab; and therefore look not sour.
Kate:	There is, there is!
Petruchio:	Then show it to me.
Kate:	Had I a glass I would.
Petruchio:	What, you mean my face?
Kate:	Well aimed for such a young one.

Maria:	You banterer! That's just like you. But how do you prove yourself to be dead. Do dead folks eat?
Pamphilus:	Yes, they do; but things that have no relish, as I do.
Maria:	What feed upon?
Pamphilus:	Mallows, leeks, and lupines.
Maria:	But you feed upon capons and partridges.
Pamphilus:	If I do, I relish them no more than beets without pepper or vinegar.
Maria:	Poor creature! But yet you're in pretty good health, for all that. And do dead folks talk too?
Pamphilus:	Yes, just as I do, with a weak voice.
Maria:	But when I heard you rallying your rival a little while ago, your voice was loud enough then. But prithee, do ghosts walk, wear clothes, and sleep?
Pamphilus:	Yes, and enjoy one another too, after their manner.
Maria:	Thou art a merry fellow.

This flirtatious and teasing tone continues, with some rather overt sexual innuendo on both sides. There is even a passage that presages the purple flower in *A Midsummer Night's Dream* describing a poison dart that causes a beautiful and wealthy young woman to fall in love with a monster, as Titania falls in love with Bottom. It is impossible to think it is not, at the very least, a flint letting off sparks that led us to the banterings of Kate, Rosalind, Beatrice, Viola, Olivia, Portia, Emilia, and Titania.

Yet another example of feminine wit, this time that of a prostitute defending her profession, finds its way from *Adolescentis et scorti* (The Teenager and The Whore) directly to Shakespeare's most lovable lowlife character, Sir John Falstaff, defending his thievery. Here Sophronius tries to persuade the prostitute Lucretia, to go give up her occupation:

Lucretia: O brave! My pretty Sophronius, have I gotten you again? It is an age methinks since I saw you. I did not know you at first sight.

Sophronius: Why so, my Lucretia?

Lucretia: Because you had no beard when you went away, but now you've come back with something of a beard. What's the matter my little heart, you look duller than you used to?

Sophronius: I want to have a little talk with you in private.

Lucretia: Ah, ah, are we not by ourselves already, my Cocky?

Sophronius: Let us go out of the way somewhere, into a more private place.

Lucretia: Come on then, we'll go into my inner bed-chamber, if you have a mind to do anything.

Sophronius: I don't think this place is private enough yet.

Lucretia: How comes it that you're so bashful all of a sudden? Well, come, I have a closet where I lay up my clothes, a place so dark that we can scarce see one another there.

Sophronius: See if there be no chink.

Lucretia: There is not so much as a chink.

Sophronius: Is there nobody near to hear us?

Lucretia: Not so much as a fly, my dear; why do you lose time?

Sophronius: Can we escape the eye of God here?

Lucretia: No, He sees all things clearly.

Sophronius: And of the angels?

Lucretia: No, we cannot escape their sight.

Sophronius: How comes it then, that men are not ashamed to do that in the sight of God, and before the face of the holy angels, that they would be ashamed to do before men?

Lucretia: What sort of alteration is this? Did you come hither to preach a sermon? Prithee, put on a Franciscan's hood and get up into a pulpit, and then we'll hear you hold forth, my little bearded rogue.

Sophronius: I should not think much to do that, if I could but reclaim you from this kind of life, that is the most shameful and miserable life in the world.

Lucretia: Why so good man? I am born and I must be kept; every one must live by his calling. This is my vocation; this is all I have to live on.

(Echo) *Henry IV Part I* re: Falstaff's thievery

Prince Hal: I see a good amendment of life in thee; from praying to purse-taking.

Falstaff: Why Hal, 'tis my vocation, Hal! 'Tis no sin for a man to labor in his vocation.

I might add here another echo, from Othello. When Sophronius says, "Can we escape the eye of God here?" I can't help but hear Iago: "In Venice they do let heaven see the pranks they dare not show their husbands; their best conscience is not to leave't undone, but keep't unknown."

The sparrings of saucy women also appear in the colloquy *Puerpera* (The New Mother) quoted earlier. Eutrapelus, a painter, engages a young woman with a new baby boy in a clever banter about child-rearing that covers everything from the importance of nursing one's own child to education in civility and the classics. Fabulla, the new mother, puts up a spunky defense on both sides of the argument of "custom" when questioned by Eutrapelus. What emerges from the discussion are Erasmus' humanist views on childcare. Fabulla stands up for women too! Here she counters his suggestion that she was fortunate to have had a boy rather than a girl:

Fabulla: What men think most urgent may seem insignificant to God. But let's exclude God from this cast, if you will. Tell me: what are your reasons for believing it's more blessed to have a lad than a lass?

Eutrapelus: It's a duty to consider this the best because God, who is beyond question best, gave it. Now if God gave you a crystal cup, wouldn't you thank him heartily?

Fabulla: I would.

Eutrapelus: What if he gave you one of glass instead? You wouldn't thank him quite so much, would you?—But I fear I'm a bother rather than a comfort wrangling over these questions with you.

Fabulla: Not at all! Fabulla is in no danger from fables. I've been in bed a month now, and I'm strong enough to wrestle.

Eutrapelus: Then why don't you fly out of the nest?

Fabulla: The king forbade.

Eutrapelus: King who?

Fabulla: A tyrant rather.

Eutrapelus: Who, I ask?

Fabulla: In a word, custom.

Eutrapelus: Ah, how many unjust demands that king makes! Let's go on discussing crystal and glass then.

Fabulla: I suppose you think man is naturally better and stronger than a woman.

Eutrapelus: So I believe.

Fabulla: On the authority of men, to be sure. Men aren't therefore longer lived than woman, are they? Not immune to disease?

Eutrapelus: Not at all. But they generally excel in strength.

Fabulla: But they themselves are excelled by camels.

Eutrapelus: Well, but the male was created first.

Fabulla: Adam was created before Christ. And artists usually surpass themselves in their later works.

Eutrapelus: But God made woman subject to man.

Fabulla: A ruler's not better merely because he's a ruler. And it's the wife, not the female, who's subject. Again, the subjection of the wife is such that, though each has power over the other, nevertheless the woman is to obey the man not as a superior but a more aggressive person. Tell me, Eutrapelus, which is the weaker, the one who submits or the one to whom submission is given?

Eutrapelus: I'll yield to you in this. . . .

And who wouldn't yield? Her last question is a powerful one that resonates through the whole history of suppression and oppression, right up to the current #MeToo movement.

Another particular favorite of mine is the maidservant Margaret, who plays a small but hilarious part in a colloquy called *Convivium poeticum*, or The Poetic Feast. Erasmus himself asserted that this colloquy was "to show what sort of feast scholars should have: frugal but gay and mirthful; seasoned with learned stories; without quarrels, bickering, or slander." His assembly of poets is served by Margaret, who apparently doesn't think a feast without bickering is worth the effort. She puts them all in their learned, scholarly places. Here Hilary, the host, calls her out of the kitchen to demand why she has served beet tops instead of lettuce:

Crato: If one's allowed to speak the plain truth at a poetic feast, what you call lettuce here are beet tops.

Hilary: Heaven forbid!

Crato: It's a fact. Look at their shape. And where's the milky flavor? Where's the tender tips?

Hilary: You rouse my suspicions. Ho there: send for the maid. [She comes] Margaret, you fury, what came into your head to serve us beet tops for lettuce?

Margaret: I did it on purpose.

Hilary: What are you talking about, you witch?

Margaret: I wanted to find out whether, among so many poets, there was one who could tell lettuce from beet tops, for I know *you* can't. Honestly now, who noticed they were beets?

Guests: Crato.

Margaret: I could easily guess *he's* no poet!

Hilary: If you contrive anything like this hereafter I'll call you Blitea [Latin for tasteless trash] instead of Margaret.

Guests: Ha ha!

Margaret: Calling me names doesn't hurt me one way or the other. Often he changes my name twenty times a day. When he wants to coax something from me, he calls me Galatea, Euterpe, Calliope, Melissa, Venus, Minerva, and I don't know what. When he's out of sorts, suddenly I turn into Tisiphone, Megara, Alecto, Medusa, Baucis, or whatever else his ill humor fancies.

Hilary:	Off with you and your beets, Blitea.
Margaret:	What did you summon me for?
Hilary:	To send you back where you came from.
Margaret:	There's an old saying, "It's easier to call up the devil than to get rid of him."
Guests:	Ha! A good hit! As the matter stands, Hilary, you will need a magic charm to get rid of her.
Margaret:	I've one already.
Hilary:	Away with you beetle, a wolf is after you!
Margaret:	What's that you say, Aesop?
Crato:	Careful Hilary, you'll feel her fists. So you've exorcised her with your Greek spell. A fine magician!
Hilary:	What do you suppose this creature is, Crato? With a spell like that, I'd have exorcised ten devils.
Margaret:	I don't give a damn for your Greekish verses.
Crato:	My dear Margaret, you know poets are an inspired—I don't dare say infuriating—tribe. I beg you to postpone this bickering until some other time and behave decently to us, for my sake, at this supper party.
Margaret:	What do I care for his snatches of verse? Time and again when I go to the butcher's he hasn't a penny—yet he recites bits of verse!
Crato:	Poets are like that. But come on; do as I say, please.
Margaret:	Well, for your sake I'll do it, since I know you're an honest man who's never beaten his brains over this sort of nonsense—but I wonder however in the world you fell in with this crew.
Crato:	But do oblige me, my sweet, by getting over your ill humor.
Margaret:	I'm leaving. I don't ask any of the others to thank me for it. (Exits)
Hilary:	Is she really gone?
Margaret:	(Shouting from the kitchen): Not so far that she can't hear you!
Crato:	You have a maid who is anything but deaf and dumb.
Hilary:	They say a good maidservant should be endowed with three qualities. She should be trustworthy, ugly, and bold—or what's commonly called "saucy." A trustworthy one doesn't steal your substance; and an ugly one isn't sought by suitors. A bold one looks readily after her master's interests, for sometimes that must be done with hands as well as eyes. This servant of mine has two of the three virtues: she's both ugly and saucy. As for her honesty, I have my doubts.

Could Shakespeare have picked up tips for some of his colloquial heroines and termagants—Mistress Quickly, Mistress Overdone, Doll Tearsheet, the Bawd in Pericles—from the saucy, ugly, suffering-no-fools Margaret?

A colloquy written in a more reflective vein is *Convivium religiosum* (The Religious Retreat), in which we find a group of men in retreat from the smoke and corruption of the city. It is strikingly similar to the group of men who leave the corrupt court and follow Duke Senior into the Forest of Arden in *As You Like It*. Note particularly the references to deceitful humanity and the voices of wisdom in nature:

Eusebius: I admire that anybody can delight to live in smoky cities, when everything is so fresh and pleasant in the country.

Timothy: All are not pleased with the sight of flowers, springing meadows, fountains or rivers: or if they do take pleasure in 'em, there is something else in which they take more, for it is with pleasure as it is with wedges, one drives out another.

Eusebius: You speak perhaps of usurers, or covetous traders; which, indeed, are all one. In my opinion, nature is not dumb, but talkative enough, and speaks to the instruction of a man that has but a good will and a capacity to learn.

Timothy: I do speak of them; but not of them only, I assure you; but of a thousand other sorts of people, even to the very priests and monks, who for the sake of gain, make choice of the most populous cities for their habitation, not following the opinion of Plato or Pythagoras in this practice; but rather that of a certain blind beggar, who loved to be where he was crowded; because, as he said, the more the people the more the profit.

Eusebius: Prithee let's leave the blind beggar and his gain: we are philosophers.

Timothy: So was Socrates a philosopher, and yet he preferred a town life before a country because he, being desirous of knowledge, had there the opportunity of improving it. In the country, 'tis true, there are woods, gardens, fountains, and brooks that entertain the sight, but they are all mute, and therefore teach a man nothing.

Eusebius: I know Socrates puts the case of a man walking alone in the fields; although, in my opinion, there nature is not dumb, but talkative enough, and speaks to the instruction of a man that has but a good will, with a capacity to learn. What does the beautiful face of the spring do, but proclaim the equal wisdom and goodness of the Creator? And how many excellent things did Socrates in his retirement, both teach his Phaedrus, and learn from him?

Timothy: If a man could have such pleasant company, I confess, no life in the world could be pleasanter than a country life.

(Echo) *As You Like It*

Duke Senior:. . . Hath not old custom made this life more sweet
Than those of painted pomp? Are not these woods
More free from peril than the envious court?
Here we feel but the penalty of Adam,

> The seasons' difference; as the icy fang
> And churlish chiding of the winter's wind,
> Which, when it bites and blows upon my body
> Even till I shrink with cold, I smile, and say
> This is no flattery; these are counselors
> That feelingly persuade me what I am.
> Sweet are the uses of adversity,
> Which like the toad, ugly and venomous,
> Wears yet a precious jewel in his head;
> And this our life, exempt from public haunt,
> Finds tongues in trees, books in the running brooks,
> Sermons in stones, and good in everything.
>
> Act II, Scene i

The setting is so similar: a group of men with a leader, choosing to return to nature and to find wisdom and comfort there. And Duke Senior is speaking of the Forest of Arden, where Shakespeare may have many times sought wisdom and comfort himself.

More than any of the other colloquies, it was *Naufragium* (The Shipwreck) that convinced me beyond a shadow of a doubt that Shakespeare was intimately familiar with the colloquies of Erasmus. Scholars have long noted it as a source that fed the imagination of the author of *The Tempest*. It was based on a real occurrence, a shipwreck off of the coast of Holland on its way from Scotland to Italy with a papal legation on board. It recounts what was probably an actual conversation Erasmus had with someone who was aboard that ship, and it is fraught with descriptive language that that rivals the terror of Miranda's cries:

> The sky, it seems, would pour down stinking pitch,
> But that the sea, mounting to th'welkin's cheek,
> Dashes the fire out. O, I have suffered
> With those I saw suffer: a brave vessel
> Who had, no doubt, some noble creature in her,
> Dashed all to pieces.
>
> Act I, Scene ii

One may well image the impact the following passage must have had on an impressionable child:

Adolph: Those mountains are mole hills, if they be compar'd to the waves of the sea. As oft as we were toss'd up, one might have touched the moon with his finger; as oft as we let fall down into the sea, we seemed to be going directly down to hell, the earth gaping to receive us.

(Translated from the Latin original)

The same boy later sent Prospero's books "deeper than did ever plummet sound," wrote Clarence's nightmare dream of drowning in *Richard III*, and gave to Ariel the most haunting of songs, "Full fathom five thy father lies/Of his bones are coral made."

Another, more comic but similar description of a shipwreck appears in the voice of the Clown in *A Winter's Tale*:

> *Clown:* I would you did but see how it chafes, how it rages, how it takes up the shore! But that's not the point. O, the most piteous cry of the poor souls, sometimes to see 'em, and not to see 'em; now the ship boring the moon with her main-mast, and anon swallowed with yeast and froth, as you'd thrust a cork into a hogshead.
>
> Act III, Scene iii

Set side by side, the specific image most frequently cited from *The Tempest* is the description of Saint Elmo's fire, a weather phenomenon which happens sometimes at sea, in which a strong electrical field illuminates plasma in the atmosphere and creates the illusion of fire. Shakespeare may have observed this himself or heard of it. Set side by side, note how precisely his description of fire rolling down the masts and across the decks mirrors that of Erasmus:

Erasmus' *Naufragium*	Shakespeare's *The Tempest*
Adolph: A certain ball of fire . . . sliding down by the ropes, roll'd itself all around the sides of the ship; after that slipping through the hatches, it vanished away.	**Ariel:** Now in the beak, now in the waist, in the deck, in every cabin/I flamed amazement. Sometimes I'd divide/And burn in many places. On the topmast, / The yards and bowsprit would I flame distinctly. (Act I, Scene ii)

But there are many shipwrecks in Shakespeare's plays, and anyone who doubts that Shakespeare performed this colloquy as a child would have to explain the startling similarity of the image of a mother and baby tied to the mast of a sinking ship in both *Naufragium* and *Comedy of Errors* or the similar rescue of Sebastian in *Twelfth Night*:

Erasmus' *Naufragium*	Shakespeare's *The Comedy of Errors*
Adolph: We set her upon a broad plank, and tied her on so fast that she could not easily fall off, and we gave her a board in her hand to make use of instead of an	**Aegeon:** . . . My wife, more careful of the latter-born, / Had fasten'd him unto a small spare mast, / Such as sea-faring men provide for storms: / To him one

Erasmus' *Naufragium*	Shakespeare's *The Comedy of Errors*
oar, and wishing her good success, we set her afloat, thrusting her from off the ship with poles, that she might be clear of it, whence was the greatest danger. And she held her child in her left hand, and row'd with her right hand. **Antony:** O, Virago!	of the other twins was bound, / Whilst I had been like heedful of the others. / The children thus dispos'd, my wife and I, / Fixing our eyes on whom our care was fix'd, / Fasten'd ourselves at either end of the mast / And floating straight, obedient to the stream, / Were carried towards Corinth . . . (Act I, Scene i)

Erasmus' *Naufragium*	Shakespeare's *Twelfth Night*
Adolph: . . . Casting about I finally thought of the stump of a mast. Since I couldn't pry it loose by myself I enlisted the help of another man. Supporting ourselves on this we put to the sea, I holding the right end and he the left.	**Captain:** . . . I saw your brother, Most provident in peril, bind himself, — / Courage and hope both teaching him the practice, — / To a strong mast that liv'd upon the sea; / Where, like Arion on the dolphin's back, / I saw him hold acquaintance with the waves / So long as I could see. (Act I, Scene ii)

Are we to assume that Shakespeare pulled this exact image—a rescue at sea involving a man or woman tied to a mast, in one case even clinging to a baby—*twice* in his career? Or is it more likely that he encountered it, in Latin, as a schoolboy with a mother at home nursing an infant sibling?

Perhaps worthy of note: It is probably more than a coincidence that in *Naufragium* Adolph is speaking to a character named Antony, and there is an Antonio present in the shipwrecks of both *The Tempest* and *Twelfth Night*. Indeed, the colloquy includes a long discourse on the despair of a merchant at losing his treasure, and it is Antonio, the merchant in *The Merchant of Venice*, who learns that he has lost his fortune in a shipwreck.

There are examples even from the very earliest of the colloquies, the ones Erasmus wrote for his students in the 1490s. Most of them were simple greetings with a comic twist or a moral lesson, and because of their brevity and simplicity they may have been introduced as early as the first or second form. He wrote a series of examples of courteous greetings, involving travelers returning from various parts of the world. In one of them, again based on Erasmus' own painful experience of a robbery he endured on the coast of England, the traveler, Ciprian, bemoans an encounter he had had with thieves. His friend Maurice comforts him:

Cyprian: My life and reputation are safe, but my purse is lost.
Maurice: The loss of life never can be repair'd; the loss of reputation very hardly.

In Othello, the situation is reversed. Cassio regrets the loss of his reputation, and Iago seems to comfort him by belittling the loss:

Cassio: Reputation, reputation, reputation. O, I have lost my reputation! I have lost the immortal part of myself and what remains is bestial. My reputation, Iago, my reputation!
Iago: As I am an honest man, I thought you had received some bodily wound; there is more sense in that than in reputation. Reputation is an idle and most false imposition: oft got without merit, and lost without deserving: you have lost no reputation at all, unless you repute yourself such a loser.

Act II, Scene iii

And then here is one more: the comically inverted greeting that seems to inspire the silly exchange when Kate, in *The Taming of the Shrew*, finally gives in to her outrageous husband and decides to play by his rules:

Greeting: God save you, little old woman of fifteen years of age.
Reply: God save you girl, eighty years old.

You can just hear the silly voice of a precocious schoolboy in Stratford playing the confusion of a little old woman 15 years of age. In *Shrew* Petruchio and Kate greet the ancient traveler Vincentio, and Petruchio tests Kate's new compliance thus:

Petruchio: Tell me, sweet Kate, and tell me truly too, Hast thou beheld a fresher gentlewoman? . . .
Kate: Young budding virgin, fresh and fair and sweet.
Whither away, or where is thy abode?
Happy the parents of so fair a child;
Happier the man, whom favourable stars
Allot thee for his lovely bed-fellow!

Act IV, Scene iv

Shakespeare is revisiting that youthful fun in confusion.

These examples only begin to touch on the wealth of textual resonances to be found. There is the long and sententious speech in *Monita paedagogica* (The School-Master's Admonitions) quoted earlier, sounding like Polonius. There is a raucously funny colloquy called *Exorcismus, sive spectrum* (The Exorcist), in which a "ghost" trick played in a country setting, at night, upon a credulous and foolish man presages the night-time tricks played on Falstaff in both *Henry IV* and *The Merry Wives of Windsor*. And for me, reading *The Old Men's Dialogue*, it is impossible not to hear the voices of Silence and Shallow in the one of the funniest and sweetest scenes in *Henry IV Part II*.

Most of the echoes from the colloquies appear in the comedies, but I am also reminded of them in the strong scent of corruption in *Hamlet*, the "something rotten in the state." Scholars have noted the Lutheran connection to *Hamlet*. The Diet of Worms is called up by Hamlet's instruction to Claudius to seek the dead Polonius "Not where he eats, but where he is eaten: a certain convocation of politic worms are e'en at him. Your *worm is your only emperor for diet*." Also, Hamlet's father, the ghost, digs under the ground, and Luther's father was a miner. Of course Shakespeare would have had many opportunities to contemplate the corruption that provoked the Reformation, which was ongoing and all around him, but Erasmus "laid the egg," as we have seen, and many of his colloquies have monks or clergymen, like the abbot portrayed at the beginning of this chapter, as characters that point up the egregious corruption of the un-reformed Catholic clergy. This is an example of how the custom of using colloquies brought contemporary issues into the classroom. Erasmus had more in mind than teaching correct Latin speaking when he wrote his colloquies. Ever the instructor, ever the thinker, ever the communicator, he was giving small boys a grounding in humanism and the contentions leading up to the Reformation.

There are also numerous passages that might not remind us of a specific connection but that just sound so Shakespearean in the way they play with logic that if they hadn't been written years before he was born we might think them parodies. These—pillaged from colloquies involving shopkeepers, feasters, householders, liars and cheats, vacuous holy men and corrupt lawyers, women and men of all stations—begin to reveal a world of material for an endlessly acquisitive imagination. Besides the ones already mentioned, here are just a few of the translated titles of the more than fifty colloquies to whet the curiosity: *Family Discourse, Of Rash Vows, Of a Soldier's Life, Of Various Plays* [games], *The Art of Hunting, The Virgin Averse to Matrimony, The Uneasy Wife, The Alchemist, The Horse-Cheat, The Beggars' Dialogue, The Lying in Woman*, and *The Poetical Feast*. Each of these embodies the spirit of the setting and the age, and it does so in a way that irresistibly evokes Shakespeare. T.W. Baldwin points out that, "To Erasmus, as to Shakespeare, words were glittering toys, with which everlastingly to play." As thinkers and as writers, they were surely kindred spirits. It is Shakespeare's colloquial characters—his clowns, his mechanicals, his tinkers, tailors, and thieves—who light up his plays with their wit and wisdom, and I can only think he remembered and relished his boyhood performances of the folks he met in the *Colloquia familiaria* of Erasmus.

★ ★ ★

I regret that Shakespeare never wrote a scene of schoolboys rehearsing for plays like he wrote for the mechanicals in *Midsummer Night's Dream*, but as it is, the colloquies get us the closest to what that playful activity might have looked like. They were certainly performed, but there is no evidence that they ever reached an audience beyond the schoolroom. Here the historical fiction imagination must take over. Their practice, being somewhat extracurricular, was probably not closely overseen by the classroom authorities. The boys might have been on their own much of the time, and they must have put the "play" into playmaking. They didn't need a lot of direction. Erasmus made it easy for them by using stock characters, often giving them names that made playful or ironic reference to their personalities so that the young actors could get into character effortlessly. All of the saucy humor and innuendo would have given them tantalizing parameters for improvisation.

Knowing how much emphasis was put on collaboration in all of the writing exercises students did in school, I would even venture a guess that little classroom troupes of Thespians developed their own material, wrote their own scenes pulled from their own experiences and observations of their own town. Shakespeare was an accomplished playwright by his mid-twenties, and he lived in an age when adult occupations were usually determined in youth. It is entirely possible that he was taking the lead with his classmates in Stratford, writing colloquies of his own, and that Kate, Falstaff, Mistress Quickly, Mistress Page, Bardolph, Nim, the carters, the apothecaries, the innkeepers, Peter Quince and company, and the common folk that enliven all of his plays, had their origins in Shakespeare's classroom in Stratford. In fact, as I've said earlier, I would not be at all surprised to learn that the first draft of *The Taming of the Shrew* was the playful work of Stratford schoolboys.

It wasn't just Shakespeare who performed colloquies in school from the first form on; it was his entire generation. It was the first generation coming out of the humanist schools that took firm root in England in the second half of the 16th century, at exactly the time that English took flight as a literary language. They were the generation that made us fall in love with the sounds and expressive genius of our language. Researching this book was one confirmation after another of my original hunch, that Elizabethan elementary school education, rich in the performing arts—music, dance, and theatre—along with the daily exercise of the rhetorical muscle, was in large part responsible for modern English literature.

10
THE LITTLE EYASES
Professional Boy Actors

FIGURE 10.1 Pageant wagon.

The Early Boys' Companies

All during the century in which the Reformation was expanding educational opportunity and embracing the curriculum of Erasmus, while schoolboys were practicing the physical rhetoric prescribed by Quintilian, while grammar school students throughout the realm were providing village entertainments for holidays, and while those same students were performing comic scenes from Plautus and Terence and the *Colloquia* with their peers, there were small islands of boys' companies going about the business of entertaining the aristocracy.

This chapter is a bit of a digression, although, hopefully, a fascinating one. Writing a book about dramatic activity in Elizabethan classrooms and focusing instead on the famous boys' companies is a little like writing a book about the Little Leagues and focusing on the all-star players in the Majors. The boy actors in the Children of the Chapel and the Children of Saint Paul's were the cream of the cream, a far cry from grammar school students spouting Ovid, although their talents were, most likely, first noticed by a schoolmaster in a classroom. If I may be forgiven for writing it, you, my reader, may be forgiven for skipping over it if your primary interest in this book is limited to arts education and cognition. If, however, you are also interested in the vital contribution of playacting children to the glorious history of English theatre, do, please, read on! It will be well worth the effort.

In fact the entire history of the boys' companies is so neglected that it is almost forgotten. In researching it I relied heavily on two books published early in the last century that tell their history: *The Evolution of the English Drama up to Shakespeare* by Charles William Wallace and *The Child Actors* by Harold Newcomb Hillebrand. So far as I've been able to ascertain, not much new information has been added since. This is an odd silence. If Wallace and Hillebrand are correct in the assertion of their importance, the Globe Theatre would never have existed without them. The fact that boy actors and the choirmasters and playwrights who provided their material had so huge an impact on the history of theatre had never occurred to me before reading these old books. Clearly, those remarkable young performers were the ultimate manifestation of an educational culture that incorporated performance into the everyday experience of a schoolboy, in school and out.

Despite reams of documentation citing dates and titles of performances, writs for impressment, expenditures for costumes and props, and lawsuits (more on that one later), there are only tiny glimpses into the day-to-day lives of the boys in the boys' companies. We know, for instance, that visitors to Saint Paul's sometimes complained about children scampering about begging for coins, which they actually had permission to do. The court impressed talented boys into service and funded them because they had to be trained and well-rehearsed at all times to provide the royalty with diversion; but the provisions were inadequate to their needs, so the boys were allowed to ask church visitors for more. (Some things never change in the theatre: actors still pass the hat, literally or figuratively, even on Broadway, where they regularly beg the audience to contribute to the Actors' Fund!) We know that their education was in the care of their choirmasters, but we know very little about the conditions of their housing. In the way of fiction, which often gives us more insight into history than the dry records, I would recommend Penelope Fitzgerald's delightful book *At Freddie's* to get a sense of what their tiny theatre world was like. The century is wrong, and the genre is light comedic, but boys really do not change that much over time and Fitzgerald's time teaching at the Italia Conti Stage School in London, in the early 1960s, gave her a chance to observe closely the habits and antics of little drama princes. (Aside from that, the book is a totally fun read!)

It is hard to know when boy choristers first became play actors. There are fleeting references to children performing at court as early as the 14th century, and in time child actors were favored above their adult companions in courtly entertainments. They became expert at performing, first allegorical interludes and eventually elaborately produced comedies and dramas. As noted earlier, the Children of the Chapel has a centuries-old history and still exists today, although it no longer incorporates playacting into its regular duties. Other children's companies were formed in the 16th century, principally the Children of Saint Paul's, and because the cultural aesthetic of the court set the standard for rest of the realm, those much loved boy actors became a part of the evolution of Elizabethan drama.

Several other boys' companies came and went over the years, entertaining the aristocracy in seats of power all over the realm, but only the Children of the Chapel and the Children of Saint Paul's had long, well-documented histories. The fortunes of these two companies rose and fell over the years but they remained essentially intact and were sustained, as were the later men's companies, primarily by royal patronage and the aristocracy's insatiable appetite for amusement and display.

Wallace was the first to draw from the original records, compiling an exhaustive list of hundreds of plays performed at court, both by the boys' companies and by grammar school boys from Eton, Merchant Taylors', Saint Paul's, and Westminster among others. Hillebrand's book corrects some of Wallace's assumptions and adds exhaustive detail covering their activity. He sites evidence of the use of children in dramatizations going back at least to the Middle Ages and documents endless performances celebrating holidays, foreign visitors, royal births and weddings, journeys, and, most especially, coronations. He then relates their history all the way through the first two decades of the 17th century, and finally their demise.

Both Wallace and Hillebrand convincingly show that the immense popularity of child actors that peaked in the 16th century was not a passing fad. The use of children in the performance of music and drama had deep roots going back hundreds of years. But because of royal favor and the historic currents that favored theatrical entertainments, it reached its full flowering during the Tudor Age. The nature and frequency of the children's performances during that fertile century varied according to the sovereign on the throne, and the history of theatre owes much to the youth of three of them. Henry VIII was a teenager when he was crowned, Edward a mere child. Then, as now, the young crave entertainment, and they both embraced all varieties of diversion: pageantry, dance, music, comedies, and the kind of chaotic hilarity provided annually at Christmas by the Lord of Misrule. Then came Elizabeth! She was only 25 when she became queen, and she never lost her love of theatre as she aged. In fact, she and her playmakers matured together.

Both Henry and Elizabeth maintained close friendships with the masters of their favorite acting groups: Henry with William Cornish and Elizabeth with Sebastian Westcote. This promoted a constant engagement with the content and the aesthetic of their dramatic interludes. Henry's enthusiasm for spectacle wearied as other concerns overwhelmed him, but his court entertainments continued unabated. Edward's patronage died with him when he was still an adolescent, but Elizabeth's never waned. Henry VIII's early years were particularly busy ones for performers, and they, in turn, were surpassed by those of Elizabeth.

So for most of the 16th century, even during the turmoil of Henry's multiple marriages and religious conflicts, even during reign of the sober Mary, the ever increasingly loved children's troupes were the chief providers of entertainment at court. To quote Hillebrand, "Indeed, from the ascension of Henry VIII until 1590 the English drama was mainly in their hands."

Once in awhile we can be grateful to Hamlet's dreaded "insolence of office." Theatre history owes a debt to the record keeping maintained by the court's Office of the Revels. There are many gaps, and in some years the entries are more meticulous than others, but they give more than enough evidence to support a clear pattern. A parallel history of the hundreds, probably thousands, of popular, native plays performed for the public by traveling adult acting companies in the streets, squares, and inns of London and in rural villages is mostly lost to us—plentiful but patchy and anecdotal. The realm of the children's companies, however, was primarily the court, where for decades they eclipsed their adult competition. Careful records of their performances and associated expenses remain to this day.

Beginning late in the 15th century, during the reign of Henry VII, child choristers in the Children of the Chapel Royal began to take speaking roles in royal entertainments. At first their small, light bodies and exquisite voices complemented adult actors in pageants, where they could easily perch atop wagons constructed as castles, fortresses, dragons, or forests. These wagons were more elaborately constructed than our Rose Parade floats are today, and the small bodies that animated them were popular favorites. The splendor of some of them was truly jaw dropping. There are plenty of contemporary descriptions of public processions and private interludes, and there are bookkeeping accounts of the lavish expenditures incurred for costumes, sets, wagons, and payments to musicians, dance masters, and playwrights. Just one description of a pageant wagon designed for a "Joust of Honor" in 1511 will give a glimpse into the prodigality of the courts and the excesses of their devisors. A wagon representing a forest with a castle was drawn by great lions and antelopes and was topped by maidens, with knights coming and going below. In another, called The Golden Arbor, the arbor was a huge, moveable stage:

> adorned with purple and gold, having branches wrought of roses, lilies, marigolds, gillyflowers, primroses, cowslips, and other kindly flowers, with an orchard of rare fruits, all embowered by a silver vine bearing 350 clusters of grapes of gold. It contained thirty persons, and its great weight broke the floor as it moved up the hall. On the sides were eight minstrels with strange instruments, and on the top, the Children of the Chapel singing.

It was William Cornish, Master of the Chapel during the early years of Henry's reign, who first produced little plays drawn from history and legend, to be performed by the Children of the Chapel as interludes between musical performances: thus the occasional reference to boy actors as "interluders." At first their scenes were little more than dialogue intertwined with song and dance, but they had rudimentary structure and each one told a story. They were in English, which was already replacing French as the preferred language of the court. These insignificant but much loved playlets gradually grew into longer works, and Cornish's play *Troilus and Pandor* was said to be the first to be presented by a cast made up of children. This play was followed by others, by both Cornish and his successor John Heywood: among them *Johan, The Four P.P., The Four Elements*, and *The Pardoner*. They were not enduring works of literature, but they were good enough that Wallace actually credits Cornish with being the father of English theatre.

Serving the royal court, the boys' company choirmasters were the finest musicians and composers of the realm, the precursors of the British poets laureate. Starting with William Cornish in the court of the lusty young King Henry VIII there is an astonishingly fertile list of creative geniuses supplying the boys' companies with material. The list includes John Heywood, Nicholas Udall, Richard Edwards, Richard Ferrant, William Hunnis, John Lyly, Robert Greene, George Peele, Christopher Marlowe, George Chapman, John Marston, John Webster, Ben Jonson, Anthony Munday, Thomas Dekker, and Thomas Middleton. In other words, just about every playwright of any note, all the way through the early Jacobean period, wrote occasionally—and lucratively—for boy actors to perform at court. Even the Earl of Oxford, the favorite candidate of the Shakespeare deniers, wrote for them. It would have been beneath him to write for the public theatres, but the boys' companies were private and had a better class of clientele. What is more, if the highly credible theory that we have already explored, that a boys' company first performed *Love's Labors' Lost*, is correct, the list would include William Shakespeare.

Many of the writers and producers grew up in the ranks. They were influenced by the plays they had performed and, in turn, they influenced new generations, forming a continuing link in the critical development of dramatic style.

This was often the best paying employment there was for dramatists, in good times and in bad. In the plague years, when the public theatres were closed, the children's troupes, even those from grammar schools, were exempted from the ban. (A relevant note: the justification for exempting grammar school plays was that they were deemed to be educational!) The courts still required entertainment, and the children provided it. Even in the final decade of Elizabeth's life, when common opinion has it that the children's companies had fallen out of favor at court, there is mention of a performance of Marlowe's *Dido, Queen of Carthage*, being performed by the Children of Her Majesty's Chapel, and children's companies were constantly employed in aristocratic homes outside of London. The very best dramatic and musical talents were continually engaged to produce the best of royal entertainments.

Unfortunately we don't know much about the early children's company plays aside from their titles and some broad descriptions written by observers. They were mostly light fare, comedy and farce, with a few histrionic historical dramas, and spectacle was probably valued over content. Of the scores of plays we know of from the first three-quarters of the 16th century, only a few remain to us as published works. Most scripts were prepared for specific occasions, were topical, and were performed only once then discarded. Only their titles remain for us, carefully logged, with accompanying dates and expenses, in the records of the Office of the Revels.

One thing we *do* know is that they were not morality plays! According to Wallace, the day of the old morality plays ended in 1514, when young King Henry stood up in the middle of one, yawned, and walked out of the room. Two years earlier, during a celebration of Twelfth Night (the holiday, not the play), Henry VIII's Sergeant of the Revels had introduced a brand new style from Italy: the "Meskaler": "called a masque, a thing not seen afore in England." The sets, the dress, the colors, the music, the wit, and especially the dance that the noble observers always joined at the end, all imported from the seat of the Renaissance, quickly displaced the old religious dramas that had dominated English theatre for centuries. This new style, mixing music and dance with interludes of dialogue, had a huge impact on theatrical productions during Henry's reign. There was a brief attempt during Mary's reign to revive morality plays performed by children, but that did not go over well. Masques, comedies, and tragedies, with all their fun, pathos, and spectacle had spoiled audiences for piety.

Choirmaster playwrights ransacked Plautus, Terence, Chaucer, Aesop, classical history, and mythology for story fodder. Some of the plays were allegorical and came straight from debate topics suggested by Erasmus for schoolboys. One performed for the Revels in 1527 depicted a debate between riches and love, arguing which one was more valuable in choosing a spouse, a topic suggested by Erasmus in *De copia*. The rhetorical device of prosopopoeia was very much in evidence in boy characters impersonating every known variety of virtue, vice, fortune, poverty, divine wisdom, the muses, the worthies, the seasons, the elements, and all manner of abstractions. The titles seem to be an endless series of Somebody and Somebodys or Something and Somethings: *Appius and Virginia, Damon and Pythias, Troius and Pandor, Palaemon and Arcyte, Cloridon and Radiamante, Predor and Lucia, The Pardoner and the Friar, Sir Clyomon and Sir Clamydkes, John the Husband and Tyb the Wife, Loyalty and Beauty, Wit and Will, Jack and Jill,* etc. One can detect a clear line between grammar school curriculum and the boys' company's plays.

The fact that so many of the scripts were discarded or lost after they were performed should not be a reflection on their quality, only on the ephemeral nature of the culture of the court. There are indications that many of the now forgotten entertainments were excellent. Contemporary audiences raved about them. As the century wore on and as the plays became more sophisticated in style and structure, many of them did survive the neglect of time. Some were revived by popular demand, re-staged for the public by grammar school boys, and some were published because their auditors and authors valued them. But it was not until the first half of the reign of Elizabeth that plays written for boys took on an artistry of their own, especially those of John Lyly.

The Golden Age of Boys' Companies

The young Elizabeth of the 1560s did not yet have available the outstanding men's companies that formed in the succeeding generation, and she had an abiding love for performances by boys. The Children of the Chapel had been allowed to go somewhat fallow under Queen Mary, but when Elizabeth became queen she recruited an old friend, Sebastian Westcote, to take over the mastership of the Children of Saint Paul's, which was a long standing choir only loosely associated with the grammar school. Almost immediately they began performing plays at court. Then in 1561 the master of the Children of the Chapel died, and she was able to hire the finest dramatist of the time, Richard Edwards.

Edwards was said by Barnaby Googe to be the greatest poet who had ever written in the English language or who ever would: "Far surpassing Plautus and Terence and not likely to be equaled by any poet in the future!" Poor fellow. Just his luck to be equaled and surpassed within a few years by Shakespeare and company. Only one of his plays, *Damon and Pythias*, has survived, and he was followed by so many other greats that today he is unfairly remembered, if at all, only as a rather musty predecessor. In his day he was a star, and his actors were boys!

Elizabeth also patronized a children's company at Windsor to entertain whenever her court was there, so for awhile there were three robust companies competing and thriving in the welcoming environment she provided. Westcote's boys performed at court twenty-nine times, more than any other troupe, child or adult; and, as we shall see, the Children of the Chapel and the Children of Windsor were successful enough eventually to move into a venue of their own.

> *Indeed, between the children's companies and the grammar school scholars, the first thirty years of the "Golden Age" of Elizabethan theatre was entirely dominated by boy actors.*

Elizabeth had been welcomed into London upon her coronation by an elaborate pageant that featured great numbers of schoolboys performing as singers and orators, and she was always a supporter of academic theatre as well. As Queen, whenever she went on progress to Oxford, Cambridge, or other rural communities she spent much time listening to young scholars recite in Latin and Greek, and in the evening she enjoyed seeing them perform plays in both Latin and English. In addition, she regularly invited players from the grammar schools to perform at court, especially during Christmas celebrations. As we have seen, students of Richard Mulcaster, from Merchant Taylors' school, were frequently invited, as were the boys of Westminster, Eton, Saint Paul's, and others. Indeed, between the children's companies and the grammar school scholars, the first thirty years of the "Golden Age" of Elizabethan theatre was entirely dominated by boy actors.

Curiously, from the very beginning, many of the plays performed by children were satirical and politically charged—even dangerously so. Like court jesters, small harmless, innocent children could be forgiven for spouting lines that pushed barriers and that would cause offense if spoken by adults. In 1527, Cardinal Wolsey arranged for the Children of Saint Paul's to perform a play in French and Latin, which was unusual for the court because by then the courts had adopted English for its amusements. The language was appropriate, because the play was performed for certain visiting noblemen from France who knew no English. In it, the boys satirized the character of "the heretic Luther" and exalted Wolsey as the rescuer of the church. This must have raised some sly eyebrows. At the time Wolsey was teetering at the pinnacle of his seemingly absolute power, but there were those in court who smelled blood and sensed the truth: that he was soon to die in miserable exile.

Knowing the witty nature of some of their playwrights, there were certainly other edgy and custom-challenging performances. One or more of Edwards' early "toying plays" gave offense, for instance, because "to some he seemed too much in young desires to range," and he was admonished to rein in his border-pushing humor. But it was not until performances by the children's companies moved beyond the courts and into the public arena that their satirical vein began to give them real fame and real trouble. That happened when they started performing at the Blackfriars Theatre.

Blackfriars

When Elizabeth came onto the throne, theatre, performed by both men and boys, was liberated from Queen Mary's moralizing expectations, and a lively new era of drama was born. During the first twenty years of her reign, the private theatre of the court spun off on into countless public ventures which were hugely popular. In time, inevitably, public theatres became profitable, and men's adult companies began sprouting up all over the country. In London, the situation got so noisy and chaotic that there was an outcry by some of the more puritanical elements of the population, so in 1572 Elizabeth issued a restrictive statute that allowed performances only by companies under noble patronage. This turned many players outside of the city into vagabonds and beggars, but in London, ironically, it lead to the establishment of the first two permanent playhouses, Burbage's Theatre and the Blackfriars.

Noble patronage had a crucial function. The court needed their favorite companies to be available at all times. This meant they had to have a place to rehearse. In 1576 Richard Farrant, then the master of the Children of Windsor, leased a section of an old, abandoned monastery that had belonged to the Dominican's before Henry VIII turned them out. They were known as the black friars because of the color of their robes, and their monastery was called Blackfriars. There Farrant proposed to train his own boys and invited William Hunnis, Edwards' successor as master of Children of the Chapel, to join him. Together they prepared their young players for their court appearances, gaining some financial advantage by charging admission to the public for their rehearsals. Their first play, *The History of Mutius Scevola*, was performed at Blackfriars and then at court for the following Twelfth Night in 1577. They continued this productive relationship with the court for the next six years.

Also in 1576, the very same year, James Burbage, theatre impresario and father of the famed actor Richard, opened The Theatre, to house his company, the Lord Leicester's Men. This was the first permanent home for the burgeoning industry developing around men's companies, and it made all the difference. Before 1573 there were almost no performances at court by men. After the Queen's restrictions that empowered the men's companies that had noble patronage, they became a constant, and no year passed without at least one play, then more and more. The race for the Queen's favor between the men and the boys was on. As we know, by the time Shakespeare arrived on the scene, the race was over and the men had won. But for several years the boys at Blackfriars gave them spirited competition.

Farrant died in 1580 and three years of legal squabbles followed, with Farrant's widow and William Hunnis trying to keep the venture alive. The landlord of Blackfriars was dismayed by the amount of traffic caused by the large audiences coming and going to the so-called "rehearsals," and he was desperately trying to cancel the lease. To the rescue came Edward de Vere, the Earl of Oxford—the very man who is today credited by some with writing Shakespeare's plays. Wallace describes him as a noted "swaggerer, roisterer, brawler, coxcomb, musician, poet," but with his noble title he was able to hold the landlord at bay and take over the lease of Blackfriars.

Oxford was a noted patron of the arts, and the children's company became known, briefly, as Oxford's Boys. He brought along his favorite playwrights: the scathingly witty young men, John Lyly and George Peele. Together they set about turning their new real estate into a profitable venue that could compete with the new public theatres. It was private only in the sense that it was indoors and more expensive than the Curtain, the Fortune, or Burbage's Theatre, all of which by now housed men's companies. The new impresarios still received patronage from the court, but in addition they increased the number and price of performances for the more well to do public. Unsurprisingly, that public ate it up.

Their collaboration at Blackfriars was a brief flare, lasting little more than a year. Landlord squabbles eventually succeeded in a long-fought quest to revoke the lease of the rowdy band of children, and for the next fifteen years Blackfriars was silent. But a new style had been launched and continued to thrive. John Lyly wrote at least eight plays presented at court by the boys, including *Compaspe, Sapho and Phao, Endymion, Gallathea, Midas,* and *Love's Metamorphosis*. Of these, apparently only the first two and George Peele's *The Arraignment of Paris* were offered first to audiences at Blackfriars, but the plays continued. After Blackfriars went dark, Peele returned to the public theatre, but Lyly continued to write for the boys at Saint Paul's, using their traditional venue attached to the Cathedral. Several more of his plays were presented at court, and audiences continued to enjoy them. Other playwrights got into the action too. Robert Greene contributed *A Looking Glass for London and England, Orlando Furioso,* and *The Scottish History of James the Fourth*. The public could not get enough of the brisk and lively dialogue, the gossipy allusions to public figures, and the poking of fun at topical issues. For a short but history-making moment, Oxford's Boys, first formed at Blackfriars, were the hottest ticket in London.

According to Wallace, it was at Blackfriars that the highly stylized aesthetic of the court merged with that of the more earthy native theatre that had been growing in popularity, and this merging launched a hybrid: the clamorous, riotous, and exuberant age of Elizabethan drama. Native English drama had been narrating its own, parallel history for decades, beyond the purview of the court but reflecting its passions. Short, farcical amusements, not unlike Italian commedia dell'arte, had been performed for popular audiences in English, in streets, innyards, and town squares for many decades. These shows were probably hilarious, but they were essentially formless. Most of them were improvised, and we have very few actual scripts on which to base a study; but with a new fascination with our language came translations of the great Latin plays, and gradually classical structure was adapted into home-grown theatre.

In the mid 1550s Terence's *The Girl of Andros* appeared in English, then in about 1560, translations of the plays of Seneca and Plautus began to appear. Schoolmaster scholars, who read the originals in Latin, borrowed from them plays for their scholars, like *Jack the Juggler*, which was a very London-like version of Plautus' *Amphitrio*. Udall freely adapted *Miles Gloriosus*, again by Plautus, in his play *Ralph Roister Doister*, which was probably written first for his students at Eton. *Grammer Gurton's Needle*, a play of unknown authorship first performed at Cambridge in 1566, is commonly referred to as the first purely English comedy with no classical model. Although it is not based on an ancient play and is coarse and vulgar, full of slapstick humor, buffoonery, and lusty language, it observes the classical unities: all the action performed in one day, taking place in one location, and structured in five acts with the appropriate preparation, climax, and close. In 1561 *Gorboduc*, now cited as the first English language play written in verse, was performed at the Lincoln's Inn. Others followed at the Inns of Court, at Oxford, and at Cambridge. Plays like *Jocasta*, *Tancred and Gismunda*, and *Misogonus* were written for university students and lawyers, not courtiers.

Stylistically, what distinguished these dramas from those performed at court was the lack of the expensive adornment required by the masques. Without the dazzling spectacle, they had to rely on good stories and clever dialogue to maintain the interest of the audience. The authorship of some of them was obscure. Some were apparently performed by students, some by adult actors. Most were loosely derived from Latin originals, but their characters, their settings, their topics, their humor, and their dialogue were all 100% English.

Wallace sees a direct line of evolution from the children's companies to the magnificent era of Elizabethan drama. These early plays at Blackfriars created the template, and he believes that it was there that the court collided with the street and a new dramatic genie was unleashed. He cites 1584 as the pivotal year that everything changed. Lyly and Peele took over for Farrant and Hunnis and found the courtly theatre as it was, with song and dance and masques and pretty dialogue. They just chopped it into five acts and gave it space to include the tropes of native English theatre. They added thunder, fencing, battles, blood, buffoonery, and constant, rapid action, and voila! Shakespeare!

Well, it was not quite as simple as that, but in time, academic theatre, with its classical structure, was taken over by native storytelling. Stock characters in those early plays—among them the braggart soldier, the unscrupulous companion, the nurse, the clown, the rude mechanical, the jealous suitor, and Poor Tom the beggar—were all derived from the Latin originals; but they became native Englishmen and made their way into popular stereotypes. The plays of Lyly and Peele were the first five-act plays not modeled on any classic drama ever to be performed in public before an English audience. The playwrights known as "the university wits," Nashe, Greene, and Marlowe, soon followed suit, and Shakespeare and his peers came after. Taste follows taste: entertainers always give an audience what it wants, and what the audience at Blackfriars wanted was witty, gossipy, rowdy, locally sourced, topical, satirical, native English theatre.

After Blackfriars was closed in 1584 the records become elusive. We know that Lyly continued to write plays for the Children of Saint Paul's and they continued to perform at court and for the public, but records are spotty. There are very few records of performances by the Children of the Chapel, but the payments for their upkeep and the permission for the impressment of boy singers to replenish their numbers continued every year. It is supposed that in the last decade of her life the boys' companies fell out of favor with the Queen, but there is no definitive explanation for this, and it is unknown whether the cause was internal or external or whether they were simply overwhelmed by the brilliance of the men's companies performing plays by the likes of Shakespeare.

There is one hint, however, that suggests the boys were silenced because they performed a play that gave great offense, either to the church or to the crown. In 1589 there is a record of the Children of Paul's being "put down" after John Lyly got them tangled up in a political kerfuffle between the state and a group of anti-episcopal Puritans. It was called the Marprelate controversy. Someone, or a group of persons, all going by the name of Martin Marprelate, began publishing pamphlets that attacked the Church of England and individual priests. They were so persistent and so contentious that the court asked their wittiest playwrights, Lyly among them, to help them respond. We don't have the play that Lyly wrote for them and that the boys performed. It was certainly written on the side of the state (Lyly was no fan of the Puritans) but apparently it was a double-edged attack and insults were flung freely in all directions. The over-stepping must have been very grave because the reaction to it was severe. In the following months the government issued a strict decree that no play could be performed without first being approved by a state censor. The boys ceased playing at court almost completely, and Lyly's career was over.

So for most of the end of the century, the boys' companies went dark. They were still active in the provinces, but the records of their travels are meager. Of course the court itself was not silent. The men's companies were churning out play after play in the public theatres and they were constantly invited to perform at court. They were profiting greatly by their ever more secure first place in the heart of their Queen.

A Short-Lived Rebirth

But the story did not end there. Indeed, there was a second flowering, which, though brief and controversial, was more dazzling than anything we have seen thus far. The turn of the century, and especially the ascendance of a new monarch, brought new life to the Children of the Chapel and the Children of Saint Paul's. But it was a life sustained by a different breath—the breath of commerce. By the Jacobean Age theatre in England was at the height of its most robust flowering in history, and there were impresarios eager to capitalize on the nostalgia for the past glory of the boys' companies.

The exact dates aren't available anymore, but by the beginning of 17th century both companies were up and running under new management. There was by this time a growing public passion for drama, and there was enough nostalgia for the heyday of Blackfriars for investors to believe they could turn a profit by re-opening it. James Burbage had purchased the property in 1596 to create an indoor home for his successful company, of which Shakespeare was a co-owner. He had remodeled a section of it to build a handsome new theatre, but the neighbors had protested and prevented the opening. At some point, in order to defray the cost of keeping it open, he had leased it to what was essentially an incorporated body of profiteers, who used the old ruse of opening it as a "private" theatre to house the Children of the Chapel. As for the Children of Saint Paul's, the records are scant, but we do know that they were performing at Saint Gregory's Church with their new Master, Edward Pierce, dusting off old favorites and soliciting new material.

Since there was no daily *London Times* archiving the doings of the city back then, most of our information about the boys' companies from 1600 to 1616 comes from one of four sources: records of performances at court; the licensing and publication of plays, in which there is usually a phrase telling where and by whom they were first performed; the written accounts of individual audience members; and lawsuits. Especially for the Children of the Chapel, the last source is perhaps the most fruitful.

The first lawsuit of note came right away, in 1601, when Henry Clifton, Esq. sued Henry Evans, the new manager of Blackfriars, and Thomas Gyles, the Chapel master, essentially accusing them of kidnapping his son Thomas. The rebuilding of two new companies after a decade of silence had required aggressive recruitment tactics, and young Thomas had been recognized as a talent at his grammar school. He had been impressed into service by the use of Gyles' customary writ from the crown. The suit succeeded and young Thomas was released, but for our purposes, some interesting facts emerged from it. First of all, the suit gives us the names of a several boys who were impressed at that time and it makes it clear that the plaintiffs were guilty of over-stepping by capturing a boy from a family of substance: the son of a gentleman. Even more interesting: Clifton emphasized that the boys captured were "in no way able or fit for singing." The purpose of the writ was, and had been for centuries, for the impressment of chapel boys to augment the choir, but these boys were not singers—they were *actors*! It wasn't long before Gyles' writ was re-*writt*en with clear wording stating that boys could not be impressed for the purpose of playing on the stage, "for that it is not fit or decent that such as should sing the praises of God almighty should be trained up or employed in such lascivious and profane exercises."

Lascivious and profane or not, when James I became king, the boys' companies were, at least for a while, well received. The Children of the Chapel were re-named the Children of the Queen's Revels, and along with Saint Paul's boys there were two other minor companies formed, one for the Prince and one for the Princess.

Without going into fine detail, let us look at what distinguished these new boys' companies from those that preceded them. From their inception, they were commercial ventures. Their material was not written by their choirmasters or playwrights internally associated with them, but by hired, well-paid, professional dramatists. The boy actors did not exhibit the light, charming, playful style of their own: they were awkwardly, and often unsuccessfully, competing with and aping a new generation of brilliant adult thespians. Despite their princely names, these companies were ultimately not indebted to royal patronage: they were indebted to investors taking risks and hoping to reap huge profits.

The boy actors had exited the Elizabethan era and entered the Jacobean, which for drama meant that the themes and topics that whetted the appetite of the audience were darker and more morally complex and ambiguous. The most noted of the playwrights from the first decade of their existence were Samuel Daniel, John Day, Thomas Middleton, George Chapman, John Marston, and Ben Jonson. They wrote dangerous comedies and satires to be performed by children for sophisticated and decadent adult audiences.

Here is just a sampling of the titles that came from the pens of these titans to be performed by children at Blackfriars and Saint Paul's. I've seen and read only a few of these plays, but just the titles are enough to know that they were acerbic and witty in tone, and they trespassed on forbidden ground. Chapman wrote *Bussy D'Ambois*, *The Gentleman Usher*, *May Day*, *Monsieur d'Olive*, and *The Widow's Tears*. Thomas Middleton wrote *A Mad World My Masters*, *A Trick to Catch the Old One*, and *Your Five Gallants*. John Marston wrote *Parasitaster*, *The Malcontent*, and *The Dutch Courtesan*, the latter honored by a performance at court for the King of Denmark's visit. Ben Jonson wrote *Cynthia's Revels*, *The Poetaster*, and *Epicoene, or the Silent Woman*, which was the most famous comedy of its time (which I can easily believe because I had to giggle just reading the synopsis). He also collaborated with Chapman and Marston on the ill-fated *Eastward Ho*, as we shall see.

All of these were excellent plays and enjoyed great success, but they may have been a stretch for boy actors. They were filtered through a new aesthetic. Audiences had changed. Educated by Shakespeare and his peers, these audiences were as brilliant as the plays they were observing. They were not satisfied with the old song and dance and delight of the masques. They wanted intellectual spice and a touch of danger, and the great playwrights knew how to give it to them.

There is one other expert source of information about those years. In *Hamlet*, Shakespeare tells us much about the children of Blackfriars and Saint Paul's. In this exchange between Rosencrantz and Hamlet, Rosencrantz reports from the city and explains why the traveling theatre company visiting Elsinore is on the road and not performing at home:

Hamlet: How chances it they travel? Their residence, both in reputation and profit, was better both ways.
Rosencrantz: I think their inhibition comes by the means of the late Innovation.
Hamlet: Do they hold the same estimation they did when I was in the city? Are they so followed?

Rosencrantz:	No, indeed, are they not.
Hamlet:	How comes it? Do they grow rusty?
Rosencrantz:	Nay, their endeavour keeps in the wonted pace: but there is, sir, an aery of children, little eyases, that cry out on the top of question, and are most tyrannically clapped for't: these are now the fashion, and so berattle the common stages—so they call them—that many wearing rapiers are afraid of goose-quills and dare scarce come thither.
Hamlet:	What, are they children? Who maintains 'em? How are they escorted? Will they pursue the quality no longer than they can sing? Will they not say afterwards, if they should grow themselves to common players—as it is most like, if their means are no better—their writers do them wrong, to make them exclaim against their own succession?
Rosencrantz:	'Faith, there has been much to do on both sides; and the nation holds it no sin to tar them to controversy: there was, for a while, no money bid for argument, unless the poet and the player went to cuffs in the question.
Hamlet:	Is't possible?
Guildenstern:	O, there has been much throwing about of brains.
Hamlet:	Do the boys carry it away?
Rosencrantz:	Ay, that they do, my lord; Hercules and his load too.

Act II, Scene ii

For the modern reader, just to make it easy, I'll highlight and translate the salient points made here. Hamlet [Shakespeare] is concerned that the reputation and profit of the men's companies are suffering because of the boy actors, whom he characterizes as squawking little eyases [eaglets]. He also demonstrates a very real concern for the boys themselves—I would guess because the abuse of the writ for impressment of choirboys, for acting instead of singing, meant that there was no provision made by the crown to send them to university. They were being poorly housed and once their voices broke they would have no choice but to grow into "common players" (a reflection of his opinion of his own profession?). He refers to a battle being waged between playwrights and adult players over payment for the best scripts, implying that the boys' companies could pay more and get better material. He infers that the boys are winning the battle.

He further notes that "the nation holds it no sin to tar them to controversy," meaning that the public is not offended by seeing children dabble in political mockery. Their plays are so satirical and topical that people of influence—those "wearing rapiers"—are afraid to attend for fear of being mocked by the playwrights—those with "goose-quills." (Here he seems to be acknowledging the ever-true maxim that the pen is mightier than the sword.)

That was roughly 1603. Very soon there were other battles being fought in the courts and in taverns, with opponents occasionally even coming to blows. The profits that had been promised the naive investors in Blackfriars were nowhere near the reality, and endless legal squabbles were inevitable. Hillebrand tries to untangle a mare's nest of suits that went on for years and cost the Children of the Revels dearly. The eventual results of most of the suits were lost in the warehouses of paper records that had not yet been examined when Hillebrand wrote his book, and, indeed, may still lie neglected somewhere. But they don't matter here. The trail of suits, even without their closure, gives us a vivid glimpse into the times for our boys.

It was the daring characteristic of the boys (or, in truth, their playwrights) to "cry out at the top of the question" that did them in at the end. Four plays in particular "berattled" the stage, although there were certainly others.

In 1604 the Children of the Queens Revels performed Samuel Daniel's *Philotas*, which closely paralleled the career of the popular Earl of Essex, only recently hanged for treason. That play was banned for seeming to meddle in the affairs of the state, and Samuel Daniel was called to account for it, but he managed to talk his way out of trouble by convincing the judges that he had started it long before Essex's rebellion.

Then early in 1605 they performed *Eastward Ho*, the play mentioned earlier, by Jonson, Chapman, and Marston. That play mocked the Scotsmen who surrounded the Scottish King James and were much disliked by the old guard. Chapman and Jonson spent some time cooling their heels in prison for that one, but Marston, who was probably the one most responsible, got away. More significantly, the boys lost their connection to the Queen and were henceforth simply called the Children of the Revels. The Queen apparently wanted nothing more to do with them and had her title removed.

Jonson and Chapman were pardoned and released after some chastened pleading, but apparently they hadn't learned their lesson, The very next year Jonson collaborated with John Day on *The Isle of Gulls*, in which two characters titled "Duke" and "Duchess" were thinly veiled caricatures of James I and Queen Anne. It portrayed the court as a bawdy house of crooks, where bribes were taken for favors and advancements. This was indeed an impudent over-stepping of the boundaries: Clearly the potential for profit outweighed the danger.

Somehow the boy players had thus far survived, either because the courts were not paying close attention or because some liberality was still extended due to their youth. But then came the last straw: Chapman's *The Conspiracy and Tragedy of Charles, Duke of Biron*. In this play King James and his Scottish favorites were again targeted, and the king was portrayed as a drunkard, striking gentlemen and cursing the heavens over a hawking mishap. This time he had had enough, and he closed all the theatres in London. Blackfriars remained closed for a long time, and when it re-opened it was not for boys—it was for Burbage's company, now called the King's Men.

In hindsight, it is hard to imagine how the boys' companies got away with their daring for as long as they did and why they kept it up despite censure. Here again, I suspect that part of the reason was commercial. There is a necessary element of risk present in all successful theatre that pushes the boundaries and asks an audience to examine its beliefs and values, and one must again remember that the Jacobean audience was voracious. They had come to expect, even demand, a healthy touch of risk in their entertainment. The child actors couldn't act with the same subtlety and skill that the audience had come to expect from the men's companies, so in order to draw crowds they had to specialize in what had worked for them so well in the past, which was satire. And they had to do it in excess.

When the end came the king's harshness was certainly intensified by his reaction to the Gunpowder Plot. It was in 1605 that a group of Catholic conspirators came within a hair's breadth of changing the course of history by blowing up the entire court and most of the aristocracy of England. It didn't happen, and today it is mostly remembered by the bonfires and fireworks that make up the gleeful celebration of Guy Fawkes Day; but the danger was very real. James Shapiro's *The Year of Lear* describes wonderfully how the exposure of the plot turned the king into a paranoiac and his court into a bastion. What he tolerated before November 5, 1605, he could never tolerate again.

In 1609 Burbage took back the lease at Blackfriars, which had been closed for several months, and at the same time he paid off Edward Pierce, then the choirmaster at Saint Paul's, to stop performing. The Children of the Revels and the Children of Saint Paul's were finished. Some of the boys were re-constituted briefly in yet another abandoned monastery, called the Whitefriars, as a short-lived company called the King's Revels, and they limped along for a few years performing minor works by minor playwrights, but by 1616 that ended as well. For several years thereafter there were traveling companies of boys, claiming to be the Revels, but they were strictly provincial and only a wisp of smoke from the ashes of their glory days.

But to conclude, try to transport your imagination back to a time when boys' voices filled the schools, courts, churches, cathedrals, and theatres with the "sweet airs" described in the loveliest lines in *The Tempest*, spoken by Caliban, its most monstrous character. As quoted earlier, boys sang with voices

> That, if I then had waked after long sleep,
> Will make me sleep again: and then, in dreaming,
> The clouds methought would open and show riches
> Ready to drop upon me that, when I waked,
> I cried to dream again.
>
> Act III, Scene ii

Again! Music falling from above: the voices of Angels. And each of the angels and each of the eaglets took his first flight learning the arts of language and presentation at a Latin grammar school.

The Boy Players at the Globe

And then there were the boy actors who performed with their adult counterparts in the professional theatres of London. Think about it.

The summer of 1998 I participated in the "Teaching Shakespeare Through Performance" program at the Globe, where we were able to work on the stage two or three mornings a week. Our call was at 7:00 AM, before the professionals arrived to rehearse. We were American English teachers, not actors, and at first we were like pilgrims stepping on to holy ground. But after awhile we grew comfortable enough to occupy our space, however briefly, and explore.

The Globe stage feels vast when you stand on it, like a field at the bottom of a huge, cylindrical well, and yet it feels surprisingly intimate. The audience standing in the pit is right at your feet and those seated line the sides. In Shakespeare's day, two thousand people could be packed into that theatre, and in the daylight, the actors could see every face. As auditors, we placed ourselves at different levels and different sides to check for acoustics. As performers we roamed about the stage, speaking our lines, to see if we could find power spots where the sound could be produced more effectively.

What we found was an acoustical marvel. Sound levels were uniform throughout the space. One would expect that a theatre shaped like a well would be an echo chamber, but the Globe is built of natural materials—wood and horse hair plaster—that absorb sound and soften the decay, so the reverberations amplify clearly. Some of the men among us with lower voices could be heard anywhere on the stage by any member of the audience, even in normal conversation. They didn't have to throw their voices from a proscenium stage to the back of a huge auditorium. It was different for voices in the higher registers, of course. We women had to work harder to be heard, but for a well-trained voice it would not have been difficult. Shakespearean blank verse did not have to be shouted. Quiet conversations were possible, and the audience could detect small, subtle gestures and facial expressions easily. This realization helped me to understand how it might have been possible for a boy of 14 to project his voice without amplification. Indeed, we were fortunate to be there for a magical scene-by-scene performance of *Merchant of Venice* by children from several local schools, and, standing in the pit or setting in the balconies, we had no difficulty hearing them. But it took more than a loud voice to play those staggeringly complex roles. I still spin at the thought of it.

The acoustics held true for music as well, which explains how a boy playing Desdemona could stirringly sing *The Willow Song*, or the boy playing Glendower's daughter could sing in Welsh next to a campfire: quiet songs, requiring exquisite voices and great emotional control. Then I imagined the songs in *The Tempest*, that most musical of Shakespeare's plays. James I's court brought masques back in vogue, and the wedding masque in the Tempest would have been in a style that boys' companies had adopted so successfully in the previous century.

The boys singing the songs of the goddesses would have sounded ethereal. But earlier in the play, I imagine that Ariel was also played by a boy, singing the achingly beautiful song:

> Full fathom five thy father lies;
> Of his bones are coral made;
> Those are pearls that were his eyes:
> Nothing of him that doth fade,
> But doth suffer a sea change
> Into something rich and strange.
>
> Act I, Scene ii

Boys at the Globe were pretty phenomenal. Anyone interested in learning more about them would enjoy Joy Leslie Gibson's *Squeaking Cleopatras*, which describes their recruitment, their training, their housing, their legal status, and the times they lived in. She also demonstrates the great care with which Shakespeare tailored their speeches with well-placed pauses to accommodate their smaller lung capacity.

But just pause for a moment and consider how fantastically, incredibly, astonishingly amazing they must have been. Think of it! Think of the huge range of female roles in Shakespeare's plays. Older women, especially the comics such as Mistress Quickly and Juliet's nurse, would have been played by adult, male character actors; but even among the spirited young women there is an infinite variety. Think of Desdemona, Rosalind, Lady Macbeth, Beatrice, Kate, Ophelia, Viola, Helena, Isabella, the French Princess Katherine, etc. etc. etc. all played by pre-pubescent boys. Think of all of the plays of Shakespeare that are totally carried by women. Not just comedies. Not just *As You Like It*, *Much Ado*, *The Taming of the Shrew*, *Measure for Measure*, and *All's Well that Ends Well*. What kind of play would *Romeo and Juliet* be without its incandescent heroine? What about *Cleopatra*? Where would the heart of *King Lear* be without Cordelia? These young actors had to be the equals of the men in every way. They had to have the same genius, to be able to act highly nuanced scenes with both subtlety and clarity. They had to be nimble and believable with both their voices and their gestures. They were the ultimate expression of the training of boys in performance.

11
THE LEGO SNAP OF LEARNING

FIGURE 11.1 Erasmus and Will play with Legos.

All learning comes from a state of wonder.

—*Plato*

The source of all creativity is yearning.

—*Eric Booth*

DOI: 10.4324/9781003344919-12

You need fertile soil to nurture the seed of an unfamiliar idea. This chapter will look at learning theory through the lens of Erasmus' writings on education to provide justification for the radical idea that the education of Shakespeare and tens of thousands of his peers—rich as it was in the arts of performance—contributed to the brilliance of their generation.

Education for the Benefit of the Commonwealth

If, indeed, humanist education in Shakespeare's day produced smarter, more flexible thinkers, more discerning minds, and more intelligent citizens, it is worth our effort to identify what elements of that education could be simulated in schools today. In this book we will examine two relatively short spans of time during which unimaginable changes occurred: the Reformation and the dawning of modern English literature. What changes would I like to see in our current generation, emerging from a pandemic and an oppressive era of standardized testing?

Of course I would not advocate the return to the required seven years of the study of Latin, and I doubt I'd make much headway in promoting the idea that students should be able to identify and use well over a hundred figures of speech in their speaking and writing (although I don't think the first of those innovations would do harm, and I believe the second could do enormous good—even if they only learned half that many!). I certainly do *not* think we should go back to educating only propertied and/or precocious male children. The cultural milieu today is so vastly different from that of Tudor England that it is ridiculous to contemplate anything like a return to the day of one hundred students from ages seven to seventeen vs. one headmaster with a birch switch at the ready. But we have wandered far afield of the core purpose of education, which, yet again, is *for the benefit of the commonwealth*: the training up of citizens with the courage to think creatively and critically, to problem solve, and to exhibit what the famous 16th-century pedagogue, Richard Mulcaster, would have called good behavior and audacity.

I like the word audacity because I like words that can take you in many different directions. It often implies boldness to a degree of rudeness, but it had a different connotation in Shakespeare's day—a much more positive one. Boldness was still a part of it, but a similar meaning today might be a word that means the courage and capacity to persuade and to influence change. *Agency* is a much-used word in educationese right now, and may not be the perfect equivalent, but it's close. I am writing this particular paragraph shortly after the student-organized "March for Our Lives" protests that happened across the country after the shooting of seventeen students and teachers in Parkland, Florida. The Parkland students, who subsequently led a national movement squaring off against the National Rifle Association, were drama students from their high school theatre program. No teenager has ever exhibited audacity/agency more effectively than Emma Gonzalez did, standing before half a million protesters in our nation's capital and stating the names of each of the dead, followed by the words, "will never," then standing with tears streaming down her face for six and a half minutes of agonized silence. Six and a half minutes—the time it took the shooter to exhaust his killing spree. Her repetition of the words "will never" showed her grasp of rhetoric and elevated two words to the affective realm that King Lear reached when he repeated "never" five times over his murdered daughter. Ms. Gonzalez may not have known that she was using the rhetorical figures epimone and aposiopesis, but, either through instinct or through training, she knew the dramatic power of repetition and silence. The audience squirmed, laughed nervously, and chanted, but they finally submitted to silence and contemplation. I truly do believe that history will show that the world shifted a bit on its axis in those six and a half minutes.

As for good behavior, a more resonant modern word would be empathy, which in an ideal world would be the root of good behavior. To empathy and agency I would add what I deeply hope my own students acquired to some degree: the love of learning, the tools to acquire it, and the judgment to use it well. Something in humanist education gave all of the above to students, and Erasmus deserves enormous credit for that.

I include all of arts instruction in everything I say about its importance. The creative process offers similar learning benefits in all of the disciplines. Would anyone argue that dance is not a visual art? Doesn't a visual artist paint or draw or sculpt to communicate a story to an audience? Doesn't music offer an immediate connection to memory? Of course! to all three. I focus on the dramatic arts here partly because of all the arts disciplines they are the most democratic and the most adaptable to any classroom. Music is skills-based, and proficiency in music demands a long-term commitment to regular and sustained practice (which, in fact, was a constant in Elizabethan schools). Dance, too, in its advanced study, is skills-based and practice-dependent, and when it is practiced as creative movement, by young children, it overlaps with drama. Engagement in visual arts is usually more solitary and involves less collaboration. But another reason for my focus is that when connecting directly to the development of linear thinking—or story—in cognition, there are aspects unique to drama.

This chapter will address the following questions. None has a clear answer, but all three are well worth the pondering:

- What is creativity and how is it related to critical thinking?
- Can creativity be taught?
- And, if the answer to the second question is yes, did the humanist education in the Elizabethan classroom teach creativity?

Creativity and Can It Be Taught?

Whenever educators speak of the arts, inevitably the subject of creativity comes up. This is understandable given that the arts provide fuel for our imaginations—the human being's chief producer of new ideas and divergent thinking. The arts stimulate the idea production process and offer multiple pathways to express them.

Flexible thinking is required to make connections between and among all ideas offered and extrapolate something new and useful, or meaningful, to the person who had the idea and, even, perhaps, to others. This could be to one other person or hundreds, thousands, or millions of others. And this doesn't just occur in the arts. Creativity permeates society and culture across the human spectrum, in all aspects of emotion and experience.

Having said that, the intersection of the arts, creativity, and cognition is a vital juncture in intellectual development and critical thinking. A critical thinker explores many points of view and alternative, logical pathways, which leads to choices about which are the most promising ones to explore further (convergent thinking). The practice of critical thinking underpins the creative classroom in any subject.

In a creative classroom, teachers and students are all learners. When this happens, learning becomes a process of discovery. And this answers the question: can creativity be taught? *Yes*, and it can be cultivated, practiced, amplified, and welcomed. In the same sense that Plato says that all learning is already within us and good teaching provides the conditions that allow for its realization and expression, good teaching provides the structure and the exercise to allow for the *practice* of our innate creativity.

As for the third question: in this chapter I will step into Erasmus' shoes (excuse me, sir) and exercise my audacity to its limits. (I know he liked audacious women, so I feel safe.) Did humanist education teach creativity? And if yes (as will be seen, I obviously believe), in this day of data worship, can we prove it?

Theatre or Drama

Before continuing, for the sake of clarity, let us tease out the meanings of the words *theatre* and *drama*, or to be precise and relevant, the difference between a theatre program and a drama program. The two are intricately interrelated, of course, and in many contexts they are interchangeable under the overarching study of the performing arts, but in the context of classroom practice there is a fine distinction to be made. In *Drama for Learning* the renowned teacher and practitioner of process drama, Dorothy Heathcote, points out that *drama* comes from the Greek word for experience. A theatrical performance is a rehearsed, artistic expression observed by an audience. Drama, on the other hand, derives from the *experience* of the expressive artist. Theatre is an art form undertaken with an audience in mind, whereas drama activities may be undertaken in any classroom, for any age, with no audience expectation required—its goal being to contextualize a situation and simulate an authentic experience. A drama program is inclusive for any student and adaptable to any study.

> **Theatre is an art form undertaken with an audience in mind, whereas drama activities may be undertaken in any classroom, for any age, with no audience expectation required.**

The skills of theatre are performance skills: projection, vocal control, expressive movement, and emotional authenticity. Drama, however, may be undertaken without emphasis on polished performance skills. Students may participate in drama activities—such as improvisation, mirroring games, or sequential tableaux to illustrate a story—in the study of any subject, in problem-solving, or in the development of social skills. A simple way to view the difference would be to say that *drama is process* and *theatre is product*. A polished theatrical production is always the end result of a long and rigorous process of dramatic exploration, but the process is also valuable in and of itself, with no end-product necessary.

> *Drama is process* and *theatre is product*.

The study of theatre arts embraces both drama and theatrical performance, but the skills of putting on a play involve a heightened level of collaboration and polish, with a limited number of participating playmakers and a greater focus on the final show. Drama, as practiced in the classroom, can involve everyone. When schoolboys in the humanist classroom practiced oratorical recitation of their daily, memorized lessons, they were *experiencing* the words they spoke and learning to embody their meaning. In that they were practicing drama. When they were performing scenes with their classmates as an exercise for learning Latin conversation, they were engaging in drama. But when a select few were rehearsing and performing plays for presentation to the community, they were doing theatre. Both are valuable in education. Both involve crafted language and, above all, story.

Skilled theatre educators know when they are engaging their students in drama, or process, and when in theatrical performance, or product. But *any* teacher, elementary or secondary, can, with some training, incorporate drama activities to illuminate their curriculum. We humans have brains that are wired to follow stories, and all of the most powerful and enduring lessons make use of that unique characteristic. Story is at the root of all artistic expression, but in both drama and theatre, it is root, branch, and everything.

For a story to have impact and to remain in memory, it is best presented artfully. In the elementary theatre curriculum that we developed for the Los Angeles schools, the first kindergarten lessons introduce two foundational concepts: "theatre brings stories to life" and "body, voice, and imagination are the tools of the actor." Everything else derives from these two lessons. Body, voice, and imagination are all it takes to develop the artistry of presentation, or "presence." They are tools that we all have. Think about the power of this for a moment. Young, old, tiny, tall, male, female, fat, thin, abled, disabled—we all have a body, a voice, and an imagination at our disposal if we choose to develop them. We are all capable of being effective storytellers, communicators, or actors. It all boils down to those three tools today as it did for Shakespeare and his peers. Strip away the Latin, the Ovid, the scores of rhetorical devices, the birch-twig-wielding headmaster, and all the pedagogical practices that have vanished in the past four centuries, and you still have *presence*. It is taught through different literatures and different strategies, but the end result is the same. Today, as they did then, drama students learn how to be *seen and heard* and *how to tell a story well*, and that is a skill that will serve them for their entire lives.

Drama in the Classroom

It is painful that after spending a career in arts education and arts advocacy, after designing and implementing a highly regarded elementary theatre program in Los Angeles schools, after observing the profound impact of the program where it was implemented in full, after attending and presenting in dozens of local, state, and national conferences focused on performing arts in schools, after reading scores of research results proving irrevocably that classroom dramatics reaps benefits in and beyond school, and after spending months researching this book I am watching my grandchildren and millions of their peers heading into schools across the nation, with fine teachers and thoughtful administrators but with minimal instruction in speech or drama. Why, with all the evidence out there, is this still true?

In the introduction of her book, *Drama in Mind*, Patrice Baldwin describes an experience that is all too maddeningly familiar to me. She was participating in a conference focused on the teaching of thinking skills, and a presenter, who was a well-established educational theatre practitioner, demonstrated a methodology derived from his own practice. She found it odd that he never once mentioned the words "drama" or "theatre." When she approached him after his presentation and asked about this, he said, "I advise you not to call what we do 'drama.'" When she protested, saying that that was exactly what it was, he suggested, in a confidential tone, that she instead call it "accelerated learning." He believed that promoting good practice in the classroom was more important than naming it. It was as though the mere mention of the word "drama" would elevate the art at the expense of the science, and that would diminish its relevance.

> *With all we know about the world of good that comes from pedagogy that incorporates drama, we should be shouting the news from the rooftops.*

I pointed the passage out to my friend and colleague, Dr. Sherry Kerr, who is involved in research on the impact of the arts in schools, and she emailed back the following:

> This really resonates. One of my graduate students wrote a grant using a "Drama In Education" focus and it was declined. We wrote the *exact same* grant using "Active Learning" and we got $125,000. Of course we taught DIE for two years under the grant. It's infuriating!!!

WHAT!!!??? Accelerated Learning? Active Learning? Call a spade a spade. It's drama! With all we know about the world of good that comes from pedagogy that incorporates drama, we should be shouting the news from the rooftops. Why be coy? Why the whispering? Why, as a literacy expert who attended one of our meetings in the Arts Branch suggested, does a filter go up in the minds of so many educators every time the subject comes up—a filter that implies that performing arts are a lovely but dispensable, *extra*curricular "enrichment," for after-hours, for the few but not the many?

I am still bewildered by this dilemma, although having observed the initial caution exhibited by teachers and administrators when we launched the pilot Arts Prototype Schools program twenty-three years ago, I have come to understand it. Certainly it is partly fear of the unfamiliar. Elementary school teachers used to be trained in arts instruction. When I went through my teacher training years ago all credential candidates were required to take two semesters of arts education: one in music and the other a choice of visual arts, dance, or theatre. That requirement is long gone, and two generations of young teachers have entered the field with zero training in artful instruction and no memory of the arts-rich curriculum that was common in California schools well into the seventies. There is also spotlight anxiety: the very real fear, on the part of both students and teachers, of embarrassment or humiliation when asked to perform unsheltered and unprepared, even for an audience of one. And, too, of all the arts, theatre may be the most encouraging of individual expression and the most fun. Dramatic improvisation opens a door to a freedom that can be worrisome in a group of students for whom classroom management is an issue.

The combination of fear on the part of teachers and exuberance on the part of students might feel like recipe for chaos. That is why our arts program was at its core a professional development. We required the participation of classroom teachers, who taught alongside the arts instructors and learned their methodology. Despite some initial resistance, thousands of classroom teachers have learned basic, trust-building and community-building improvisation techniques that can help students explore text, subtext, and nuance in literature. They have seen that training in drama skills is not just about a select few brave souls putting on a play. It is about discipline, time management, exploration, empathy, and attention. Contrary to chaos, performing arts classes are focused and rigorous, and teachers who have witnessed that have stepped in to try out the methods for themselves. They have discovered, as I have many times, that students who are disruptive in other subjects are engaged and cooperative in drama, where they are able to *move* with purpose and intent.

Even so, the fear obstacle has never gone away, even in Los Angeles Unified, which, large as it is, is just one district among thousands. This is a measure of how exceedingly daunting it is. Overcoming it will require a supportive approach to ongoing professional development to diminish the resistance to risk, and that approach will need to be fully backed by all administrators. Cautious teachers brave enough to give classroom dramatics a try need an underpinning of confidence that it will make a difference in the cognitive development of their students. That is why we need the contemporary evidence that confirms the view of theatre education advocates that their work is essential for the healthy development of every child. There is plenty out there. It comes from two fields: the field of arts education research and the field of neuroscience.

Arts Education Research

There is no shortage of research connecting the performing arts to achievement and to social and emotional health. There's more than enough to silence any doubter if they read it all. This chapter must be dedicated to the late James Catterall, who died in 2017, suddenly and unexpectedly, leaving unfinished a huge body of research in the field of arts education. More than anything else, it was Catterall's contribution to *Champions of Change: The Impact of the Arts on Learning*, published in 1997, which launched Los Angeles and other school districts on the slow but steady effort to restore the arts to their rightful place in schools. Author of a great many books and articles, documentation that is desperately needed to support the agenda of arts education advocates, he moved our field forward immeasurably. A few years ago, after retiring from the University of California, he started the Center for the Research on Creativity, and when he died he was deeply invested in gathering and analyzing data from arts education programs all across the country. He was also developing a tool that could assess creative ability in K-12 students, which would have been the holy grail of the data gatherers among arts education advocates. His was a terrible loss, but his work continues in the hands of the many researchers that he trained, two of whom, Dr. Kerr and Kim Zanti, have been enormously helpful to me in accessing the research I need for this chapter.

Since the national Arts Education Partnership was founded in 1995, it has published numerous exhaustive studies, starting with *Champions of Change* and followed by *Critical Evidence* and *Critical Links*. Catterall, Steve Seidel and Dennie Palmer Wolf of Harvard's Project Zero, and Eliot Eisner and Shirley Brice Heath of Stanford are just a few of many giants in arts education research that have produced scores of studies. Indeed, it is hard to keep track of them all. The research page of the AEP, ArtsEdResearch, is a great place to start, sortable by discipline, by age, by programs structured in school and out, and by student outcomes.

There is plenty of documented proof that an arts-rich educational environment will absolutely enhance academic achievement in literacy and numeracy. One particular study: In the year 2000, Harvard's Project Zero published the *Reviewing Education and the Arts Project*, known as the REAP Report. It did not conduct its own investigations, but instead analyzed the results of hundreds of research projects carried out over the past century, hoping to find irrefutable links between classroom arts and academic scores. In the executive summary the editors caution the reader, pointing out that 1) It is difficult to establish *irrefutable* links because of the infinity of variables in education and 2) It is a shallow task because it implies that academic achievement in the three R's is the only reason that the arts should be taught. In fact they needed this caveat because in some ways the project was a disappointment. They were only able to find irrefutable links in two of the ten areas they had identified. That said they did find moderate links between the study of music and spatial and temporal awareness; *and, significantly, they found a strong link between classroom drama and verbal test scores*. Again, statistically, it was an *irrefutable* link, and, what was more important, the increase in achievement was transferable from subject to subject. So theatre was the winner in that particular study.

Sadly, however, that narrow focus on achievement in math and literacy is a double-edged sword. It is what the educational policy makers of today want to see: solid evidence that engagement in the arts will produce higher test scores for the glory and financial benefit of schools. Most of these studies, therefore, were necessitated by policy and funded by policy makers, whose concern was driven by the belief I've heard stated far too often: "If we don't test it, they won't teach it." This is frighteningly true for those of us in the field who do not countenance the idea that test scores, not thinking skills, are the ultimate goal of education.

There are other, better, reasons that education in the performing arts should be considered the birthright for every student. If the researchers had been around in the 16th century, with their charts and their precision measurements, they would have had a phenomenal opportunity. If they were asked to show that universal instruction in drama could reap positive benefits for literacy, they could have gathered the data from the humanist curriculum at the time—anecdotes of dozens of thespian-inspired school masters; statutes of scores of Latin grammar schools; purchases of thousands of texts of colloquies, Latin comedies, and Senecan tragedies; surveys of tens of thousands of theatre goers—and charted all that along with the results: the nurturing of the most discerning and critical audience in theatre history and the birth of modern English literature. *How's that for evidence?*

> **If the researchers had been around in the 16th century, with their charts and their precision measurements, they would have had a phenomenal opportunity.**

Accountability

Here is where I permit myself a tirade. Testing. I have the chops to say what I am going to say. I've spent years in the classroom, and I share my concern with tens of thousands of teachers who have observed classrooms numbed by incessant test preparation. I've witnessed the terror in 7-year-old faces, the tears, the vomiting, the quivering chins, and the shaking hands (as though today's children did not have enough cause for stress in their innocence). I've seen teenagers wilt with boredom after hours of studying test-taking skills and simply disappear into daydreams or rebel with outrageous behaviors. I know brilliant adults who have internalized a "below average" assessment of their own intellect for their entire lives because of one totally irrelevant SAT or IQ score. I've attended days of professional development, with free lunch provided, teaching me how to legally boost test scores. I know all the tricks. It's legal but it's still cheating! None of it, not one second of it, constitutes what I consider education.

It goes without question that there must be accountability, which is why educators have embraced academic standards. Standards give teachers, students, and their parents an observable measure for developmentally appropriate achievement, and as such they provide guideposts for instruction. The problem comes with their marriage to standardized tests and the elevation of these tests to a level far beyond what was intended by their developers. There are many ways to assess achievement, but authentic assessment is expensive and time-consuming. Standardized tests are easy and relatively cheap (and the word "relatively" should be used with a footnote here, because educational testing is a billion dollar industry), but they do not differentiate for learning modalities and give only a very narrow slice of the picture of learning. They are tools that serve a limited purpose in narrowly focused studies to be used by educators in the context of their own practice in schools or classrooms. But making their results public, exposing innocent children to them, broadcasting them on banners on school fences, using them as bludgeons to punish struggling schools and hard-working teachers, and making them the basis for financial rewards and the data for research in achievement is unconscionable abuse. Schools trying to educate under a shadow of accountability anxiety based on standardized tests abandon what they know about authentic instruction and resort to drill and kill. Classrooms suffer. Teachers suffer. Children who are turned into data points and who internalize the deceptive message of their test scores may suffer damage that is irreversible.

Erasmus would have been mystified. Nowhere in his hundreds of pages of writing about the education of elementary age children is there any mention of a report card. Nowhere does he discuss school accountability. Data is a Latin word that he certainly knew, but never applied to education. As far as I've been able to ascertain, the ultimate assessment of a student's learning was in debate: the successful display of in utramque partem, argument pro et contra, on both sides of an issue. The best grade, one would assume, went to the winner, at least until the next debate. As for accountability, everything Erasmus wrote addressed what today we would call the whole child, a holistic approach to learning based on good sense and a profound awareness of child development. What is foundational to all of his philosophy of education is the nurturing of a person with the knowledge and judgment to engage productively and thoughtfully in public life, something that cannot be assessed in real time. Most educators would argue that that is what they are trying to do, but from my perspective, it is arts educators who do it best.

Thinking Better

The first year that we launched our new arts program in the first prototype elementary schools in LAUSD, I invited a *Los Angeles Times* education reporter to spend a day observing classes. We watched lessons in visual arts, dance, and theatre, in four different schools. In each school the teachers and the principal fell all over themselves in their eagerness to share their enthusiasm. One ebullient fourth grade teacher, who exuded love for her students and her profession, told us with a refreshing urgency, "You have no idea how much easier it is to teach math after a dance class!!!" I did have an idea, and so did she. After all, from one perspective, just as music is math made audible, dance, which explores measurement, space, value, and time, is math embodied in movement. It was her joy in the realization that remains with me.

But my best memory from that day was an exchange between the reporter and an entire class of fourth grade students in a school in East Los Angeles. They had just taken part in a drama lesson in which the teacher, Carol Tanzman, had shared with them a trickster story from Mongolia, *The Merry Prank of Pa 'leng T'sang*. She stopped the story right before the trick, which was how a poor peasant boy got a fat, wealthy, and pompous district bureaucrat to dismount from his horse. The students, working in small groups, came up with possible improvised endings and acted them out. They were inventive and lively, totally engaged, and excited to share.

The reporter had heard administrators and teachers extol the program, but now he wanted to interview the students. After asking if they had enjoyed the class, which, of course, the students answered with a resounding *yes!*, he asked what they had learned. Their answers were precise: "We've learned what makes a good story." "We've learned how to create an interesting character." "We've learned about suspense." "We've learned the importance of surprise."

Then he asked a question that worried me. He asked them how they felt when they went back to class, to their regular, daily lessons. I was afraid that the question was a set-up and that they would say, in front of their teacher, that school, as a whole, was boring. But that never came up. One boy raised his hand and said, "When we go back to class, we are more relaxed," and then another added, "When we go back we can *think better.*"

This takes me right back to my 500-year-old friend, Richard Mulcaster, who himself referred back again and again to Plato. Engagement in the arts "prepares the mind for learning." *It helps us to think better.*

> *Another way of saying that the arts prepare the mind for learning is to say that they help build a better brain.*

This is old news for any experienced teacher, but today, when everything must be proven through statistical evidence, how to prove it? Ultimately the research that best validates the argument for an arts-rich curriculum in schools is not coming from the field of arts education research with its narrow focus on achievement in literacy and numeracy. It is coming from the explosion of evidence revealed to us over the past generation from the study of neuroscience. Arts education research is rooted in the modern world, which looks nothing like the world of Erasmus or Shakespeare, but the human brain evolves slowly over the millennia, and that of a student five hundred years ago is not significantly different than that of one today. Another way of saying that the arts prepare the mind for learning is to say that *they help build a better brain.*

Representation

While I was in the LAUSD Arts Branch, James Catterall became a friend and mentor, a person I turned to on many occasions for advice. I was counting on him for guidance in the deep dive into the research that I planned for this chapter. That won't happen, but he shared insights with me in casual conversation over the years that I can still draw upon. One example was when he pointed out to me the importance of *representation* in the student experience of art making.

One of my challenges over my years as an arts education administrator and advocate was to explain a mystery. What is it that happens in the mind and soul of a student engaged in artistic exploration? How is that connected to cognition? How is it connected to lasting memory, critical thinking, emotional health, social confidence, judgment, discipline, empathy, love of learning, agency, impulse control, etc. etc. etc. We make vast claims, we observe and document and publish the startling evidence, but how do we explain it?

The ability to understand, articulate, and clearly communicate cognition, of course, is a complicated stew of elements interwoven into an ever-active and changing mind, which is at work all the time, awake and asleep, conscious and unconscious, reactive, and reflective. We know a great deal about it, but much still remains in a realm beyond our understanding. Because of this complexity, making a concise and convincing argument for an arts-rich curriculum that is based on cognitive development is like building a sand sculpture at low tide. Every new incoming wave erodes the edges, and the teachers and administrators who need to be convinced are experiencing wave after wave from the reform agenda coming from the ocean of educational policy.

In my experience, when teaching teenagers something difficult to grasp, I always tended to start with a few simple ideas, preferably not more than three, not to dumb down the content but to provide a comfortable framework through which to explore complexity. It was a habit hard to break, and when I was chatting with James about the difficulty of explaining the interconnection of arts and cognition to an audience of educators, I suggested that cognition might be explained by a simple three-step sequence of *wonder* (curiosity, inquiry, yearning) plus *exploration* (creativity, experimentation, trial, and error) plus *reflection* (pondering, assessment, analysis). I was so fixated on limiting myself to *three* steps on the road to cognition that I missed the most important and obvious one: *representation*! Catterall pointed out that it is in representation that lasting learning happens. Reflection is crucial to cognition and is, in fact, built into every step in the creative process, but it is in the representation, the articulation, the voicing, the showing, that cognition is locked in. In representation, the artist shares a piece of his or her very being. It takes courage. Call it audacity. It can take the form of speech or writing, and it powerfully takes the form of representational performance: painting, sculpting, composing, singing, dancing, or dramatizing.

Memory, a key element of cognition, is provably reinforced by performance. It is not rote memorization that best locks in long-term memory, it is the performance or voicing of what is memorized, which is why Erasmus was right in his frequent suggestion that the best way to learn something well is to teach it to others. I've taken the time to memorize many favorite passages from poems and plays, but when I've tried to recover them weeks or months later they're gone; and yet I can remember every word of Joyce Kilmer's *Trees*, which I was required to memorize in the seventh grade and nervously recite in front of the entire class. My husband, who has a laughably bad memory, can recite the Gettysburg Address word for word sixty-five years after he had to recite it in the eighth grade. My grandmother could recite hours of poetry well into her nineties because she was educated in the 19th century, when students were still, like Shakespeare, expected to recite memorized lessons before an audience of their peers. Something about the adrenalin rush of performance locks in the cadences, the phrases, and the meanings.

Here, however, we will go beyond memory and explore another crucial element of cognition: affect.

Affect and Doctor Greasepaint

Eric Booth gave me the title for this chapter. I asked him once about a phrase he had used in a professional development he did for our LAUSD theatre teachers several years ago. He had led us through an activity designed to open us up cognitively to the emotional center of a Yeats poem, and he defined the moment of connection—the moment that our emotional intelligence grasped the deeper meaning of the poem—as an "isomorphic match." I loved the sound of that and never forgot it, but when I looked up *isomorphic* it was all about matching patterns in math and science. Confused, I gave him a call, and of course as soon as we began talking, the match happened. The patterns connected. The isomorphic match is when the content being taught *matches* the receptivity of the learner. The patterns, mental models of knowledge already in the mind, match the new information to create new learning. We've heard it called the "aha moment." Eric called it the "Lego snap."

In his book *The Feeling of What Happens*, the neuroscientist Antonio Damasio demonstrates that in the infinite workings of our amazing brain, learning never happens without emotion. Parmenides, Pythagoras, and Plato all had it wrong when they elevated reason above emotion. In cognition, logic and emotion are never separate from each other. Damasio pointed out that early neuroscience had ignored emotion because it was not observable and measurable, and he took it upon himself to assert both its ubiquity and its priority. His mantra is, "We are not thinking machines that feel, we are feeling machines that think." In essence, Damasio sees emotion as the embodiment of the logic of survival. We encounter every new experience with our feelings first, and our brain instantly determines if the experience is a threat (to run away from or attack), something to engage with (to eat or examine or play with), or just another ordinary, easily forgettable event.

Whatever that mysterious something is that happens inside of us when we deeply and lastingly learn something, it is always accompanied by emotion, and it often happens in the very act of presenting something of ourselves to the world, of revealing ourselves in all our vulnerability, of being *seen and heard*. This takes us into the affective realm of our memory. Here someone will certainly point out that there are things that we all remember in detail all of our lives, such as the assassination of President Kennedy or the bombing of the twin towers, and we know that the vividness of our memories is connected to an emotional shock which sends waves of sensory impulses coursing through our brains and etching in the details, but here we are talking about something that goes beyond emotional shock and into the realm of secondary emotion, or *affect*.

With all people, but especially with children, the receptivity of the learner is connected to affect. Emotion and affect are so closely related that the words are often used interchangeably, even here, and, indeed, emotion underlies affect; but there is a nuanced distinction that is highly relevant in the context of our exploration of arts and cognition. In *Shakespeare's Classroom*, Lynn Enterline gives etymological definitions to distinguish passion, emotion, and affect. Passion is a corporeal response to a situation: lust, rage, extreme joy, intense grief, etc. Primary emotion would be what you feel when you hold a new baby or watch a loved one die. It is a commonsense response to a real event. *Affect* is a *second-hand* emotion, one that frequently derives from an artificially devised experience such as a work of literature or art. Drama lives in the realm of affect. Listening to a story or to music, or watching a play or film, will induce an affective response, but the most immediate and intense connection to affect occurs in performance.

The best way I can explain this is by example. I will tell a story.

I once participated in an educational theatre activity that was designed to help students comprehend the trauma experienced by immigrants. Being citizens of a nation of immigrants, we were all asked at the beginning of the activity to write a story in the form of a monologue, describing the experience of a relative who had come to this country in the past. We were to write it in the first person and practice it to be performed in character. We were then asked to face a central circle, or stage, lined up at a port of entry representing New York, Los Angeles, San Francisco, the Mexican or the Canadian border. We were to enter one by one and begin anywhere we liked in our monologue, narrating until the leader said to freeze. Each of us got to relate a portion of our story for about twenty seconds. We could shift positions whenever another speaker was asked to freeze, so we did not get uncomfortable, but we always had to stay in character.

I narrated a story that my husband's grandfather had told many times. It was told as a joke. He was a Jew who had fled Poland early in the century to avoid enlistment in the Russian army. He caught a cargo ship and traveled first to China, then around the rest of the world, finally ending up in New York City. He was sixteen years old. There was recession at the time and very little chance of finding work, but he was clever. There was a factory nearby that would post a sign if they were hiring, and always, by six o'clock in the morning after a sign went up, there would be a line of men hoping to be taken on. Moishe went out late every night and waited to see if the sign would go up. One night it did. He took it down, took it back to his boarding house, went to bed, got up at five, went back to the factory, and put the sign back up. He was the first in line and he got hired.

I had heard the story several times and Grandpa would laugh and we would all laugh with him, but he had the familiar habit of an older person of repeating himself, so after a few hearings my laughter was a willing courtesy. This time was different. When I walked onto the stage in character and started *my* story, I was a teenage boy, scarcely out of puberty, alone in New York City with no family, no money, and no friends, unable to speak the language. It wasn't funny this time. To my surprise, because I was not prepared for it, my voice broke. I began to cry.

One by one, as others began telling their own stories, the same thing happened. At the end of the activity at least half of us were moist-eyed.

When I listened to Grandpa Morris telling the story it obviously had an emotional impact on me, otherwise I would not have remembered it. But when I performed it, the story entered my very being. That is affect. It is the *secondary* reflection of the emotion of another, often by an actor or a storyteller. Affect happens most powerfully when one goes into role.

No one has ever described this realm better than Shakespeare himself, when, as Hamlet, he marvels at the authenticity of the fictional passion conveyed by the actor reciting Aeneas' tale to Dido, describing Hecuba's anguish at the death of Priam and the fall of Troy—a passion he himself, with much more immediate and genuine cause for grief—is unable to access.

> O, what a rogue and peasant slave am I!
> Is it not monstrous that this player here,
> But in a fiction, in a dream of passion,
> Could force his soul so to his own conceit
> That from her working all his visage wann'd,
> Tears in his eyes, distraction in's aspect,
> A broken voice, and his whole function suiting
> With forms to his conceit? and all for nothing!
> For Hecuba!
> What's Hecuba to him, or he to Hecuba,
> That he should weep for her?

He then works himself into something close to the very passion that has eluded him, finishing the soliloquy in a fevered despair:

> . . . for it cannot be
> But I am pigeon-liver'd and lack gall
> To make oppression bitter, or ere this
> I should have fatted all the region kites
> With this slave's offal: bloody, bawdy villain!
> Remorseless, treacherous, lecherous, kindless villain!
> O, vengeance!
>
> Act II, Scene ii

The actor here described by Hamlet has performed the scene hundreds of times, and yet each performance arouses in him the same intensity of feeling. In recalling his performance, the actor who is playing Hamlet accesses a heightened state of intensity that is almost unbearable; and if he is worth his pay, the audience follows him.

The research we need is the research that explains the physical changes in the body and the mind that happen within a person in role. That is the mystery. I know there is a change because I have felt it myself, and I've seen it happen in actors and students countless times. Certainly it helps when an actor can readily access emotion (I recall my brother joking in an interview, describing what a wuss he is, saying, "I weep at life insurance commercials"), but how does a performer do it day after day, night after night?

Ask any working actor and they will tell you that they have gone on stage hung over, exhausted, sick, even in pain, and found that once in role the weariness and pain drop away for the duration of the performance. This transformation is not permanent and it may leave one even more spent once it has passed, but it's something they can rely on. The same curiosity has been known to occur with actors who are chronic stutterers but who never stutter when on stage. My brother tells me they even have a name for it. They call it Doctor Greasepaint.

There is a mounting body of evidence, for instance, from the study of students with spectrum disorder: autism or Asperger's syndrome. Teachers and parents have often been amazed to see students on the spectrum perform, fully in role. They make eye contact, speak clearly, respond correctly to cues and show no gestural evidence of their difficulty in social situations. It is as though within the confines of the character that they temporarily inhabit, they have a safe structure that dictates correct behaviors. One of the first times I observed this in a student, I chatted with his mother, commenting on how remarkable I found it. I mused aloud that it might be possible for someone with Asperger's simply to go through life in role. She took me seriously, and pointed out that functioning adults on the spectrum are doing exactly that, but cautioned that it is physically draining. She said it would be much better for her child if the world could simply accept him exactly as he was. I was never so cavalier about the subject again.

As we shall see, this physical phenomenon can be explained in part by neuroscience. The brain is still a vast mystery to us, but we are getting closer to understanding its extraordinary potential.

Attention: Active Listening

I happened to be working on this chapter in 2021, during the early summer emergence of the seventeen-year locust (actually a cicada—an extremely loud one!). I live in California and I didn't get to hear it this time, except on Zoom calls with friends from the Midwest, but when I was nine, in 1953, in Ohio, oh boy did I hear them then! That was the summer I learned to *listen*. I *had* to. It was the second year of the Antioch Shakespeare Festival, outside, on a stage built over the steps of the main hall of the college. The cicadas filled the trees on the campus and the glen across the road with a deafening, high-pitched drone that rose and fell and nightly drowned out the voices on the stage. The actors had to shout and the audience had to strain to hear. Night after night, I would sit on the edge of my seat, leaning forward, my shoulders hunched, alert, piecing out the words. I watched the actress playing Hermione in *A Winter's Tale* take a few relaxing breaths before entering the stage to plead with her jealous husband for her life, breathe in a flying cicada, spit it out, and still manage to let her beautiful voice soar with the poetry. I gasped, watching *Titus Andronicus*, when the raped and mutilated Lavinia was brought before her violators, her hands bloody stumps, her tongue cut out, her mouth gushing blood; and I wept when her uncle Marcus cried out to her above the buggy cacophony. It was an elemental battle between the bugs and the Bard, and *listening*, straining to *hear* above the din allowed me to be led as deep into the human heart as language would ever take me.

In Shakespeare's day they didn't use the verb to "see" a play. It was always to "hear" it. We still use the word attend when speaking of seeing a performance. To attend a play was to *hear* it. Eric Booth defines the word "attend" as the *act* of listening. He calls the process of art, "the act of world making." He is well known for his fascination with semantics. To *attend* is to stretch out, to stretch into a new idea, a new world. Attending an arts experience allows you to "enter that world and know what to do when you get there." His highest calling for the teaching artist is "to let people know what to do when they don't know what to do." The counter balance to attend is to reflect, which means "to bend back toward," recalling John Dewey, "If we do not reflect upon our experiences, we do not learn from them."

I've always had a problem with the label "learning disabled," used ubiquitously in special education. Human beings are learning machines. It is impossible to *disable* learning. One can make choices and judgments about what should be learned and how this should happen, but not about the presence of learning itself. Of course the problem is that children can learn things that inhibit academic learning. Children can learn fear. They can learn, or *attend* to, anxiety, hopelessness, shame, distrust, hunger, aimlessness, and rage. There is a passage in Eric Booth's book, *The Every Day Work of Art* that speaks to this:

> People are shaped by what they extend themselves into. We must be very careful with the objects we present to ourselves and to our children because we are changed by them. Art lends shape to yearning. Art is the best container for yearning because it is so rich, so human, so satisfying on so many levels. Art gives serious outer shape to serious inner yearning. And if these yearnings are informed by less rich objects, they will go to sleep, will die, or will eventually express themselves in the harmful symptoms of search that fill the pages of the daily newspaper.

Plato says essentially the same thing in *The Republic*, and, as we shall see, Richard Mulcaster says it in his *Positions*. It is the whole point of Erasmus' *De copia*, which, with his *De ratione studii*, was the what-to and how-to teach standard that was followed faithfully for one hundred years after his death. Young people should be exposed to the best humanity has to offer. What we extend ourselves into, what we pay *attention* to, matters.

In a presentation that the LAUSD Arts Branch arranged for administrators several years ago, the Stanford University linguist Shirley Brice Heath described research she was conducting in the area of attention. She had research assistants observe classrooms in subject areas across the curriculum, and all they had to do was to clock the seconds that students in the class made eye contact with the lesson—either with the instructor or with the task assigned. Obviously, eye contact is not the only indicator of attention, but it is one that is easily observable and measurable. In eye contact alone, attention in arts classes far exceeded that in any other subject. Students were attentive and engaged, and engaged learners are open to new ideas that mesh with the patterns of knowledge they already have inside of themselves: the isomorphic match, or the Lego snap.

Neuroscience, too, tells us that the mere act of paying attention, or extending into an idea, alters the brain. This is an elevation of the idea of attention. We teachers constantly expect and implore students to *pay attention* in order to learn, frequently because their attention is flying in other directions, and the exhortation to "pay attention!" is often heard in classroom control; but what the most experienced teachers know is that the best lessons are those in which the lesson itself actively and authentically *holds* attention. That is what arts lessons do.

> *Neuroscience, too, tells us that the mere act of paying attention, or extending into an idea, alters our brains.*

Neuroscience: The Brain and the Mind

I recently attended an exhibit called *The Beautiful Brain* at a gallery at New York University, where they displayed drawings done in the 19th century by Santiago Ramón y Cajal, the Leonardo da Vinci of neuroscience. The catalog from that show still sits on my coffee table and is one of the most beautiful books I own. Cajal was able to make use of new technologies of the time: greatly improved microscopes and the ability to color-dye cells for greater visibility. He spent decades making thousands of drawings of neurons from different parts of the brains of humans and animals. His exquisite pictures look like ethereal gardens of infinite variety. He claimed to be on an almost spiritual search for "the organ of the soul":

> Like the entomologist in pursuit of brightly colored butterflies, my attention hunted in the flower garden of gray matter [the cerebral cortex], cells with delicate and elegant forms, the mysterious butterflies of the soul, the beating of whose wings may someday—who knows?—clarify the secret of mental life.

In the century that has passed since Cajal opened the microscopic world of the brain to our view, much has been learned, and the growth of knowledge continues exponentially in a seemingly inexhaustible field of exploration. Our human brain, about the size of a grapefruit, contains about one hundred billion neurons, each with branching dendrites (little fingers) which multiply with stimulation and take in impulses or information and send them along single, stem-like axons, which transmit them across microscopic synapses to more dendrites on more neurons, creating neuronal pathways that process information from the world around and within us. The possible neuronal pathways in your brain are as infinite as the stars in the sky or the sands of the earth.

A fun story: When Dr. Kerr was working with us in the Arts Branch, she was still working with James Catterall as a senior researcher. We incorporated her research into our drama curriculum for elementary students, and Sherry had pins made for all of her students that said "Drama Develops Dendrites." In explaining to them that the simulated experiences they did in drama class would nurture the healthy development of their dendrites, she cautioned that some experiences, such as those that cause stress, could do the opposite and cause them to wither. One day she was walking through the yard and heard a little third grader responding to a bully who was larger than him. He puffed out his chest and called out, bravely, "You do not have the right to shrink my dendrites!"

Throughout life, but especially in youth, there is a constant process of pruning that is happening in the brain, as pathways that do not get used wither and those that are used frequently are strengthened and coated with a protective layer of a substance called myelin. This pruning and strengthening is especially active in the early, language acquisition years, which is why young children, in the right circumstances, can learn several languages and why we are encouraged to begin the study of music and other highly sense-related skills at an early age. New neurons can be produced through neurogenesis in the memory-sorting area of the brain, called the hippocampus, but with tens of billions to start with, there is little danger of neuronal power running low. The only danger is in the withering of neuronal pathways that lead to healthy cognition and the strengthening of those that do not.

In addition to neurons, the brain has billions of glial cells called astrocytes ("star cells," named for their shapes) that wrap around the neurons and seem to provide them with care and feeding. They release chemicals onto synapses that modulate the neurotransmitters, electrochemical impulses, and the responses of neurons. They also apparently release other chemicals that regulate blood flow to the brain. Today neuroscientists can use Magnetic Resonance Imaging (MRI) that can illuminate energy flow and mental activity in the brain. I like to think of astrocytes as tiny stars lighting up our mental processes. We cannot yet read thoughts, thank goodness, but with MRI we can see where in the brain and to what extent they are taking place. MRI scans that map the activity of the brain are known to light up when participants are focused and engaged in creative activity.

It has been said that the brain is the hardware and the mind is the software. Those infinite and ever-changing neuronal pathways constitute the mental processes of the conscious and unconscious mind—our short-term, long term, and procedural memories, our deeply embedded behaviors, our habits, our values, our enthusiasms, our phobias, and our addictions. The mind extends well beyond the brain and interacts with the world through sensory input. It also interacts with other minds and can be highly suggestible, which is why we see both highly effective collaborations and, sometimes, dangerous groupthink occurring in social groups.

Here let's take a brief tour of the brain and the nervous system that connects the mind to the world around it and to the workings of the body. What we usually see in pictures of the brain is the folded and wrinkled outer layer, the cerebral cortex or "gray matter," which wraps around the interior limbic system. The symmetrical cortex has a left side and a right, and both are made up of lobes that have specific functions, although these functions overlap and are in constant communication with each other. The two halves of the brain are also in communication, through a mass of nerve fibers called the corpus callosum. On either side, around the ears, are the temporal lobes, which process sound, taste, and smell impulses. Behind the temporal lobes are the occipital lobes, which process visual information. Above and center are the parietal lobes, which interpret sensory information such as temperature and touch. All of these lobes play a role in memory, as they connect sensory information to existing mental models in the brain.

In the front of the cerebral cortex are the frontal lobes, where thinking, planning, organizing, problem-solving, short-term memory, and impulse to movement happen. If you make a fist and hold it up in front of you with your fist tilted, imagine that your arm is your spine and your fist is your brain. Your knuckles, then, would be the frontal lobes, and your fingernails, tucked against your palm, would be the inferior frontal lobe, which houses the area of Broca, the center of speech. The frontal lobes are not fully developed in children, and they go through a rapid process of maturation during adolescence and early adulthood—causing a good deal of mental, emotional, and social chaos in the process.

The frontal lobes are where reasoning and logic take place. That is the seat of the reflection, evaluation, judgment, and problem-solving. It is where the sensory processing lobes send the information to be analyzed and acted upon in the context of existing knowledge and memory. Sensory information that ends up in what I'll call here the "thought" zone first enters the brain through the thalamus, which sends the impulses to the hippocampus, where memories are sorted out by importance and are then sent along to the appropriate lobes in the cortex for processing and possible long-term storage. They are then accessible by the frontal lobes, to be made use of by reason and be articulated by speech. This makes up the *reflective* mind. Reflection takes time. Not always a lot of time, but always some. The reflective brain does not act instantaneously.

The *reactive* brain, however, is a remnant of the primitive brain stem, or the "lizard brain," which is part of the limbic system cradled within the protective outer cortex. On each side of the brain, deep within the temporal lobe, there is a little organ called an amygdala, which is about the size and shape of an almond. Amygdala, in fact, comes from the Greek word for almond. All sensory information heading from our eyes, ears, nose, tongue, or skin has to check in with the amygdala on its way to the thalamus, and the amygdala lets most of it pass innocently by. But if there is something new—some novel, unexpected, and unaccustomed sensory impulse—the amygdala springs into action and makes an instantaneous determination. If it senses danger or attraction, it signals to the hypothalamus, which regulates body temperature and hormones like adrenalin. Blushing, sweat, flinching, heart palpitations are all signals that the hypothalamus is at work. These are involuntary functions, like breathing and heartbeat, and they are not within our control. The amygdala monitors the flight or fight impulse. It's also responsible for the exhilarating rush of love at first sight. A typical teenager's brain, with its still maturing frontal lobes, is highly susceptible to, and often at the mercy of, the signals from the amygdala and thus highly prone to impulsive behaviors.

The reactive and reflective brain functions are sometimes referred to as fast-processing and slow-processing. Nicholas Carr, in his hair-raising book, *The Shallows: What the Internet is Doing to Our Brains*, shows throughout history how each new tool that humanity has adopted has altered brain function. The astonishing digital tools that we have today are no exception. We can now say "Hi" and anything else we wish to millions of people on Facebook. We can tweet foreign policy impulsively at four in the morning if we happen to be the President. We can use Snap Chat to send naughty pictures to friends, and they'll disappear before anyone else finds out. If we are researching a book like this one, we can go on the Internet and, with a few punches of our fingertips, order Xerox copies of tomes that have been out of print for five hundred years, and they'll be on our front porch within a few days, eliminating the need for expensive travel to dusty archives. We have access to museums, encyclopedias, and music from all over the world. We can type in any question to Google and get an answer. Most all information known to humankind, translated into any language, is accessible instantly with an iPhone. We don't need memory anymore. We hardly need to think. *But what is this doing to our brains?* Our children, digital natives, are developing fast processing skills that could only be dreamed of a generation ago, but at what expense?

> *A typical teenager's brain, with its still maturing frontal lobes, is highly susceptible to, and often at the mercy of, the signals from the amygdala and thus highly prone to impulsive behaviors.*

One of the must urgent arguments for arts education is that engagement in creativity, in art making, requires the slow processing functions of the brain. It cannot be done without linear thinking, aesthetic valuing, judgment, empathy, problem-solving, focus, and concentration. These are all qualities of the frontal lobes, which are in the process of maturation throughout the years of traditional schooling.

> *One of the must urgent arguments for arts education is that engagement in creativity, in art making, requires the slow processing functions of the brain.*

Drama slows down the moment. It gives students the opportunity to explore ideas with deeper understanding. Drama gives us valuable tools for the development of the slow processing brain. If the digital age is developing brains brilliant at fast processing at the expense of slow processing, and we as educators are doing nothing to counter that, we are headed for real trouble.

Mirror Neurons: "The Organ of the Soul"

If Santiago Ramón y Cajal had ever found what he said he was looking for, "the organ of the soul," it would certainly have been intertwined in some way with mirror neurons. Let's call them the "empathy neurons," because that's pretty much exactly what they are. The amazing thing is that with MRIs, neuroscientists can actually *see* them. They light up when they encounter something they care about. In other words, neuroscientists actually *can* observe emotion after all. The fascinating thing about them is that they fire when one is experiencing something, but they also fire, in exactly the same way, when that something is not experienced directly but is observed or enacted as a fiction. The neurons mirror the authentic experience. In other words, it is the answer to Hamlet's question, "What's Hecuba to him or he to Hecuba that he should weep for her?" The brain responds to an emotion that is observed or performed *exactly* the way it responds to one that is experienced firsthand. That is why we cry at the sad scenes in a movie. It is why I wept when I performed Grandpa's story as a monologue. It is why an imaginary kitten that had been passed around a kindergarten drama class that I observed and ended up in the arms of one little girl, was so real to her that she asked, as she left the class, "Can I keep it?"

The way mirror neurons were first identified is a funny story. About thirty years ago neurophysiologists in Italy were studying the hand-to-mouth motions of macaque monkeys. They put electrodes in the brain of one monkey and were surprised a bit later when they brought in lunch for themselves, and the electrodes in the monkey started going haywire. The neurons that were lighting up while the monkey watched them eat were the exact same ones that lit up when he himself was eating. Since then mirror neurons have been found in the brains of mammals and even birds. In humans they are found in the Broca area, the center of speech, but also in the premotor cortex, the supplementary motor area, the primary somatosensory cortex, and the inferior parietal cortex, all areas that have to do with motion and emotion. In other words, they seem to be part of a network that connects all areas of the brain.

> *When a young person dramatizes something in a game, a rehearsal, or a performance, the brain processes it exactly as though it were an authentic experience.*

The important thing to understand about mirror neurons in the context of this study is that when a young person dramatizes something in a game, a rehearsal, or a performance, the brain processes it exactly as though it were an authentic experience. Drama is becoming authentic, making a context where things feel real, and the same transmitters are fired as if they were. Theatre educators know how to contextualize a situation and make it a dramatic experience. When a drama teacher asserts that one of the primary things that her students are learning is empathy, she is absolutely right. Her students are developing their mirror neurons. They are learning to care.

And So . . .

Someday, and it can't come soon enough, educational policy makers will crash on the rocks of their delusion that standardized test scores tell us anything worth knowing, and they will end their romance with data. When that happens, if there is even a tiny sliver of a possibility that they will turn to weary old teacher warhorses like me (and there are legions of us), we need to be ready to guide them back to authentic pedagogy.

Maybe I'm a bit like Erasmus. I like old ideas. (We have seen that what Erasmus called "New Learning" was mostly the un-burying of the ancient Greeks.) I'm tired of hearing about innovation in education and have long ago become suspicious of every new instructional flavor du jour that guarantees to turn our kids into little Einsteins and bring up their scores in the process. Maybe we don't need new ideas. Maybe we need to learn from our elders.

To summarize let us start with a few basic things we know about the developing brains and minds of young people, and reflect on how the archaic and long-abandoned underpinnings of humanist education might have contributed to that development.

Young people are fanatically social. Even if they appear to be shy or antisocial, that is simply the frightened flip side of a profound, underlying need for connection.

When my granddaughter walks in the door, inevitably the first thing she says to me is, "Play with me." That primal need for social connection and play will be dominant for at least the next twenty years and, in fact, it will never go away completely. Our minds develop in a social context. Children learn from playing with each other far more than they learn from schooling, which, for better or for worse, opens a wealth of opportunity. Is it any wonder that the most ancient and authentic form of communicating a story is called a *play*?

The humanist classroom was, by necessity, built on collaboration. Large classes and few textbooks meant that students had to rely on each other, and their daily structure for learning was social. There might have been one hundred or more students in a classroom with one headmaster and one usher, but each student had to recite his daily lessons to someone, so that someone was often an older student called a praepositore, who took the role of instructor, making corrections, and giving encouragement. (To quote Erasmus again: "The surest way to learn something is to teach it.") Collaboration was emphasized in writing exercises, in memorization, in translations, and, most definitely, in playacting.

Today we see students engaged in structured cooperative learning clusters, pair-shares, editing groups, feedback loops, all to their benefit. In the most successful classrooms you see students encouraged to work together and help each other. All this is great, but there is no more demanding collaborative endeavor than dramatics. Whether it is informal community-building games that improve classroom morale, scene work, monologues, dramatic improvisation, active exploration of literature, class presentations, or full productions, students working in drama are constantly engaged in collective problem-solving. This is because of the huge amount of on-site, real-time decision-making they must do collaboratively, often with no help from teachers. Collaborative problem-solving and successful achievement in groups leads to accelerated maturity and *audacity*, in the Elizabethan sense of the word.

Young people are tribal. They seek the gratification of belonging to a sympathetic confederacy. The Elizabethan classroom presumably had to function like a family tribe in which everyone had a role to play.

Something used to amuse me every semester at the beginning of a new drama class. Secondary teachers will recognize the confusion of the first days of a new term, when students are coming and going, being reassigned, having their programs adjusted by counselors to meet their graduation requirements and balance class size. Because of that, we teachers tend to fill the first two or three days with valuable but nonessential activities, and in theatre we fill it with team-building improvisation games. What I always found astonishing was how quickly these games would turn a class of radically diverse students who hardly knew each other when they first walked into the room into a tribe. When the next day would come and new students would enter the room, there was an immediate, though subtle, resistance. The tribe was already formed after only one day, and there was a primal need to repel intruders. This had to be overcome by more team-building before we could move on.

Gangs are tribes. Cliques are tribes. Tribes can be competitive and cruel—even dangerous. But theatre tribes form with the intention of telling a story to an audience, and there is an implied responsibility for the story to be meaningful. *Theatre students become messengers of possibility—messengers of hope.* Look again at the drama students who led the response to the Parkland massacre and turned it into a national movement.

It is beginning to dawn on us that social media is almost an oxymoron. We have Facebook, Instagram, and TikTok but teens are lonelier than they've ever been and teenage suicide rates are climbing. Tribal groups have a magnetic appeal. There is a need for safe and healthy tribes in which young people can learn social skills, empathy, and discipline. The Internet provides infinite possibility for tribal connection that is abstract, impersonal, detached, faceless, and thus open to inhumanity. It can leave a person seeking connection feeling more isolated than ever. But nothing fills the need for personal, human connection more satisfyingly and healthily than the tribes that develop in a drama class.

Emotional intensity is a characteristic of youth. Any parent or teacher who has observed the emotional rollercoaster of an adolescent knows that there is really no such thing as a teenager who is not at risk. Truthfully, adolescence is a perilous passage for everyone. Erasmus was wise to recommend highly charged passages from the classics for young boys to enact with full emotional delivery. This gave them an opportunity to channel their own wildly fluctuating emotional engagement with their peers.

It would be difficult to find a theatre teacher who does not have a single story about seeing a dangerously at-risk student whose life was changed, even saved, through drama. This is because engagement in drama gives definition to one's character and aspirations. Engaging in drama gives students voice and self-knowledge in a collaborative context like no other.

Young people test the parameters of risk and safety. Just walking onto a stage, or any performance space, takes courage. It's been said that for many people, speaking in public is as terrifying as falling out of an airplane. Teenagers, especially, are both drawn to and frightened by the risk of being singled out and the intimacy of being *seen*. Spotlight anxiety can be crippling for anyone who has had no experience. In his book *New Discovery of the Old Art of Teaching School*, the 16th-century schoolmaster Charles Hoole cited the importance of playacting in training students to "expel that subrustic bashfulness and unresistable timorousness" characteristic of young persons, so that they may grow into adults able to present themselves persuasively in public. The daily exercise Elizabethan students had in oral presentation emboldened them and gave them essential tools to use throughout their lives, to have impact or be heard in a public forum: to "hold court."

The Elizabethan exercise of in utramque partem, argument on both sides, was sustained practice in the examination of the consequences of one's actions. Drama activities provide a context in which students can safely explore risk. They benefit from a sheltered and structured learning environment where the testing of parameters can take place with feedback and can then be replayed for objective analysis. The nurturing of mirror neurons and emotional intelligence, with its accompanying development of empathy, gives substance to the experience of being a feeling human.

Young people seek novelty and creative exploration. Here is where we can circle back to the study of rhetoric. Students are drawn to creative language: rap poetry, spoken word, and verbal jam sessions. The study of rhetoric gave to Elizabethan schoolboys tools that could be applied to persuasive, inventive language and provided constant practice in elastic and nimble thinking. We have seen examples of how Shakespeare reveled in these gifts. He was not alone. A cornucopia of literary genius emerged from his generation.

21st-Century Competencies and STEAM

After expressing my disdain for some of the data-based innovations coming from contemporary educational policy, I would be remiss if I wrote this book without giving a vigorous nod to two of the innovations that I find encouraging: the emphasis on 21st-century competencies and STEAM.

Depending on which document you read, you will find a selection of the following competencies listed among those core to the concept of what 21st-century education must teach our students:

Creativity collaboration
Problem-solving
Visioning
Team-building
Emotional intelligence
Empathy
Judgment
Relationship management
Critical thinking
Citizenship
Self-confidence
Social awareness
Civic literacy
Communication skills
Leadership skills
Self-awareness

Is there a single competency in this list that is not taught by engagement in theatre and drama? Of course I would add to the list courage, agency, good behavior, and audacity.

Then there is the growing movement to add A (arts) to STEM science, technology, engineering and math) to generate STEAM. Back in the days at the district when we did interdepartmental workshops, our most satisfying and invigorating were with the science folks. We speak each other's language. Our pedagogy is often identical. Study in the sciences explores the unseen and follows the paths of wonder, exactly as we do in the arts.

Niente Senza Gioia: Nothing Without Joy

It's common sense. If there is no other reason to include a daily dose of arts in a student's education it is the simple fact that pleasure helps a person learn what you want them to learn and stress does the opposite. *Niente senza gioia*, nothing without joy, is the philosophy of the Reggio Emilia approach to early childhood education. It is the belief that joy fuels learning. Reggio Emilia has its origins in Bologna, Italy, but I'm told that Americans who go there to study the approach are greeted with the bewildered question, "What are you Americans doing *here*? The entire pedagogy comes from America!" It is based on our own John Dewey!

> *Pleasure helps a person learn what you want them to learn and stress does the opposite.*

There must be a place for joy in every school. The most successful schools have it. What if you could assess joy? Arts educators have long wished that they could take the lead in the accountability movement. Assessment is embedded in the creative process: both self-assessment at every step and public assessment in what is finally presented to an audience. When the curtain goes up or the orchestra tunes up or the gallery opens, everything the student artist has done or not done to train and communicate artfully is there to be seen by the world. In the classroom setting, arts projects are best assessed by a rubric which students are familiar with before they embark, and in the highest levels of learning the students themselves are capable of creating their own rubrics to assess their own success. This happens in schools where learning thrives naturally through inquiry, experimentation, collaboration, and collective reflection. It is woven into every decision and every judgment at every stage in the process, and if students in all disciplines could internalize, even design, rubrics to grade themselves against the standards, they would be deeply invested in their own success and would take great pleasure in it. Call it joy. In successful schools, students are engaged, and the joy is palpable.

Wonder and Yearning

I have never written an entire book before and apparently I could never have written this one without a habit I have tried all my life to suppress without success: the crippling (or so I'd always thought) habit of daydreaming. I was delighted a few years ago to read an article in *The New Yorker* by Jonah Lehrer called *The Virtues of Daydreaming*. The opening sentence is: "Humans are a daydreaming species." He continues citing Harvard psychologists who actually measured the average percentage of waking minutes that people spend letting their minds wander: 47%! That means that if I spend half of every hour daydreaming, I am perfectly normal. What a relief! What liberation! He goes on to show that "mind-wandering is an essential cognitive tool." He quotes Virginia Woolf's description of daydreaming as a state in which "scenes, names, sayings, and memories" are thrown up from the depths of the subconscious mind "like a fountain spring," producing novel ideas. He cites experiments in laboratory conditions that prove that daydreaming, even in short spells, improves cognitive function. Armed with that information, I took to taking long walks every time I got stuck on a problem. It helped me as an arts administrator and it has helped me as a writer, to think through the sometimes-snarled logic of my perceptions.

Children daydream. Those budding cartoonists and drummers sitting in the back rows of any classroom are daydreamers. The window gazers and the clock-watchers are daydreamers. The hormonal spring fever of teenage romantics derives from daydreaming. Mind wandering is built into our story-loving DNA, and since educators cannot fight it, they should embrace it as the fountain of imagination that it is. Remember, too, how deeply satisfying, comforting, even addicting art making is. The urge to create is a human need as profound and nurturing as food and sleep. It exists everywhere, in every culture and throughout all time. Exquisite music and art emerged even from the death camps of World War II. Erasmus would have seen daydreaming as a search for beauty and harmony in a chaotic world.

"Chaotic" would certainly describe the world we live in today. All the evidence I see daily is that our political and economic leadership has been entirely disconnected from the anxieties of childhood. It scarcely even registered in the national conversation that urban public schools across the nation had to bring in counselors the day after the 2016 election to address the terrors of children, and during the past administration we witnessed horrifying stories of children cruelly separated from their immigrant parents seeking asylum at the border. It isn't only immigrant children who were traumatized. Children are profoundly aware of how their own families are affected by injustice and inequality. They are terrified by the consequences of global warming on their own fragile futures. Subtly, step-by-step, these fears, unaddressed, are being etched into their brain development. If building a healthy and well-educated population is a priority, as it certainly should be, the fact that we are raising a generation of frightened children should be considered a national disaster.

We need to support, comfort, and nurture our daydreamers more than ever. The arts define us and allow us *self*-definition. Engagement in drama, dance, music, and visual arts gives shape to daydreams, structure to aspirations, vision and hope for the future, comfort for hearts, and fuel for minds. We urgently need to bring creative exploration and expression back into the very core of learning. Our survival as a culture demands it.

Shakespeare, too, was raised in the deeply and sometimes dangerously divided social and cultural milieu emerging from the Reformation. I would posit that the education of his generation gave him and his peers significant cognitive tools to navigate their era, and elements of it could do the same for ours

12
CONCLUSION

FIGURE 12.1 Will sleeping.

Here I have addressed my concern about the state of education today by looking to the past. In so doing I've had to wrestle a simple story out of one that has been obscured by complexity. How does one find a clear pathway between two vastly different worlds? The education of children and adolescents in Shakespeare's day was entirely in Latin. It was based on the ancient trivium of grammar, logic, and rhetoric. Its focus in literature was on the Greek and Roman classics. It was for propertied boys only. It relied on corporal punishment for discipline. It was emerging from centuries when it was conducted almost entirely, orally, through what Erasmus described as "the endless tedium of memorization." It was so vastly different from conditions now, how can we possibly find a linking thread? How does one see an arc of complex pedagogical issues clearly through the circuitous windings of time? The answer lies in something left out of this grim list: fun!

These were boys, after all! Goofy, playful boys! And as it turns out, Erasmus knew a lot about the antics of boys from his own experience of being one. In all of his voluminous writings about education, he emphasized the importance of pleasure, and Mulcaster, as we have seen, agreed with him. Erasmus believed it was possible for children to *enjoy* learning. I know Shakespeare made fun of his education, and we have "the whining schoolboy" of his Seven Ages of Man soliloquy in *As You Like It* to thank for the common conviction that he hated school. I don't believe it. I think he had a great time at Stratford Latin Grammar School, and his rigorous education there prepared him well for his career as the most entertaining poet and dramatist in our history.

In Elizabethan schools, a huge part of the pleasure students enjoyed was due to the vibrant presence of the performing arts. It is so deeply embedded in the history of humanist education that it has often gone unnoticed. When you are able to brush away the clouds you can see that students at that time were engaging daily in the artful presentation of elegant language and the performance of dance, music, and drama. Instruction in music is listed in all the statutes, and dance was taught with music. Per the existing statutes of schools in England, performance of plays by Terence, Plautus, and Seneca were regular fare, as were, of course, the humble colloquies. I have endeavored to reveal here my conviction that that active, engaged involvement in presentation led to the emergence of an age of creative minds and cognitive brilliance.

Desiderius Erasmus was my guide in this. The more you read of him the more you realize that his genius was to see things clearly. Fortunately he makes it easy by being such an engaging and humorous thinker. When I first read his colloquies, what jumped out for me was the laughter, and the more I searched the more I found a mind that was finely attuned to the ways that we humans learn.

My plea to everyone concerned about the physical and emotional health of young people in this post-pandemic, digital age (and I would hope that is everyone) is to make room for joy in our schools. Not just joy in play: joy in *learning*. My greatest hope as an educator is that the era of drill, kill, test, and repeat will end. If you think "kill" is too strong a word in the context of educating children, consider that one can kill enthusiasm. One can kill exploration, motivation, and joy. The testing industry has made a fortune off of our innocent kids. It's time for a re-examination of the purposes and parameters of standardized testing, opting instead for authentic assessment that is supportive of growth.

We are living through unprecedented times of both anxiety and possibility. It is stressful, and the stress is evident in our children. We should be making the relief and redirection of that stress our top priority. Our children and our young adults need to be heard. They need more drama on the stage than in real life. They need to be witnessed. They need ways to contain and redirect their wildest emotional searching. They may need to cry, and they absolutely need to laugh. They need to express themselves, to define, process, and verbalize their concerns. They need a safe place to explore the outer reaches of emotion and experience that illuminates their own humanity. They need the arts!

APPENDIX I

Performing the Colloquies in Latin and in English

Here are five of Erasmus' colloquies chosen for the frequency of resonances in Shakespeare's plays, especially his comedies. The adapted translations are my own. I've used both Nathan Bailey and Craig R. Thompson as a guide, and the hilariously garbled Google translator when it helped clear up some confusion. But I've also used my own sense of what the speakers might be saying in today's linguistic customs. They are translations from rather archaic Latin, so any teacher or student playing these roles should feel free to adapt as well, to reveal the wit and suggestive language wherever possible. Erasmus would appreciate that!

Proci et puellae
Boys and Girls: Courtship

Naufragium
The Shipwreck

Uxor
Marriage

Abattis et eruditae
The Abbot and the Learned Woman

Herilia
A Master's Commands

Proci et Puellae

Boys and Girls: Courtship

Personae: Pamphilus and Maria

Pamphilus: **Salve crudelis, salve ferrea, salve adamentina.**
Hello, you cruel, hardhearted, unrelenting creature!

Maria: **Salve tandem & tu Pamphile, quoties & quantum voles, & quocunque libet nomine. Sed interim mihi videris oblitus nominis mei. Maria vocor.**
Hello back to you, as often as you like, but you seem to have forgotten who I am. My name is Maria.

Pamphilus: **At Martiam dici oportuit.**
It should have been Martia!

Maria: **Quid ita, quaeso? Quid mihi cum Marte?**
Why, what has Mars got to do with me?

Pamphilus: **Quia quemadmodum illi deo pro ludo est, homines interficere; ita & tibi: nisi quod tu Marte crudelior occidis etiam amantem.**
Because just as Mars makes a sport of killing, so do you. But you are even more cruel. You'll even kill one who loves you.

Maria: **Bona verba. Ubinam strages ista mortalium, quos ego occidi? Ubi sanguis interfectorum?**
Is that so? Where is the great slaughter of men that I've made? Where are all the bloody bodies?

Pamphilus: **Unum cadaver vides examine, si modo me vides.**
You can see one corpse right in front of you. Just look at me!

Maria: **Quid ego audio? Moruus loqueris, & obambulas? Utinam mihi nunquam occurrant umbrae formidabiliores!**
What, are you joking? Does a corpse walk and talk? I hope I never see a more frightful ghost!

Pamphilus: **Ludis tu quidem; tamen interim miserunt exanimas, & crudelius occidis, quam si confoderes telo. Nunc longo cruciatu excarnificor miser.**
Sure, you can make fun of me, but for all that, you're still killing me. And you're doing it more cruelly than if you stabbed me with a dagger because now, poor me, I die a slow, lingering death.

Maria: **Eho, dic, quot gravidae ad tuum occursum abortierunt?**
Oh my! Tell me, please, how many pregnant women have miscarried at the sight of you!?

Pamphilus:	**Atqui pallor arguit exsanguem magis quam ulla fit umbra.**
	But look how pale I am! I have no more blood in my body than a ghost.
Maria:	**Atqui iste pallor tinctus est viola. Sic palles ut cerasium maturescens, aut uva purpurascens.**
	Oh yes, I see! You're as pale as a violet! You're as pale as a ripe cherry or a purple grape!
Pamphilus:	**Satis procaciter rides miserum!**
	You're laughing at my misery.
Maria:	**Atqui si mihi non credis, admove speculum.**
	Just look at yourself in the mirror.
Pamphilus:	**Non optarim aliud speculum, nec arbitror esse clarius ullum, non optarim aliud speculum, nec arbitror esse clarius ullum, quam in quo me nunc contemplor.**
	I don't need a mirror. There's no better mirror in the world than the one I'm looking at now.
Maria:	**Quod speculum mihi narras?**
	And what mirror is that?
Pamphilus:	**Oculos tuos.**
	Your eyes!
Maria:	**Argutator, ut semper tui similis es! Sed unde doces esse exanimem te? An cibum capiunt umbrae?**
	You flirt! That's just like you. Prove to me that you're dead. Do dead people eat?
Pamphilus:	**Capiunt, sed insipidum, qualem ego.**
	Yes, but nothing I eat tastes any good.
Maria:	**Quibus igitur vescuntur?**
	Why, what do you eat?
Pamphilus:	**Malvis, porris, & lupinis.**
	Nothing but mallows, leeks, and bitter lettuce.
Maria:	**Atqui tu non abstines a capis & perdicibus.**
	But I've seen you eat capons and partridges.
Pamphilus:	**Verum; sed interim nihilo plus sapiunt palato meo, quam si malvis vescerer, aut betis absque pipere, vino & aceto.**
	True, I eat them, but to me they don't taste any better than beets without salt or vinegar.
Maria:	**O te miserum! & tamen petobesulus es. An & loquuntur exanimes?**
	Oh, you poor thing! It's amazing how healthy you look! And do dead people talk as well?

Pamphilus: **Sic ut ego, voce perquam exilis.**
Yes, but just as I do: their voices are very weak.

Maria: **Atqui nuper cum audirem te conviciantem rivali tuo, vox non erat admodum exilis. Sed obsecro te, num etiam ambulant umbrae? Num vestiuntur? Num dormiunt?**
Hmm! When I heard you bellowing at your rival a little while ago you seemed to have a sufficiently loud voice. But tell me, do ghosts walk about? Do they wear clothes? Do they sleep?

Pamphilus: **Etiam coeunt, sed suo more.**
Yes, and they enjoy each other too, in their way.

Maria: **Nae tu suavis nugator es.**
Oh, I see. You are a smooth operator.

Pamphilus: **Sed quid dices, si argument . . . evincam, & me esse mor . . . homicdam.**
What would you say if I proved undeniably that I am dead, and that you are the murderer?

Maria: **Absit omen, . . . aggredere sophisina.**
Perish the thought!

Pamphilus: **Primum illud mihi donabis, opinor, mortem nihil aliud esse, quam abductionem animae a corpore.**
First of all, I think you'll agree that death is just the soul leaving the body.

Maria: **Largior.**
OK.

Pamphilus: **Sed ita, ut ne reposcas, quod dederis.**
Don't change your mind now.

Maria: **Non fiet.**
I won't.

Pamphilus: **Tum haud inficiaberis, eum qui alteri adimit animam, homicidam esse.**
I assume you won't deny that a person who takes away another's life is a murderer.

Maria: **Accedo.**
Yes, your point?

Pamphilus: **Concedes et illud, quod, a gravissimis auctoribus dictum, tot seculorum suffragiis comprobatum est, animam hominis not illic esse ubi animat, sed amat.**
Then I suppose you will agree to what the greatest men of the ages say, that the soul of a man is not where he lives, but where he loves.

Maria: **Istuc explana crassius: non enim satis assequor, quid velis.**
Could you explain that again, in plain language?

Pamphilus: **Et hoc sum infelicior, quod istuc non aeque sentis atque ego.**
Oh I wish you could see it as clearly as I do.

Maria: **Fac ut sentiam.**
Just try to explain it to me.

Pamphilus: **Eadem opera fac ut sentiat adamas.**
I might as well try to explain it to a rock.

Maria: **Equidem puella sum, non lapis.**
I'm a girl, not a rock.

Pamphilus: **Verum: sed adamante durior.**
Yes, but you're harder than rock.

Maria: **Sed perge colligere.**
Ok, so go on. What are you saying?

Pamphilus: **Qui corripiuntur afflatus divino, nec audiunt, nec vident, nec olfaciunt, nec sentient, etiamsi occidas.**
Those who are in the grasp of love neither hear, nor see, nor smell, nor feel, even if you kill them.

Maria: **Audivi sane.**
So they tell me.

Pamphilus: **Quid coniectas esse in caussa?**
Why do think that is?

Maria: **Dic tu, philosophe.**
You tell me, professor.

Pamphilus: **Nimirum quoniam animus est in coelis, ubi habet quod vehementer amat, et abest a corpore.**
Obviously because their soul is in heaven, living in the imagination of ardent love, and it has left the body.

Maria: **Quid tum postea?**
So what?

Pamphilus: **Quid tum dura? Illud consequitur, et me esse mortuum, et te esse homicidam.**
So what? You hard-hearted creature! So it means I'm dead and you are the murderer.

Maria: **Ubi est igitur anima tua?**
Where's your soul then?

Pamphilus: **Illic ubi amat.**
It's gone where it loves.

Maria: **Quis autem ademit tibi animam? Quid suspires? Dic libere, dices impune.**
But who robbed you of your soul? Why do you sigh? Speak freely. I won't hold it against you.

Pamphilus: **Crudelissima quaedam puella, quam ego tamen ne mortuus quidem odisse possum.**
Oh you cruelest of girls! I can't hate you, even though I'm dead.

Maria: **Humanum ingenium. Sed cur illi vicissim non adimis suam animam, par pari, quod aiunt, referens?**
Ingenious man, why don't you just deprive me of my soul? Tit for tat?

Pamphilus: **Nihil me felicius, si quidem liceat facere permutationem, sic ut illius animus vicissim demigret in pectus meum, quemadmodum meus animus totus demigravit in corpus illius.**
Nothing would make me happier if your soul would migrate into my breast, just as mine would take over your body!

Maria: **At licetne mihi vicissim sophistam agere?**
But may I, in turn, play the sophist with you?

Pamphilus: **Sophistriam.**
The sophistress.

Maria: **Num fieri potest, ut idem corpus sit animatum, et exanime?**
Is it possible for the same body to be both alive and dead?

Pamphilus: **Non eodem quidem tempore.**
No, not at the same time.

Maria: **Quum abest anima, tum mortuum est corpus?**
So when the soul is gone, the body is dead?

Pamphilus: **Est.**
It is.

Maria: **Nec animat, nisi quum adest?**
And it is alive only when the soul is in it?

Pamphilus: **Esto sane.**
Right.

Maria: **Qui fit igitur, ut quum ibi sit, ubi amat animet tamen corpus, unde demigravit? Quod si animat, etiam quum amat alibi, quomodo vocatur exanime corpus, quod animatum est?**
How is it possible then, that while the soul is chasing after the one it loves, it still animates the body that it has left behind? And if it animates that body, even when the soul is somewhere else, how can the body be called lifeless?

Pamphilus: **Argutare tu quidem satis sophistice; sed me talibus pedicis no capies. Anima, quae moderator utcunque corpus animantis, improprie dicitur anima, quum revera sint tenues quaedam animae reliquiae; non aliter quam odor rosarum manet in manu, etiam rosa submota.**
That's a cunning argument, but you won't catch me in that trap. The soul that has left the body to inhabit the lover is incorrectly called a soul. It is just the remnants of a soul. Just as the scent of roses remains in your hand if the roses are taken away.

Maria:	**Difficile est, ut video, vulpem capere laqueo. Sed illud responde: Nonne agit, qui occidit?**
	Ok, I can't catch a fox with that trap, I see. But answer this: Doesn't a murderer perform and act?
Pamphilus:	**Maxime.**
	Of course.
Maria:	**Et patitur, qui occiditur?**
	And the one who is killed suffers?
Pamphilus:	**Scilicet.**
	Of course.
Maria:	**Qui fit igitur, ut quum qui amat, agat, quae amatur, patiatur, occidere dicatur, quae amatur, quuam amans potius occidat seipsum?**
	How is it then that he who loves, acts, and she that is loved, suffers. She that is loved is said to be the one to kill, when he that loves actually kills himself?
Pamphilus:	**Imo contra; qui amat patitur: quae amatur agit.**
	On the contrary. He that loves is the one who suffers, and she who is loved is the one who acts.
Maria:	**Istuc nunquam evinces apud Areopagitas Grammaticos.**
	You'll never prove that, with all your grammar.
Pamphilus:	**At evincam apud Amphictyones Dialecticos.**
	I'll prove it with logic then.
Maria:	**Verum ne graveris et illud respondere. Volens amas, an nolens?**
	Just tell me this: do you love willingly or unwillingly?
Pamphilus:	**Volens.**
	Willingly.
Maria:	**Quam igitur liberum sit non amare, videtur homicida, quisquis amat; praeterque ius accusat puellam.**
	Then since one is free not to love, whoever loves seems to be a self-murderer. To blame the girl just isn't fair.
Pamphilus:	**Atqui puella non ideo occidit quod amatur, sed quod non amat mutuum. Occidit autem; quisquis servare potest, nec servat.**
	But the girl doesn't kill by being loved but by refusing to return the love. Whoever can save someone and refrains from doing so is guilty of murder.
Maria:	**Quid si iuvenis amet inconcessa, hoc est uxorem alienam, aut virginem Vestalem? Num illa amabit mutuum, ut servet amantem?**
	Suppose a young man falls in love with someone who is forbidden, like another man's wife or a Vestal Virgin. She shouldn't return his love in order to save his life, should she?

Pamphilus:	**Sed hic iuvenis amat, quod amare fas piumque est, atque etiam aequuam et bonum, et tamen occiditur. Quod si leve est homincidii crimen, et veneficii ream peragam.**
	But this young man loves what is lawful and right and reasonable and honorable to love; and yet he is slain. If the crime of murder is trivial I'll charge you with poisoning too.
Maria:	**Istuc prohibeant superi. An Circen quampiam ex me facies?**
	God forbid! Will you make a Circe of me?
Pamphilus:	**Aliquid et ista crudelius. Nam porcus aut ursus esse malim, quam id quod id quod nunc sum, exanimis.**
	Oh, you are more cruel than Circe! I'd rather be a pig or a bear than what I am now, half dead.
Maria:	**Quo tandem veneficii genere perdo homines?**
	By what sort of enchantment do I kill men?
Pamphilus:	**Fascino.**
	You enchant with your eyes.
Maria:	**An igitur, ut posthac abs te deflectam noxios oculos?**
	Should I take my noxious eyes off you then?
Pamphilus:	**Bona verba. Imo magis afflecte.**
	No, I love it when you look at me.
Maria:	**Si mihi sunt oculi fascinatores, qui fit, ut non contabescant et ceteri, quos obtueor? Itaque suspicor fascinum istud esse in tuis oculis, non in meis.**
	If my eyes are so infectious, how come every man I look at doesn't fall ill? I think the infection is in your eyes, not in mine.
Pamphilus:	**Non sat tibi erat iugulare Pamphilum, ni insultes insuper?**
	It's not enough for you to kill poor Pamphilus but you have to insult him too?
Maria:	**O lepidum mortuum! Sed quando parabuntur exsequiae?**
	What a dashing corpse! When is the funeral?
Pamphilus:	**Opinione tua celeries, nit tu succurras.**
	Sooner than you think, if you don't resuscitate me.
Maria:	**Egon' rem tantam possum?**
	Have I so much power?
Pamphilus:	**Potes vel mortuum ad vitam revocare, idque minimo negotio.**
	You could so easily bring a dead man back to life.
Maria:	**Si quis mihi porrigat panacen.**
	Sure, if I had a magic potion.
Pamphilus:	**Nihil opus herbis; tantum redama. Quid autem facilius, imo quid aeguius? Non aliter absolveris ab homicidii crimene.**
	You don't need herbs or medicine or magic. Just love me! What could be easier than that? It's only justice. It's the only way to clear you of the crime of murder.

Naufragium

The Shipwreck

Personae: Antonius and Adolphus

Antonius: **Horrenda narras. Est istuc navigare? Prohibeat Deus, ne mihi quidquam unquam tale veniat in mentem.**
What horrors you're telling me! If that's what going to sea is like, I want nothing to do with it!

Adolphus: **Imo quod haectenus commemoravi, lusus merus est prae his quae nunc audies.**
Oh, no, what I've told you so far is sport compared to what's next!

Antonius: **Plus satis malorum audivi: inhorresco te memorante, quasi ipse periculo intersim.**
I've heard more than enough of calamities! What you're telling me makes me shudder. It's as if I were there!

Adolphus: **Imo mihi iucundi sunt acti labores. Ea nocte quiddam accidit, quod magna ex parte spem salutis ademit nauclero.**
It's the opposite with me. The troubles I've survived are entertaining! That night something happened that nearly robbed the captain of all hope.

Antonius: **Quid, obsecro?**
What!? Tell me!

Adolphus: **Nox erat sublustris, et in summon malo stabat quidam e nautis in galea; sic enim vocant, opinor; circumspectans, si quam terram videret: huic coepit adsistere sphaera quaedam ignea: id nautis tristissimum ostentum est, si quando solitarius ignis est; felix quum gemini. Hos vetustas credidit Castorum et Pollucem.**
The night was partly clear and one of the crew was in the crow's nest, as they call it, looking out for land. Suddenly a fiery ball appeared beside him. That's a very bad sign to sailors when it's a single flame, lucky when it's double. In ancient times they believed those were Castor and Pollux.

Antonius: **Quid illis cum nautis, quorum alter fuit eques, alter pugil?**
What do they have to do with sailors? One was a horseman and one was a boxer.

Adolphus: **Sic visum est poetis. Nauclerus qui clavo assidebat, Socie, inquit, (name o nomine se mutuo compellant nautae;) videsne, quod sodalitium tibi claudat latus? Video, respondit ille; et precor ut sit felix. Mox globus igneus delapsus per funes devolvit sese usque ad nauclerum.**
This is the poets' version. The captain, standing by the helm spoke up: "Mate" (that's what sailors call each other), "don't you see your companion alongside there?" "Yes, I see him," says he, and I pray he's

	a lucky one. But then this fiery ball glided down the ropes and rolled over and over, close to the pilot.
Antonius:	**Num ille exanimatus est metu?**
	Was he scared out of his wits?
Adolphus:	**Nautae assuevere monstris. Ibi paullisper commoratus, volvit se per margines totius navis: inde per medios foros dilapsus evanuit. Sub meridiem coepit magis ac magis incrudescere tempestas. Vidistine unquam Alpes?**
	Sailors are used to these terrible sights. It stopped a little there, then rolled all around the sides of the ship. After that, slipping through the hatches, it vanished away. Then, at about noon, the storm got worse. Have you ever seen the Alps?
Antonius:	**Vidi.**
	Yes!
Adolphus:	**Ille montes verrucae sunt, si conferantur ad undas maris. Quoties tollebamur in altum, licuisset lunam digito contingere: quoties demittebamur, videbamur dehiscente terra recta ire in Tartara.**
	The Alps are warts compared to the waves of that sea. Each time we were borne up to the crest, we could have touched the moon with a finger. Each time we dipped we seemed to plunge a gaping hole in the earth to hell.
Antonius:	**O insanos, qui credunt mari!**
	O what fools they are who trust themselves to the sea!
Adolphus:	**Nautis frustra luctantibus cum tempestate, tandem nauclerus totus pallens nos adiit.**
	When the crew's struggle with the storm became hopeless, the captain, pale as a ghost, came up to us.
Antonius:	**Is pallor praesagit aliquod magnum malum.**
	His pallor must have seemed a portent to some great disaster.
Adolphus:	**Amici, inquit, desii esse dominus navis meae; vicere venti: reliquum est, ut spem nostram collocemus in Deo, et quisque se parat ad extrema.**
	"Friends," he said, "I am no longer master of my ship. The winds have won. The only thing to do is for each of us to put our hope in God and prepare himself for death."
Antonius:	**O vere Scythicam concionem!**
	Truly a Scythian speech! This was cold comfort!
Adolphus:	**In primis autem, inquit, exoneranda est navis; sic iubet necessitas, durum telum: praestat consulere vitae dispendio rerum, quam simul cum rebus interire. Persuasit veritas: proiecta sunt in mare plurima vasa plena pretiosis mercibus.**

"But first," he says, "the ship must be lightened. Deadly necessity compels it. Better to save some lives at the cost of goods than for both to perish." The blunt fact convinced them. A lot of luggage filled with costly treasure was tossed overboard.

Antonius: **Hoc erat vere iacturam facere.**
This was sacrifice indeed!

Adolphus: **Aderat Italus quidam, qui legatum egerat apud regem Scotiae: huic erat scrinium plenum vasis argenteis, annulis, panno, ac vestimentis sericis.**
There was an Italian on board who had served as a legate to the king of Scotland. He had a chest full of silver plate, rings, cloth, and silk robes.

Antonius: **Is nolebat decider cum mari?**
Did he hesitate? Was he planning to negotiate with the sea?

Adolphus: **Non; sed cupiebat aut perire cum amicus opibus suis, aut simul cum illis servari. Itaque refragabatur.**
No, he wanted to go down with his treasure or be saved with it. He protested.

Antonius: **Quid nauclerus?**
What did the captain do?

Adolphus: **Per nos, inquit tibi cum tuis perire solum: sed aequum non est, ut nos omnes tui scrinii caussa periclitemur; alioqui te una cum scrinio dabimus in mare praecipitem.**
"We're willing to let you perish with your goods," he said, "but it's not fair for you to endanger all of us. If you like, we'll throw you and your trinkets into the sea together."

Antonius: **Orationem vere nauticam.**
Spoken like a true sailor!

Adolphus: **Sic Italus quoque iacturam fecit, multa mala precans et superis et inferis, quod suam vitam element tam barbaro credidisset.**
So the Italian, too, threw his goods overboard, all the while cursing heaven and hell because he had entrusted his life to so barbarous an element.

Antonius: **Agnosco vocem Italicam.**
Sounds like the voice of an Italian!

Adolphus: **Paulo post venti, nihilo mitiores muneribus, rupere funes, disiecere vela.**
Pretty soon the winds, unappeased by our offerings, broke the ropes and tore the sails to shreds.

Antonius: **O calamitatem!**
O, calamity!

Adolphus: **Ibi rursus nos adit nauta.**
So the pilot comes to us again.

Antonius: **Concionaturus.**
Another speech?

Adolphus: **Salutat: Amici, inquit, tempus hortatur, ut unusquisque Deo se commendet, ac morti se praeparet. Rogatus a quibusdam nauticae rei non imperitis, ad quot horas se crederet posse tueri navem, negavit se posse polliceri quidquam, se ultra tres horas non passe.**
He salutes us. "Friends," he says, "the time has come for us to commend ourselves to God and prepare to die." Some of the passengers who were familiar with seamanship asked him how long he thought he could keep the ship afloat. He said he couldn't promise anything, but it wouldn't be more than three hours.

Antonius: **Haec concio durior etiam erat priore.**
This speech was more frightening than the first one.

Adolphus: **Haec ubi locutus est, iubet incidi funes omnes; ac malum usque ad thecam, cui inseritur, incidi serra, ac simul cum antennis devolvi in mare.**
After saying this he ordered all the shrouds to be slashed and the mast to be sawn off at its socket and thrown into the sea, along with the spars.

Antonius: **Cur hoc?**
Why?

Adolphus: **Quonian sublato aut lacero velo erat oneri, non usui: tota spes erat in clavo.**
With the sail ruined, the mast was a useless burden. Our only hope was in the tiller.

Antonius: **Quid interea vectores?**
What were the passengers doing meanwhile?

Adolphus: **Ibi vidisses miseram rerum faciem: nautae canentes, Salve regina, implorabant matrem Virginem, appellantes eam stellam maris, reginam coeli, dominam mundi, portum salutis, aliisque multis titulis illi blandientes, quos nusquam illi tribuunt sacrae literae.**
You would have seen what a wretched plight we were in! They were all singing "Salve Regina," praying to the Virgin Mary, calling her the Star of the Sea, Queen of Heaven, Mistress of the World, Port of Salvation, and flattering her with all sorts of titles that the Scriptures never assigned to her.

Antonius: **Quid illi cum mari, quae nunquam, opinor, navigavit?**
What does she have to do with the sea? I don't recall that she ever went sailing.

Adolphus: **Olim Venus agebat curam nautarum, quia nata credebatur ex mari: ea quoniam desiit curare, suffecta est huic matri non virgini Virgo mater.**
It used to be that Venus was the protector of sailors, because she was born of the sea. Since she gave up guarding them, the Virgin Mother took over. After all, Venus wasn't a virgin.

Antonius: **Ludis.**
You've got to be kidding!

Adolphus: **Nonnulli procumbentes in tabulas adorabant mare, quidquid erat olei effundentes in undas, non aliter illi blandientes, quam solemus irato principi.**
Some prostrated themselves on the deck, worshipping the sea, pouring whatever oils they had on the waves, flattering it as though it were a wrathful sovereign.

Antonius: **Quid aiebant?**
What did they say?

Adolphus: **O clementissimum mare, o generosissimum mare, o ditissimum mare, o formosissimum mare; mitesce, serva: huiusmodi multa occinebant surdo mari.**
"O most merciful sea! O most generous sea! O most splendid sea! O most lovely sea! Have mercy on us! Save us!" Many songs of this kind they sang to the deaf sea.

Antonius: **Ridicula superstitio. Quid alii?**
Ridiculous superstition. What about the others?

Adolphus: **Quidam nihil aliud quam vomebant, plerique vota nuncupabant. Aderat anglus quidam, qui promittebat montes aureos Virgini Walsamgamicae, si vivus attigisset terram. Alii multa promittebant lingo cruces, quod esset in tali loco; alii rursum, quod esset in tali loco. Idem factum est de Maria Virgine, quae regnat in in multis locis; et putant votum irritum, nisi locum exprimas.**
Some did nothing but vomit. Many made vows. There was an Englishman who promised heaps of gold to the Virgin of Walsingham if he made it to shore alive. Some promised precious things to the wood of the cross at such and such a place. The same with respect to the Virgin Mary, who reigns in many places and they think the vow worthless unless you specify the location.

Antonius: **Ridiculum: quasi divi non habitent in coelis.**
Ridiculous! As though saints don't live in heaven.

Adolphus: **Erant, qui se promitterent fore Carthusianos. Erat unus, qui polliceretur se aditurum divum Iacobum, qui habitat Compostellae, nudis pedibus et capite, corpore tantum lorica ferrea tecto, ad haec cibo emendicato.**

	Some pledged themselves to become monks. There was one who promised to make the journey to Saint James at Compostella barefoot, bare headed, clad only in a coat of chain mail, begging for his bread along the way.
Antonius:	**Nemo meminit Christophori?**
	No mention of Christopher?
Adolphus:	**Unum audivi non sine risu, qui clara voce, ne non exaudiretur, polliceretur Christophoro, qui est Lutetiae in summo templo, mons verius quam statua, cereum tantum, quantus esset ipse. Haec quum vociferans quantum poterat identidem inculcaret, qui forte proximus assistebat illi notus, cubito tetigit eum ac submonuit: Vide quid polliciearis: etiamsi rerum omnium tuarum auctionem facias, non fueris solvendo. Tum ille voce iam pressiore, ne videlicet exaudiret Christophorus: Tace, inquit, fatue; an credis me ex animi sententia loqui? Si semel contigero terram, non daturus sum illi candelam sebaceam.**
	Oh yes, I couldn't help laughing as I listened to one guy shouting in a loud voice (for fear he wouldn't be heard) promising a wax taper as big as himself to the Christopher in the tallest church in Paris—a mountain rather than a statue. While he was proclaiming this at the top of his lungs, again and again, a friend of his who chanced to be standing near him, nudged him and warned him, "Careful what you promise. If you survive you could never pay for it, even if you auctioned off everything you own." So he lowered his voice, so Christopher wouldn't hear, of course, and said, "Shut up, you fool. Do you think I'm serious? If I make it to land I won't give him a tallow candle."
Antonius:	**O crassum ingenium! Suspicor fuisse Batavium.**
	O what a crass ignoramus. Bavarian, I suppose.
Adolphus:	**Non, sed erat Zelandus.**
	No, he was a Zeelander.
Antonius:	**Miror, nulli in mentem venisse Paulum Apostolum, qui ipse olim navigarit, et fracta navi desilierit in terram. Is enim haud ignarus mali didicit miseris succurrere.**
	I'm surprised nobody thought of calling upon the apostle Paul, who was once shipwrecked himself, and when the ship broke apart he leaped overboard and reached land. No stranger to misfortune himself, he knew to help others in distress.
Adolphus:	**Pauli nulla erat mentio.**
	Paul didn't come up.
Antonius:	**Precabantur interim?**
	So, in the meantime were they all praying?

Adolphus: **Certatim. Alius canebat, Salve Regina; alius credo in Deum. Erant, qui peculiares quasdam preculas habebant, non dissimiles magicis adversus pericula.**

Certainly! One sang Salve Regina, another the Credo in Deum. Some had certain queer beads, like charms, to ward off danger.

Antonius: **Ut afflictio facit religiosos! Rebus secundis nec deus, nec divus quisquam nobis venit in mentem. Quid tu interea? Nulli divorum nuncupabas vota?**

How devout men are made by suffering! In prosperity no thought of God or the saints ever enters their heads. What were you doing all this time? Were you promising anything to the saints?

Adolphus: **Nequaquam.**

No way!

Antonius: **Cur ita?**

Why?

Adolphus: **Quia non paciscor divis. Quid est enim aliud, quam contractus iuxta formulam, Do, si facias: aut Faciam, si facias: Dabo cereaum, si enatem: Ibo Romam si serves.**

I don't make deals with saints. What kind of bargain is that: "I'll give you this if you do that" or "I'll do this if you'll do that." "I'll give you a candle if I can swim." "I'll go to Rome if you save me!"

Antonius: **At implorabas alicuius divi praesidium?**

But didn't you call for help from any divine power?

Adolphus: **Ne id quidem.**

Not even that.

Antonius: **Quam ob rem autem?**

Why is that?

Adolphus: **Quia spatiosum est coelum. Si cui divo commendaro meam salutem, puta sancto Petro, qui fortasse primus audiet, quod adstet ostio; priusquam ille conveniat deum, priusquam exponat caussam, ego iam periero.**

Because heaven is a vast space. If I were to ask for help from any saint, like, say, Saint Peter, because he'd be the closest, standing there at the door, I might be dead before he got to the Almighty to explain my condition.

Antonius: **Quid igitur faciebas?**

So what did you do?

Adolphus: **Recta adibam ipsum Patrem, dicens, Pater noster, qui es in coelis. Nemo divorum illo citius audit, aut libentius donat quod petitur.**

I went straight to the Father himself, reciting the Pater Noster. No saint hears sooner than he does or more willingly grants what is asked.

Antonius:	**Sed interea non reclamabat tibi conscientia? Non verebaris appellare Patrem, quem tot sceleribus offenderas?**
	But didn't your conscience bother you? Weren't you afraid to entreat the Lord directly, when you were guilty of so many sins?
Adolphus:	**Ut ingenue dicam, deterrebat nonnihil conscientia; sed mox recipiebam animum, ita mecum cogitans: Nullus est pater tam iratus filio, quin si videat eum periclitantem in torrente aut lacu, capillis arreptum eiiciat in ripam. Inter omnes nullus se tranquillius agebat, quam mulier quaedam, cui erat infantulus in sinu, quem lactabat.**
	To be honest, I was a little worried. But I quickly recovered my spirits, thinking to myself, "No father is so angry with his son that if he sees him in danger, drowning in a stream or a lake, he won't grab him by the hair and pull him out." But of all the passengers, the one who remained the most calm was a certain woman who was suckling a baby.
Antonius:	**Quid illa?**
	What did she do?
Adolphus:	**Sola nec vociferabatur, nec flebat, nec pollicibatur: tantum complexa puellam, precabatur tacite. Interea dum navis subinde illideretur vado, nauclerus metuens ne tota solveretur, redentibus eam cinxit a prora et a puppi.**
	She was the only one who didn't scream, or weep, or make promises. She just prayed in silence, holding tight to her little boy. While the ship was continually battered by the sea, the skipper undergirded it with ropes both fore and aft, for fear that it might break in pieces.
Antonius:	**O misera praesidia!**
	O what pitiful protection!
Adolphus:	**Interim exoritur quidam sacrificus senex, annos natus sexaginta; nomen erat Adamus: is abiectis vestibus usque ad indusium, adiectis etiam ocreis et caceis, iussit, ut omnes itidem pararemus nos ad natandum. Atque ita stans in medio navis, concionatus est nobis ex Gersone quinque veritates de untilitate confitendi; hortatus omnes, ut se quisque praepararet et vitae et morti. Aderat et Dominicanus quidam. His confessi sunt qui volebant.**
	In the meantime, an old priest, a man of about sixty, named Adam, jumped up. Stripped to his underwear, and with his shoes and leggings removed, he urged us all to do likewise and prepare to swim. And standing in the middle of the ship he preached a sermon on the five truths concerning the benefits of confession. He told everyone to be ready either for life or for death. A Dominican monk was there too. Those who wanted to confess did so to those two.

Antonius:	**Quid tu?**
	What about you?
Adolphus:	**Ego videns omnia plena tumultus, tacite confessus sum deo, damnans apud illum meam iniustitiam et implorans illius misericordiam.**
	Seeing as everything was in an uproar, I confessed silently to God, admitting my unrighteousness before him and asking for his mercy.
Antonius:	**Quo migraturus, si sic perisses?**
	Where do you think you would have gone, if you died?
Adolphus:	**Hoc commitebam iudici Deo. Neque enim volebam esse mei ipsius index: tamen bona quaedam spes interim habebat animum meum. Dum haec aguntur, redit ad nos nauta lacrymabundus. Paret, inquit, se quisque; nam navis non erit usui ad quartam horae partem. Iam enim ocis aliquot convulse hauriebat mare. Paulo post nauta renuntiat nobis, se videre procul turrim sacram, adhortans, ut divi, quisquis esset eius temple praeses, auxilium imploraremus. Procumbunt omnes et orant ignotum divum.**
	I left that up to God, who is the judge. I would not want to be my own judge. But I was hopeful. While this was going on the captain returned to us in tears. "Get ready," he said, "because the ship will sink within the next quarter of an hour!" It was already shattered in several places and water was flowing in. Then a sailor reported that he could see a spire in the distance and begged us all to pray to whatever saint protected that church. Everyone fell to his knees and started praying loudly to that unknown saint.
Antonius:	**Si nomine compellassetis eum, fortassis audisset.**
	Maybe he would have heard if they called him by his name.
Adolphus:	**Erat ignotum. Interim nauclerus quantum potest, eo navem dirigit iam laceram, iam undique combibentem undas, ac plane dilapsuram, ni rudentibus fuisset succincta.**
	We didn't know his name. But the skipper began to steer in the direction of the spire. By now only the ropes undergirding the ship were holding it together.
Antonius:	**Dura rerum conditio.**
	A bad state of affairs!
Adolphus:	**Eo provecti sumus, ut eius loci incolae prospicerunt nos periclitantes; ac procurrentes catervatim in extremum littus, sublatis togis, et galeris in lanceas impositis, invitabant ad sese; ac iactatis in coelum brachiis significaband se deplorare nostram fortunam.**
	But soon we were close enough to land for the people there to see our plight. Groups of them rushed to the shore and urged us toward

them, sticking hats and coats on long poles and lifting their arms to heaven to show their pity for us.

Antonius: **Exspecto quid evenerit.**
I'm breathless! What happened?

Adolphus: **Iam mare totum navim occuparat, ut nihilo tutiores essemus futuri in navi, quam in mari.**
By now the ship was so full of water that we were no safer on board than off.

Antonius: **Heic ad sacram ancoram confugiendum erat.**
Now was the time to plead for divine intervention!

Adolphus: **Imo ad miseram. Nautae scapham exonerant aqua, ac demittunt in mare. In hanc omnes sese conantur coniicere, nautis magno tumult reclamantibus, scapham non esse capacem tantae multitudinis, arriperet sibi quisque quod posset, ac nature. Res non patiebantur lenta consilia: alius arripit remum, alius arripit remum, alius contum, alius alveum, alius situlam, alius tabulam, ac suo quique praesidio nitentes committunt se fluctibus.**
Indeed, it looked hopeless. The crew released the one lifeboat and lowered it into the sea. Everyone tried to hurl himself into it, the sailors protesting in the uproar that the boat wouldn't hold such a crowd, but that everyone should grab what he could and swim. One person grabbed an oar, another a boat hook, another a tub, another a bucket, another a plank; and each, relying on his own resources, jumped into the waves.

Antonius: **Quid interim accidit illi mulierculae, quae sola non eiulabat?**
What about the poor woman? The only one who didn't weep and wail?

Adolphus: **Illa omnium prima pervenit ad littus.**
Oh, she was the first one of all to make it safely to shore!

Antonius: **Qui potuit?**
How!?

Adolphus: **Imposueramus eam repandae tabulae et sic alligaveramus, ut non facile posset decider: dedimus illi tabellam in manum, qua vice remi uteratur: ac bene precantes exposuimus in fluctus, conto protrudentes, ut abesset a navi unde erat periculum: illa laeva tenens infantulum, dextra remigabat.**
We had tied her to a warped plank so she couldn't fall off. We gave her a small board to use as a paddle, wished her luck, and shoved her into the waves, pushing with a pole to get her clear of the ship, where the danger was worst. She held her baby with her left arm and paddled with her right.

Antonius: **O viraginem!**
What a brave woman!

Adolphus: **Quum iam nihil superesset, quidam avulsit ligneum statuam Virginis matris, iam putrem atque excavatam soricibus, eamque complexus coepit natare.**
Since nothing else remained, one man seized a wooden statue of the Virgin Mother, now rotten and mouse-eaten, and, embracing it, began to swim.

Antonius: **Scapha pervenit incolumis?**
Did the lifeboat make it to shore?

Adolphus: **Nulli prius periere. Porro triginta sese in eam coniecerant.**
It went down right away, with thirty people on board.

Antonius: **Quo malo fato id factum est?**
How did that happen?

Adolphus: **Prius quam posset se liberare a magna navi, illius vacillatione subversa est.**
It was swamped by the rolling of the ship before it could get into the clear.

Antonius: **O factum male! Quid tum?**
Oh no! What happened then?

Adolphus: **Ego, dum aliis consulo, paene perieram.**
I was so busy looking out for others I nearly drowned myself.

Antonius: **Quo pacto?**
How so?

Adolphus: **Quia nihil superarat aptum natationi.**
Because there was nothing left for me to hold onto.

Antonius: **Illic subera fuissent usui.**
A chunk of cork would have been useful there!

Adolphus: **In eo rerum articulo maluissem vile suber, quam candelabrum aureum. Circumspicienti tandem venit in mentem de ima mali parte: eam quoniam solus eximere non poteram, adscisco socium: huic ambo innixi committimus nos mari, sic ut ego dextrum cornu tenerem, ille laevum. Dum sic iactamur, sacrificus ille concionator narticus, medium iniecit se in humeros nostros. Erat autem ingenti corpore. Exclamamus: Quis ille tertius? Is perdet nos omnes. Ille contra placide: Sitis, inquit, bono animo; sat spatii est, Deus aderit nobis.**
At that point I would have rather had a cork tree than a golden candlestick. But casting about, I finally thought of the stump of the mast. Since I couldn't pry it loose by myself I got another man to help me, and floating on this we put to sea, me on the right end and him on

the left. While we were tossing about in the waves, the priest who had preached to us on board threw himself on our shoulders. "Who's the third?" we yelled. "He'll be the death of us!" He just said, calmly, "Don't worry, there's plenty of room. God will help us."

Antonius: **Cur ille tam sero coepit esse natator?**
Why did he get such a late start swimming?

Adolphus: **Imo futurus erat in scapha, una cum Dominicano, nam omnes hoc honoris illi deferebant; sed quanquam errant invicem confessi in navi, tamen obliti nescio quid circumstantiarum, rursus ibi in ora navis confitentur, et alter alteri manum imponit; interim scapha perit: nam haec mihi narravit.**
Oh, he was supposed to be in the lifeboat, along with the Dominican (everyone showed this much deference to them), but although they had confessed to each other on the ship, some condition—I don't know what—had been left out, so they were standing on the edge of the ship confessing anew, each laying hands on the other, when the lifeboat sank. Old Adam told me about it.

Antonius: **Qui actum est de Dominicano?**
What happened to the Dominican?

Adolphus: **Is, ut idem narrabat, implorata divorum ope, abiectis vestibus, nudum se commisit natationi.**
According to Adam, after begging the saints to protect him, he threw off his clothes and began to swim.

Antonius: **Quos divos invocabat?**
Which saints did he invoke?

Adolphus: **Dominicum, Thomam, Vincentium, et nescio quem Petrum, sed in primis fidebat Catherinae Senensi.**
Dominic, Thomas, Vincent, and I don't know which Peter, but mostly he put his trust in Catherine of Siena.

Antonius: **Christus illi non veniebat in mentem?**
Christ didn't come to mind?

Adolphus: **Ita narrabat sacrificus.**
That's what the priest told me.

Antonius: **Melius enatesset, si non abiecisset sacram cucullam: ea deposita, qui potuit illum agnoscere Catherina Senensi? Sed Perge narrare de te.**
He'd have been better off if he hadn't thrown off his sacred cowl. With that gone, how could Catherine of Siena recognize him? But go on. What happened to you?

Adolphus: **Dum adhuc volveremur iuxta navim, arbitrio fluctuum huc et illuc se volventem, clavus illisus fregit femur eius, qui tenebat laevum cornu. Sic ille revulsus est; sacrificus precatus** illi requiem aeternam, successit in locum illius, adhortans me ut magno animo tuerer cornu meum, ac strenue moverem pedes. Interim potabamus multum aquae salsae. Adeo Neptunus nobis non balneum tantum salsum, sed potionem etiam salsam temperarat: quanquam sacrificus ei rei monstraret remedium.

While we were tossing about beside the ship, which was rolling from side to side at the will of the waves, the broken rudder smashed the thigh of the man holding the left side of the stump, so he was torn away. The priest, saying a prayer *Requiem aeternam* for him, took his place, urging me to hold on tight and kick vigorously. We were swallowing a lot of water by now. Neptune was making sure we had both a salty bath and a salty drink! But the priest had a remedy for that.

Antonius: **Quod, obsecro?**
What, pray?

Adolphus: **Quoties unda nobis occurreret, ille opposuit occipitium, ore clause.**
Every time a wave rushed upon us, he turned his head and kept his mouth shut.

Antonius: **Strenuum senem mihi narras.**
That's a brave old man.

Adolphus: **Ubi iam aliquamdiu sic natantes nonnihil promovissemus, sacrificus, quoniam erat mirae proceritatis, Bono, inquit, es animo; sentio vadum. Ego non ausus tantum sperare felicitates, Longius, inquam, absumus a littore, quam ut vadum sperandum sit. Imo, inquit, sentio pedibus terram. Est, inquam, fortassis e scriniis aliquod, quod huc devolvit mare. Imo, inquit, scalptu digitorum plane sentio terram. Quum adhuc aliquamdiu natassemus, ac rursus sentiret vadum, Tu fac, inquit, quod tibi videtur factu optimum, ego tibi cedo malum totum, et vado me credo; simulque exspectato fluctuum decessu, pedibus secutus est quanto potuit cursu. Rursus accedentibus undis, utraque manu complexus utrumque genu, obnitebatur fluctui, occultans sese sub undis, quemadmodum, solet mergi et anates: rursus abeunte fluctu promicabat et currebat. Ego videns hoc illi succedere, sum imitates. Stabant in arena, qui porrectis inter se praelongis hastilibus fulciebant sese adversus impetum undarum: viri robusti, et fluctibus adsueti, sic ut ultimus hastam porrigeret adnatanti. Ea contacta, omnibus in litus se recipientibus, tuto pertrahebatur in siccum. Hac ope servati sunt aliquot.**
After we had made some progress swimming awhile, the priest, who was very tall, said, "Be of good heart! I'm touching the bottom!"

I didn't dare hope for such great luck. "We're too far from shore," I cried. "Oh no," he replied, "I feel land with my feet." "Maybe it's something from the chests that the sea has rolled this way." "No," he says. "I feel plainly by the scraping of my toes." We swam a little farther in the same direction and he again touched bottom. "You do what you think best," he said. "I'm giving the whole mast to you and trusting myself to the bottom." After waiting for the waves to subside a bit, he went on foot as fast as he could. Whenever the waves overtook him, he clasped his knees, putting his head under water like divers and ducks do. When the waves receded he popped up and moved on. When I saw his success I imitated him. Standing on the shore were men – hardy fellows who were used to the water – who by means of extremely long poles, held out from one to the other, braced themselves against the force of the waves, until the one farthest out pushed the pole out to the swimmer. When this was grasped, all heaved toward shore and the swimmer was hauled to dry land. Several were rescued by this technique.

Antonius: **Quot?**
How many?

Adolphus: **Septem: verum ex his duo solute sunt tepore, admoti igni.**
Seven. But two of them died when brought to warm up by a fire.

Antonius: **Quot eratis in navi?**
What was the total number in the ship?

Adolphus: **Quinquaginta octo.**
Fifty-eight.

Antonius: **O saevum mare! Saltem decimis fuisset contentum, quae sufficient sacerdotibus. Ex tanto numero tam paucos reddidit?**
Oh cruel sea! It least it might have been satisfied with a tenth, which is enough for the priests. Of such a large number, so few made it to safety!

Adolphus: **Ibi experti sumus incredibilem gentis humanitatem, omnia nobis mira alacritate suppenditantis, hospitium, ignem, cibum, vestes, viaticum.**
We were treated with wonderful kindness by the people there. They looked after us with amazing eagerness and provided us with every need: lodging, fire, food, clothing, money for travel.

Antonius: **Quae gens erat?**
What people were they?

Adolphus: **Batavica**
Dutch.

Antonius: **Ista nihil humanius, quum tamen feris nationibus cincta sit. Non repetes, opinor, posthac Neptunum.**
There are no kinder people, although they have savage neighbors! I don't suppose you'll be going to sea very soon again.

Adolphus: **Non, nisi mihi Deus ademerit sanam mentem.**
No way! Unless God robs me of reason.

Antonius: **Et ego malim audire tales fabulas, quam experiri.**
As for me, I'd rather hear about such events than experience them for myself!

Uxor

Marriage

Personae: Eulalia, Xanthippe

Eulalia: **Salve multum, exoptatitissima mihi Xanthippe.**
Good morning, Xathippe. I'm glad to see you! Come in!

Xanthippe: **Salve tantundem, mihi carissiam Eulalia. Videre solito formosior.**
Good morning my dear friend. You look lovelier than ever.

Eulalia: **Itane statim me scommate excipis?**
Are you teasing me?

Xanthippe: **Non profecto; sed ita mihi videris.**
No, really. You look terrific.

Eulalia: **Fortasse nova vestis commendat formam.**
Oh thank you. It must be my new dress.

Xanthippe: **Recte conjectas. Nihil jam diu vidi elegantius. Suspicor pannum esse Britannicum.**
You're right! It's one of the prettiest I've ever seen. It's English cloth, isn't it?

Eulalia: **Lana Britannica est, tinctura Veneta.**
The wool is English, but the dye is from Venice.

Xanthippe: **Mollities byssum superat. Quam vero blandus purpurae color! Unde tibi tam egregium munus?**
It's as soft as silk! And such a lovely shade of purple! Who gave it to you?

Eulalia: **Unde decer honestas matronas accipere, nihi a maritas fuis?**
My husband, of course. Whom else should a virtuous woman receive gifts like this from?

Xanthippe: **O te felice, cui talis contigit sponsus! At ego vellem me nupsisse fungo, cum meo nuberem Nicolao.**
Oh, happy woman, to have such a good husband! I'd rather be married to a mushroom than to Nick.

Eulalia: **Quid ita, quaeso te? Tam cito male convenit inter vos?**
Why, is there already trouble between you two?

Xanthippe: **Nec unquam convenit cum tali. Vides quam sim pannosa; fic patitur uxorem suam incedere: dispergaquam, nisi saepe**

	pudet me prodire in piblicum, cum video cultae sint aliae, quae multo pauperioribus nupsere maritis.
	There's no way I can get along with the man I've got! You see what rags I'm wearing. He lets me go out looking like a bag lady. I'm embarrassed to be seen in public, especially when I see how other women look, and their husbands aren't nearly as rich as mine.
Eulalia:	**Matronarum ornatus non est in vestibus, aut reliquo corporis cultu, quaemadmodum docet divus Petrus Apostolus, (nam id audivi nuper in concione,) sed in castis ac pudicis moribus, & in ornamentis animi. Meretrices coluntur oculis multorum. Nos satis cultae fumus, si placeamus uni marito.**
	The ornament of a married woman isn't fine clothes or costly jewelry or other deckings of the body. I heard that in a sermon lately. The Apostle Peter says that the evidence of a good woman is chaste and modest behavior and the ornaments of the mind. Whores are tricked out to please the eyes of many, but we are well enough dressed if we please our husbands.
Xanthippe:	**Sed interim ille bonus vir, tam in uxorem parcus, strenue prodigit dorem, quam ex me non mediocrem accepit.**
	Well, in the meantime, this worthy fellow of mine, who is so sparing of his wife, squanders my dowry, which was not a small one, I can tell you that!
Eulalia:	**Quibus rebus?**
	Squanders it on what?
Xanthippe:	**Quibus ipsi visum fuerit, vino, scortis, alea.**
	You name it: wine, whores, gambling.
Eulalia:	**Bona verba.**
	No, really?!
Xanthippe:	**Atqui sic res habet. Deinde cum mihi temulentus ad multam noctem redit domum diu exspectatus, destertit noctem totam nonnunquam & lectum convomens, ut ne quid addam.**
	It's true! And then when he comes home, after I've been waiting up for him 'til the wee hours, he's as drunk as a lord. He does nothing but snore all night by my side, and sometimes vomits all over the sheets.
Eulalia:	**Te ipsam dehonestes, cum dehonestas maritum.**
	Stop! You disgrace yourself when you disgrace your husband!
Xanthippe:	**Emoriar, nisi malim dormire cum scropha, quam cum rali marito.**
	Let me die if I'd rather not live with a swine than with such a husband.
Eulalia:	**Non tu tum illum excipis iurgio?**
	Do you scold him?

Xanthippe:	Ita ut dignus est, sentit, me non esse mutam.
	Oh, yes, indeed I do! I use him as he deserves. He finds I've got a tongue in my head.
Eulalia:	**Quid ille contra?**
	And what does he say?
Xanthippe:	**Initio reclamabat saevissime, credens, fore ut me saevis verbis protelaret.**
	First he rages at me cruelly and tries to frighten me with big words.
Eulalia:	**Numquamne rixa incruduit usque ad verbera?**
	But did your argument ever escalate? Did he threaten to beat you?
Xanthippe:	**Semel duntaxat eo incaluerat utrinque contentio, ut minimum res abfuerit a pugna.**
	Just once. We got so angry that we were just about to start pounding on each other.
Eulalia:	**Quid ego audio?**
	What did you do?!
Xanthippe:	**Librabat fultem, saevius interim clamoribus intonans, ac dira minitans.**
	He was screaming at me and threatening me with a stick, cursing like a soldier.
Eulalia:	**Non ibi metuebas tu?**
	Weren't you scared?
Xanthippe:	**Imo vicissim ego corripiebam tripodem: si contigisset me digito, sensisset, mihi non deesse manus.**
	Not a bit! I grabbed a three-legged stool, and if he had touched me with one finger he'd have known he was dealing with a woman of spirit!
Eulalia:	**Novum clypei genus. Deerat colus lanceae vice.**
	Well, that's a new kind of shield. What did you use for a lance?
Xanthippe:	**Sensisset, sibi cum viragine rem esse.**
	He saw that he was facing a woman warrior and he backed down.
Eulalia:	**Ah mea Xanthippe, non ita decet.**
	Oh, my Xanthippe, that was not becoming.
Xanthippe:	**Quid decet? Si ille me non habet pro uxore, nec illum habitura sum pro marito.**
	What do you mean, "becoming"! If he doesn't treat me like a wife I won't treat him like a husband.
Eulalia:	**At Paulus docet, uxores oportere subditas esse viris cum omni reverentia. Et Petrus nobis exemplum proponit Sarae, quae maritum suum Abraham Dominum appellabat.**
	Saint Paul teaches that wives must be subject to their husbands and treat them with reverence. And Saint Peter cites the example of Sarah, who called her husband, Abraham, Lord.

Xanthippe: **Audivi ista. Sed idem Paulus docet, ut viri diligant uxores suas, sicut Christus dilexit sponsam suam Ecclesiam.**
I've heard those same sermons, but the same Paul also teaches that men should love their wives as Christ loved his spouse, the church. Let him remember his duty and I'll remember mine!

Eulalia: **Sed tamen ubi res in eum statum devenit, ut alteri cedendum sit, aequum est uxorem marito cedere.**
Just the same, at the end of the day, if one must submit to the other, it stands to reason that the wife must submit to the husband.

Xanthippe: **Si modo ille maritus est appellandus, wui me habet pro ancilla.**
That would be true if the man who treats me like a scrubwoman deserves to be called a husband.

Eulalia: **Sed dic, mea Xanthippe, post desiit minitari verbera?**
But tell me, Xanthippe, did he stop threatening you after this?

Xanthippe: **Desiit, et sapuit; alioqui vapulasset.**
You bet he did! And a good thing too! He was about to get a thrashing!

Eulalia: **Sed tu non desiisti rixari cum illo?**
But didn't you stop arguing with him?

Xanthippe: **Nec desinam.**
No, and I won't!

Eulalia: **Quid ille interea?**
What does he do in the meantime?

Xanthippe: **Quid? Nonnumquuam dormit, somnium hominis; interdum nihil aliud quam ridet; aliquoties arripit testudinem, in qua vix tres habet fides: eam quantum potest pulsans, mihi vociferanti obstrepit.**
Oh, sometimes he pretends to be fast asleep, sometimes he just laughs at me, sometimes he grabs his fiddle, with its three strings, and scrapes away to drown out my screaming.

Eulalia: **Ea res male urit te?**
Does that just make you crazy mad?!

Xanthippe: **Sic ut dici vix possit. Aliquando vix tempero a manibus.**
Yes! I can't tell you how much! I can hardly keep my hands off him!

Abattis et *eruditae*

The Abbot and the Learned Woman

Personae: Antronius, a venal and profligate clergyman Magdelena, a well-educated woman

Antronius: **Quam hic ego supellectilum video?**
What a mess!

Magdalia:	**Nonne elagantem?**
	You don't think my home is elegant?
Antronius:	**Nescio an elegantem; certe perum decorum matronae.**
	I don't know how elegant it is, but it's certainly not becoming, either for a maiden or a married woman!
Magdalia:	**Quam ob rem?**
	Why do you say that?
Antronius:	**Quia librorum plena sunt omnia.**
	Because there are books lying about everywhere!
Magdalia:	**Tu, tantus natu, tum Abbas, nunquam vidisti libros in aedibus matronarum?**
	What? You've lived a good long life as an Abbot and a courtier, and you've never seen books in a woman's house?
Antronius:	**Vidi, sed Gallice scriptos; hic video Graecos et Latinos.**
	Of course I've seen books, but they were French novels, not Greek and Latin classics!
Magdalia:	**An soli Gallice scripti libri docent sapientiam?**
	What? Are French romances the only ones that teach wisdom?
Antronius:	**Sed decet hoc matronas, ut habeant quo delectent otium.**
	What wisdom? Ladies don't need wisdom. They should have pleasant diversions to wile away their leisure hours.
Magdalia:	**An solis iis licet sapere et suaviter vivere?**
	Can't women be wise and also enjoy pleasant diversions in life?
Antronius:	**Male conectis sapere et suaviter vivere; non est muliebre sapere.**
	You shouldn't confuse being wise with enjoying life. Women don't need to bother with wisdom. Their business is pleasure. Girls just want to have fun!
Magdalia:	**Nonne omnium est bene vivere?**
	Shouldn't everyone strive to live well?
Antronius:	**Opinor.**
	Of course they should.
Magdalia:	**Quomodo potest autem suaviter vivere, qui non vivit bene?**
	Well, how can anyone live a pleasant life that is not also a good life?
Antronius:	**Immo quomodo potest suaviter vivere, qui vivit bene?**
	Just the opposite. How can anyone live an enjoyable life if they're trying to be good all the time?
Magdalia:	**Ergo tu probas eos qui vivunt male, modo suaviter?**
	Oh, so you approve of living a bad life as long as it's fun?
Antronius:	**Arbitror illos bene vivere qui vivunt suaviter.**
	Well, if you ask me, I think we live a good life if it's a pleasant life.
Magdalia:	**Sed ista suavitas unde proficiscitur? e rebus extraneis an ex animo?**
	Where do you think pleasure comes from? From the external world or from the mind?

Antronius: **E rebus extraneis.**
From external things, of course.

Magdalia: **O subtilem Abattem, sed crassum philosophum! dic mihi, quibus rebus tu metiris suavitatem?**
Oh subtle Abbot, but thick-skulled philosopher! Pray tell me, what do you think makes life sweet?

Antronius: **Somno, conviviis, libertate faciendi quae velis, pecunia, honoribus.**
Well, feasting and sleeping, liberty and wealth. And honors of course.

Magdalia: **Verum, si istis rebus Deus addiderit sapientiam, num vives suaviter?**
But suppose to all these things God should include wisdom. Wouldn't you be able to live more happily then?

Antronius: **Quid appellas sapientiam?**
That all depends on how would you define wisdom.

Magdalia: **Hoc est, si intellegeres hominem non esse felicem, nisi bonis animi; opes, honores, genus neque feliciorem reddere neque meliorem.**
This is wisdom: To know that a man is only happy by being at peace in his mind.
Wealth, honor, status—none of those make a man happier or better.

Antronius: **Valcat ista quidem sapientia.**
If that's wisdom, I don't want anything to do with it.

Magdalia: **Quid si mihi suavius ecrit legere bonum auctorem, quam tibi venari, potare, ludere aleam, non videbor tibi suaviter vivere?**
Well, suppose that I take more pleasure in reading a book by a good author than you do in hunting, drinking and gambling. Would you think I that I don't have a happy life?

Antronius: **Ego non viverem.**
I certainly wouldn't enjoy that sort of life!

Magdalia: **Non Quaero Quid tibi sit suavissimum, sed quid deberet esse suave.**
I'm not asking what you would enjoy. I'm asking what you ought to enjoy.

Antronius: **Ego nolim meos monachos frequentes esse in libris.**
Well, I wouldn't want my monks to spend time reading books.

Magdalia: **At meus maritus hoc maxime probat. Sed quam ob rem tandem non probas hoc in monachis tuis?**
My husband approves of my reading. Why wouldn't you want your monks to be book lovers?

Antronius: **Quoniam experior illos minus morigeoros; neque velim quemquam meorum plus apere quam ego sapio.**

	Because I wouldn't want them arguing with me. I don't want them to know more than I do.
Magdalia:	**Istud ita vitari possit, sit u des operam ut quam plurimum sapias.**
	You could avoid that by learning more than they do and acquiring as much wisdom as possible.
Antronius:	**Non est otium.**
	I don't want to do that.
Magdalia:	**Cur sic?**
	Why not?
Antronius:	**Quia non vacat.**
	Because I don't have the time.
Magdalia:	**Non vacat sapere?**
	What, you don't have the time to be wise?
Antronius:	**Non.**
	No
Magdalia:	**Quid obstat?**
	What hinders you?
Antronius:	**Prolixae preces, cura rei domesticate, venatus, equi.**
	I'm too busy with prayers, household affairs, hunting, looking after my horses, business at court.
Magdalia:	**Itane ista tibi sunt potiora sapientia?**
	And you think those things are more important than wisdom?
Antronius:	**Nobis sic usu venit.**
	That's just the way things are.
Magdalia:	**Iam illud mihi dic, si quis Iupiter hanc protestatum tibi daret, ut posses et monachos tuos et te ipsum vertere in quodcunque animal velles, illos in porcos verteres, te ipsum in equum.**
	Tell me this. If you had the power to turn yourself and your monks into any animal you chose, would you turn the monks into hogs and yourself into a horse?
Antronius:	**Nequaquum.**
	Of course not!
Magdalia:	**Atqui sic vitares, ne quis plus te uno saperet.**
	Even if by doing so, you might prevent them from becoming wiser than yourself?
Antronius:	**Mea non magni referret quod genus animalis essent monachi, modo ipse essem homo.**
	I wouldn't care what sort of animal my monks became, as long as I were still a man.
Magdalia:	**An hominem esse censes, qui nec sapiat nec velit sapere?**
	What kind of man has neither wisdom nor the desire to acquire it?

Antronius:	**Mihi sapio.**
	I'm wise enough to please myself.
Magdalia:	**Et sibi sapient sues.**
	Hogs are wise enough to please themselves.
Antronius:	**Videre mihi sophistria quaedam; ita argutaris.**
	You sound like a female sophist, you argue so cunningly.
Magdalia:	**Non dicam quid tu mihi videaris, sed cur haec displicet supellex?**
	I'm not going to tell you what you sound like to me. But tell me, what is it you don't like about my household furnishings?
Antronius:	**Quia fusus et colus sunt arma muliebria.**
	A spinning wheel is the proper weapon for a woman, not a book.
Magdalia:	**Nonne matronae est administrare rem domesticam, erudire liberos?**
	Isn't it a woman's business to take care of her family and teach her children?
Antronius:	**Est.**
	Yes, it is.
Magdalia:	**An rem tantam existimas administrari posse sine sapientia?**
	And you think so weighty an office can be done without wisdom?
Antronius:	**Non arbitror.**
	No, I didn't say that.
Magdalia:	**At hanc sapientiam docent me libri.**
	Well, I learn wisdom from books.
Antronius:	**Ego domi habeo sexaginta duos monachos; tamen nullum librum reperies in meo cubiculo.**
	I have sixty-two monks under my care in my cloister, but you won't find a single book in my chamber.
Magdalia:	**Bene prospectum est monachi illis.**
	That's a fine way to look after your monks!
Antronius:	**Fero libros, non fero Latinos.**
	I can take books all right, but I can't stand books in Latin!
Magdalia:	**Quapropter?**
	Why is that?
Antronius:	**Quia non convenit ea lingua feminis.**
	Look, Latin is not suitable for the female tongue.
Magdalia:	**Exspecto causam.**
	I'd like to know the reason for that!
Antronius:	**Quia parum facit ad tuendam illarum virtutem.**
	Because it does nothing in defense of their chastity.
Magdalia:	**Ergo nugacissimis fabulis pleni libri Gallice scripti faciunt ad virtutem?**
	Oh, but how do French romance novels, which are stuffed with the silliest nonsense, contribute to chastity?

Antronius: **Aliud est.**
There's another reason.

Magdalia: **Dic istud, quidquid est, aperte.**
Whatever it is, spit it out.

Antronius: **Tutiores sunt si nesciunt Latine.**
Women are safer from the priests if they don't understand Latin.

Magdalia: **Immo istinc minimum est periculi vestra opera; quandoquidem hoc agitis sedulo, ne sciat Latine.**
Well, that's the last thing to worry about coming from you. You'll do whatever it takes to avoid the pain of learning any Latin!

Antronius: **Vulgus ita sentit, quia rarum et insolitun est feminam scire Latine.**
Common people agree with me. It's a rare and unusual thing for a woman to know Latin.

Magdalia: **Quid mihi citas vulgum, pessimum bene gerendae rei auctorem? Quid mihi consueturdinem, omnium malarum rerum magistram? Optimis assuescendum: ita fiet solitum, quod erat insolitum: suave fiet, quod erat insuave: fiet decorum quod videbatur indecorum.**
Why tell me what the common people think! They're the worst examples in the world to follow. What do I care about custom? Custom is the mistress of all evil practice. We ought to accustom ourselves to the best things. By that means, what is uncommon would become habit, what is difficult would become easy, and what is awkward would become graceful.

Antronius: **Audio.**
I hear you, but . . .

Magdalia: **Nonne decorum est feminam in Germania natam discere Gallice?**
Is it becoming for a German woman to learn French?

Antronius: **Maxime.**
Of course.

Magdalia: **Quam ob rem?**
Why is that?

Antronius: **Ut loquatur cum his, qui sciunt Gallice.**
Because then she can converse with anyone who speaks French.

Magdalia: **Et mihi putas indecorum, si discam Latine, ut cottidie confabuler cum tot auctoribus tam facundis, tam eruditis, tam sapientibus, tam fidis consultoribus?**
Then why is it unbecoming for me to learn Latin? In Latin I can have daily conversation with so many eloquent, learned and wise authors and faithful counselors.

Antronius: **Libri adimunt multum cerebri feminis, cum parum illis supersit.**
Books destroy women's brains—what little brains they have.

Magdalia: **Quantum vobis supersit, nescio; certe mihi quantulumcumque est malim in bonis studiis consumere quam in precibus sine mente dictis, in nocturnis conviviis, in exhauriendis capacibus poculis.**
What little brain you have I cannot tell. As for myself, whatever little brain I have I'd rather spend in study rather than in prayers mumbled over without any heart in them or in staying up all night drinking glass after glass of wine.

Antronius: **Librorum familiaritas parit insaniam.**
Bookishness drives people crazy.

Magdalia: **An colloquia scurrarum tibi non pariunt insaniam?**
And doesn't the blather of your drinking buddies drive you crazy?

Antronius: **Immo depelllunt taedium.**
My buddies help me pass the time.

Magdalia: **Quomodo fiat igitur ut tam dulces sodales mihi pariant insaniam?**
How can it be then that my pleasant companions, my books, would drive me crazy?

Antronius: **Sic aiunt.**
I'm just saying . . .

Magdalia: **At aliud ipsa loquitur res. Quanto plures videmus, quibus immodica potatio et intempestiva conviva pepererunt insaniam!**
In my experience it's quite the contrary. How many more do we see driven insane by hard drinking, unseasonable fasting, and sitting up all night gambling, which destroys both health and senses. That's the road to madness.

Antronius: **Ego sane nollem uxorem doctam.**
By my faith, I would never want a learned wife.

Magdalia: **At ego mihi gratulor, cui contigerit maritus tui dissimilis. Nam et illum mihi et me illi cariorem reddit eruditio.**
Thank heavens my husband is not like you. Learning endears him to me, and me to him. It's a thing we share.

Antronius: **Immensis laboribus comparator eruditon, ac post moriendum est.**
Learning takes a lot of work. Life is too short.

Magdalia: **Dic mihi, vir egregie, si cras tibi moriendum esset, utrum malles mori stultior an sapientior.**
My brilliant sir, pray tell me. Suppose you were to die tomorrow. Would you rather die a fool or a wise man?

Antronius: **Si sine labore contingeret sapientia.**
If I didn't have to work for it, I'd rather die a wise man.

Magdalia:	**Sed nihil homini sine labore contingit in hac vita; et tamen quidquid quantisvis laboribus comparatum est, hic relinquendum est, cur pigeat nos in re omnium pretiosissima sumere laboris aliquid, cuius fructus nos in alteram quoque vitam comitatur?**
	But there is nothing to be attained in this life without working for it. Whatever we get in life, and whatever pains we take to get it, we must leave it all behind when we die. Why then should we not take the pains to attain the most precious thing of all, the fruits of which will accompany us into the next life.
Antronius:	**Audivi vulgo dici feminam sapientem bis stultam esse.**
	I have often heard it said that a wise woman is twice a fool.
Magdalia:	**Hoc quidem dici solet, sed a stultis. Femina quae vere sapit non videtur sibi sapere; contra quae, cum nihil sapit, sibi videtur sapere, ea demum bis stulta est.**
	Indeed that has often been said, but it has been said by fools. A woman who is truly wise does not think herself to be so; but on the contrary, one who knows nothing thinks herself to be wise, and that is being twice a fool.
Antronius:	**Nescio quomodo fit ut, quemadmodum clitellae non convenient bovi, ita non littarae mulieri.**
	I don't know why it is, but just as saddle packs don't look right on an ox, so learning doesn't look right on a woman.
Magdalia:	**Olim rara avis erat Abbas indoctus, nunc nihil vulgatius; olim principes et Caesares eruditione non minus quam imperio eminebant, neque tamen usque adeo rarum est quam tu putas, sunt in Italia, sunt in Anglia non paucae mulieres nobilissimae, quae cum quovis viro queant contendere. Quod nisi caveritis vos, scholis, ut contionemur in templis.**
	I suppose that's true, but you can't deny that saddle packs would look better on an ox than a miter looks on an ass or a sow. There was a time when princes and emperors excelled as much in learning as in might. But even now that isn't so rare as you think. In Spain and Italy there are more than a few women of the highest rank who can rival any man.
Antronius:	**Deus avertat!**
	God forbid!
Magdalia:	**Immo vestrum erit hoc avertere. Quod si pergetis ut coepistis, citius anseres contionaturi sunt quam vos mutos pastores ferant, videltis iam inverti scaenam; aut deponenda est persona aut agenda sunt suae cuique partes.**

No, it will be up to you to forbid. But if you keep on as you've started, geese may do the preaching sooner than put up with you tongue-tied pastors. The world's a stage that's topsy-turvy now, as you see. Every man must play his part or get off the stage.

Antronius: **Unda incidi in hane feminam? Si quando vises nos, ego te suavius accipiam.**
(Aside) How did I run into this woman?
When you visit us, I'll treat you with more courtesy.

Magdalia: **Quibus modis?**
How?

Antronius: **Venabimur, ludemus, ridebimus**
We'll dance, drink, play games and laugh.

Magdalia: **Mihi quidem iam nunc ridere libet.**
I'm laughing already!

Herilia

A Master's Commands

Personae: Rabinius and Syrus

Rabinius: **Heus, hues, furcifer, jamdudum raucesco clamore, nec tu tamen expergisceris; videre mihi vel cum gliribus certare posse. Aut ocyus surge, aut ego tibi fuste somnun istum excutiam. Quando crapulam hesternam edormieris? Non te pudet somnium hominis, in multam lucem stertere? Qui frugi funt famuli, solent exortum solis antevertere, curareque, ut herus surgens reperiat omnia parata. Ut aegre divellitur a nido tepefacto cuculus? Dum scalpit caput, dum distendit nervos, dum oscitat, tota abit hora.**
Wake up you scoundrel! I'm hoarse from calling you, and you lie there sleeping like a dormouse! Get up or I'll start beating you with this club! Aren't you ashamed, sleeping off yesterday's debauchery? A good servant gets up early to make sure everything is put in order before the master rises. This cuckoo is so hungover he won't leave his warm nest. He takes a whole hour to scratch and stretch and yawn.

Syrus: **Vix dum diluxit.**
It's hardly day yet.

Rabinius: **Credo; tibi. Nam oculis adhuc multa nox est. Tibi nox adhuc est concubia.**
Maybe for you! For you it's still the dead of night.

Syrus: **Quid me jubes facere?**
What do you want me to do?

Rabinius: **Fac ut luceat foculus: verre pileum ac pallium: exterge calceos & crepidas. Inversas caligas primum intus purga scopis, mox foris. Deinde suffitum aliquem facito purgando aeri. Accende lucernam. Muta mihi lineum indusium, ac ad ignem fumi expertem sicca lotum.**
Make a fire, brush my cap and cloak, clean my shoes and boots, take my stockings and turn them inside out, and brush them well, first within, then without, burn a little incense to sweeten the air, light a candle, give me a clean shirt, and air it well before the fire.

Syrus: **Fiet.**
I will.

Rabinius: **Atqui move te ocius. Iam haec fecisse oportuit.**
But hurry up! All this should have been done by now!

Syrus: **Moveo.**
I'm going as fast as I can.

Rabinius: **Video; fed nihil promoves. Ut incedit testudo.**
I can see how fast you're going. A fast as a turtle.

Syrus: **Non possum simul sorbere, & flare.**
I can't do two things at once.

Rabinius: **Etiam sententias loqueris, carnifex? Tolle matulam. Compone lecti stragulas, revolve cortinas. Verre pavimentum. Verre solum cubiculi. Adfer aquam lavandis manibus. Quid cessas, asine? Annus est priusquam accendas candelam.**
You rascal, do you talk back to me? Take away the chamber pot, make the bed up, draw the curtains, sweep the house, sweep the bedroom floor, get me some water to wash my hands. What are you dithering about, you ass? You'll take a year to light the candle.

Syrus: **Vix reperio scintillam ignis.**
I can't find a spark of fire.

Rabinius: **Sic heri condidisti.**
Didn't you rake the ashes last night?

Syrus: **Nec follem habeo.**
I don't have a bellows.

Rabinius: **Ut responsat nebulo, quasi qui te habeat, careat folle.**
What kind of answer is that? Do you think someone who has a servant wouldn't have a bellows?

Syrus: **Quam imperiosum haveo dominum! Vix hujus jussis decem expediti famuli fecerint fatis.**
(Aside) What an imperious master I have. Ten of the nimblest fellows int the world couldn't get all of his orders done.

Rabinius: **Quid ais, cessator?**
What's that you say, you slowpoke?

Syrus: **Nihil: omnia recte.**

	Nothing, sir.
Rabinius:	**Non ego te audio murmurantum?**
	Didn't I hear you muttering something under your breath?
Syrus:	**Equidem precor.**
	I was saying my prayers.
Rabinius:	**Credo, Paternoster inversum. Precationem opinor, Dominicam praepostere. Quid gannis de imperio?**
	You must have been saying the Lord's Prayer backwards then. What was it you were mumbling about imperiousness?
Syrus:	**Precor tibi ut fias Imperator.**
	I was just wishing that you were an emperor.
Rabinius:	**Et ego tibi, ut fias homo ex caudice. Sequere me ad templum usque. Mox domum recurrito, lectos concinnato. Haec confusa, suo quaeq; loco digerito. Fac ut niteat tota domus. Matulam defricato. Haec sordida submoveto ab oculis, fortassis invisent me quidam aulici. Si sensero praetermissum, vapulabis largiter.**
	And I wish you were a man and not a tree stump. Attend me to church and then run home and make up the beds and put everything in order. Let everything be put to rights from top to bottom. Rub the chamber pot and put the dirty clothes out of sight. I may have some important people come for a visit. If there's any mess I'll thrash you!
Syrus:	**Hic sane novi. Benignitatem tuam.**
	That kindness is nothing new.
Rabinius:	**Proinde cave, si sapis.**
	So watch out if you're smart.
Syrus:	**At interim de prandio nulla mentio.**
	But in the meantime, what about dinner?
Rabinius:	**Vah, ut hic mentem habet furcifer! Non prandeo domi. Itaq; sub horam decimam ad me transcurrito, adducturus me eo, ubi sum pransurus.**
	Ah, so that's what's on your mind! I won't be eating at home today. Come at about ten o'clock to take me to where I will have lunch.
Syrus:	**Tibi quidem prospectum, sed hic interim nihil est quod edam.**
	So you've taken care of yourself, but in the meantime there's nothing for me to eat!
Rabinius:	**Si non est quod edas, est quod esurias.**
	If you have nothing to eat, you have something to hunger for.
Syrus:	**Nemo fit esuriendo satur.**
	Fasting won't fill my belly.
Rabinius:	**Est panis.**
	There's bread.

Syrus: **Est, sed ater & furfuraceus.**
It's black, and as grainy as the bran itself.

Rabinius: **Delicias hominis! Te quidem foenum esse oportuit, si pabulum detur te dignum. An postulas, ut te asinum tantum placentis faginem? Si fastidis panem ciora obsonium, adde porrum, aut, si mayis cepe.**
Aren't you a dainty fellow! You ought to be fed with hay. That's what you deserve. You want plum cakes? If you don't want bread, eat leeks. If you don't like leeks, eat onions.

APPENDIX II

Selection of Educational Drama Resources for Teachers

The following is a short list of some of the books I've found most helpful in assisting the classroom teacher in the use of improvisation and dramatic exploration to explore content across the curriculum.

Boal, Augusto: *Games for Actors and Non-Actors*
Heathcote, Dorothy: *Drama for Learning*
Rohd, Michael: *Theatre for Community Conflict and Dialogue: The Hope Is Vital Training*
Saldana, Johnny: *Drama of Color*
Spolin, Viola: *Theatre Games for the Classroom: A Teacher's Handbook*
Spolin, Viola: *Improvisation for the Theatre: A Handbook of Teaching and Directing Techniques*
Way, Brian: *Development Through Drama*

BIBLIOGRAPHY

Angels and Eaglets

Gunther, Anke L.B., Nadina Karaolis-Dancke, Anja Kroke, Thomas Remer and Anette E. Buyken. 2010. *Dietary Protein Intake throughout Childhood Is Associated with the Timing of Puberty*. http://jn.nutrition.org/content/140/3/565.full.
Hillebrand, Harold Newcomb. 1964 (first published 1926). *The Child Actors*. New York: Russell & Russell, Inc.
Vail Motter, T.H. 1929. *The School Drama in England*. London: Longmans, Green and Co.
Wallace, William Charles. 1912. *The Evolution of the English Drama Up to Shakespeare*. Berlin: Georg Reimer, Publisher and Printer.

Good Behavior and Audacity: The Training Up of Schoolboy Orators

Ascham, Roger. Republished 1909. *The School Master*. London: Cassell and Company.
Baldwin, T.W. 1944. *William Shakespere's Small Latine & Lesse Greeke, Volumes I & II*. Urbana: University of Illinois Press.
Barkan, Leonard. 2001. "What Did Shakespeare Read?" *The Cambridge Companion to Shakespeare*. Cambridge: Cambridge University Press.
Bate, Jonathan. 2009. *Soul of the Age: A Biography of the Mind of William Shakespeare*. New York: Random House.
Baynes, T.S. 1894. "What Shakespeare Learnt at School." In *Shakespeare Studies, and Essay on English Dictionaries*. London: Longmans, Green, and Co. https://ia600404.us.archive.org/2/items/cu31924013147560/cu31924013147560.pdf
Brinsley, John. 1917. *Ludus Literarius or the Grammar Schoole* (1612). Edited by E.T. Campagnac. Liverpool: Liverpool University Press.
Charlton, Kenneth. 1965. *Education in Renaissance England*. Chatham: W. & J. Mackey & Co. Ltd.

Cressy, D. 1975. *Education in Tudor and Stuart England*. New York. St. Martin's Press.
Critchlow, Keith ed. 2010. *quadrivium: The Four Classical Liberal Arts of Number, Geometry, Music and Cosmology*. Bloomsbury: Wooden Books.
Dowden, Edward, L.L.D. 1880. *Shakespeare: A Critical Study of His Mind and His Art*. New York: Harper & Brothers Publishers.
Elyot, Sir Thomas. 1561. *The Book Named the Governor*. Edited by S.E. Lehmberg. 1962. London: Everyman's Library, Dutton.
Enterline, Lynn.2012. *Shakespeare's Schoolroom: Rhetoric, Discipline, Emotion*. Philadelphia: University of Pennsylvania Press.
Gunther, Anke L.B., Nadina Karaolis-Dancke, Anja Kroke, Thomas Remer and Anette E. Buyken. 2010. *Dietary Protein Intake throughout Childhood Is Associated with the Timing of Puberty*. http://jn.nutrition.org/content/140/3/565.full.
Hoole, Charles. 1913. *A New Discovery of the Old Art of Teaching Schoole in Four Small Treatises*. (1660). Edited by I.T. Campagnac. Liverpool: Liverpool University Press.
Kempe, William. 1588. *The Education of Children in Learning, Declared by the Dignitie, Utilitie, and Method Thereof*. Facsimile: https://play.google.com/books/reader?iEqw4AQAAMAAJ&printsec=frontcover&output=reader&hl=en&pg=GBS.PT4.
Kennedy, George A. trans. 2003. *Protogymnasmata: Greek Textbooks of Prose Composition and Rhetoric*. Atlanta: Society of Biblical Literature.
Martindale, Charles and A.B. Taylor, eds. 2004. *Shakespeare and the Classics*. Cambridge: Cambridge University Press.
Newstok, Scott. 2020. *How To Think Like Shakespeare: Lessons from a Renaissance Education*. Princeton: Princeton University Press.
Pogue, Kate Emery. 2012. *Shakespeare's Education: How Shakespeare Learned to Write*. Baltimore: Publish America.
Potter, Ursula. 2004. "Performing Arts in the Tutor Classroom." In *Tudor Drama Before Shakespeare 1485–1590*. Edited by Lloyd Edward Kermode, Jason Scott-Warren, and Martine Van Elk. New York: Palgrave MacMillan. www.academia.edu/8855538/Performing_Arts_in_the_Tudor_Classroom
Sylvester, W.D., ed. 1970. *Educational Documents: England and Wales 800–1816*. https://books.google.com/books?id=D3apayEuoZ8C&printsec=frontcover#=onepage&q&f=false
Thompson, C.R. 1958. *Schools in Tudor England*. Washington: Folger Books.
Watson, Foster. 1908. *The English Grammar Schools to 1660: Their Curriculum and Practice*. Cambridge: Cambridge University Press.

Context: The Hatch and Brood of Time: A Brief History of the English Reformation

Gottlieb, Anthony. 2000. *The Dream of Reason*. New York: W.W. Norton & Co.
Greaves, R.L. 1981 *Society and Religion in Elizabethan England*. Minneapolis: University of Minnesota Press.
Greenblatt, Stephen. 2011. *The Swerve: How the World Became Modern*. New York: W.W. Norton & Co.
Massing, Michael. 2018. *Fatal Discord: Erasmus, Luther, and the Fight for the Western Mind*. New York: Harper Collins Publishers.
Sellin, P.R. 1968. *Daniel Heinsius and Stuart England*. London: Oxford University Press.

Woodward, William Harrison. 1897. *Vittorina da Feltre and other Humanist Educators.* 1963 edition. New York: Teachers' College Press, Columbia University.
Wright, Louis B. 1935. *Middle-Class Culture in Elizabethan England.* Ithaca: Cornell University Press.

Erasmus' Egg

Dolan, John P., ed. and trans. 1964. *The Essential Erasmus.* New York. New American.
Erasmus, Desiderius. 1514. On Copia of Words and Ideas. Donald B. King and H. David Rix, trans. Milwaukee: Marquette University Press. 2007.
Erasmus, Desiderius. 1994. *In Praise of Folly.* London: Penguin Classic.
Ferguson, W.K., ed. 1978. *Collected Works of Erasmus, Literary and Educational Writings, Vol. I.* Toronto: University of Toronto Press.
Froude, James Anthony. 1896. *Life and Letters of Erasmus. Lectures Delivered at Oxford, 1893–94.* New York: Charles Scribner's Sons.
Huizinga, J. 1924. *Erasmus and the Age of Reformation.* Translated by F. Hopman. 2001. Mineola: Dover Publications.
Hyma, Albert 1930. *The Youth of Erasmus.* Ann Arbor: University of Michigan Press.
King, D. and H.D. Rix, eds. 2007. *Desiderius Erasmus on Copia of Words and Ideas.* Milwaukee: Marquette University Press.
Massing, Michael. 2018. *Fatal Discord: Erasmus, Luther, and the Fight for the Western Mind.* New York: Harper Collins Publishers.
Phau, D. 1995. "Erasmus of Rotterdam: The Educators Educator." *Fidelio Magazine,* Summer edition. www.schillerinstitute.org/fid_91-96/952_erasmus.html
Rummel, Erika, ed. 1990. *The Erasmus Reader.* Toronto: University of Toronto Press.
Sowards, J.K. 1958. "Erasmus and the Apologetic Textbook: A Study of De Duplici Copia Verborum ac Rerum." Studies in Philology, Vol. 55, No. 2 (April), pp. 122–135. The University of North Carolina Press.
Woodward, William Harrison. 1904. *Desiderius Erasmus: Concerning the Aim and Method of Education.* Cambridge: Cambridge University Press.
Zweig, Stefan. 1934. *Erasmus of Rotterdam.* New York: Viking.

The Delightful Mulcaster

DeMolen, Richard. 1971. *Richard Mulcaster's Positions.* New York: Teachers College Press, Columbia University.
DeMolen, Richard. 1991. *Richard Mulcaster (c1531–1611) and Education Reform in the Renaissance.* Den Haag: Nieuwkoop de Graaf.
Jones, Emrys. 1977. *The Origins of Shakespeare.* Oxford: Oxford University Press.
Mulcaster, Richard. 1581. *Positions Concerning the Training Up of Children.* http://members.tripod.com/bible_study/courses/training/positions.html
Mulcaster, Richard. 1582. *The Elementarie.* Scholar Press Facsimile, 1970. www.classiclanguagearts.net/Projects/WritingLessonsFromTheRenaisszance/the-elementary.htm
Oliphant, J.M.A., F.R.S.E. 1903. *The Educational Writings of Richard Mulcaster.* Glasgow: James Maclehose and Sons.
Quick, R.H. 1888. *Positions: by Richard Mulcaster, First Headmaster of Merchant Taylors' School (A.D. 1561–1586).* Translated by N. Bailey. London: Longmans, Green & Co.

Rogerton, Margaret. 1998. "Provincial School Masters and Early English Drama." Leeds Studies in English, Vol. 29, pp. 315–32.
Watson, Foster. 1893. *Richard Mulcaster and His Elementarie*. London: C.R. Hodgson & Sons.
Wilson, John Dover. 1932. *The Essential Shakespeare*. Cambridge: Cambridge University Press.

Per Quam Figuram?

Altman, J.B. 1978. *The Tudor Play of Mind: Rhetorical Inquiry and the Development of Elizabethan Drama*. Oakland: University of California Press.
Arvatu, Adina and Andrew Aberdein. 2015. *Rhetoric, the Art of Persuasion*. Glastonbury, Somerset: Wooden Books Ltd.
Austen, Gilbert. 1966. *Chironomia or, a Treatise on Rhetorical Delivery*. Carbondale and Edwardsville: Southern Illinois University Press.
Bragg, Melvyn. 2003. *The Adventure of English: The Biography of a Language*. New York. Arcade Publishing.
Bryson, Bill. 1990. *The Mother Tongue: English and How It Got That Way*. New York: Harper Collins.
Bulwer, John. 1644. *Chirologia and Chironomia*.
Carruthers, M., ed. 2010. *Rhetoric Beyond Words: Delight and Persuasion in the Arts of the Middle Ages*. Cambridge: Cambridge University Press.
Dragicevich, Milan. 2019. *The Persuasive Actor: Rhetorical Power on the Contemporary Stage*. Indianapolis and Cambridge: Focus, and imprint of Hackett Publishing Co.
Everitt, A. 2001. *Cicero: The Life and Times of Rome's Greatest Politician*. New York: Random House.
Holton, Amanda and Tom MacFoul, eds. 2011. *Tottel's Miscellany*. (First published 1557). London: Penguin Classics.
Joseph, Sister Miriam. 1937. *The trivium, the Liberal Arts of Logic, Grammar, and Rhetoric: Understanding the Nature and Function of Language*. Philadelphia: Paul Dry Books.
Joseph, Sister Miriam. 1947a. *Rhetoric in Shakespeare's Time*. New York: Harcourt, Brace & World, Inc.
Joseph, Sister Miriam. 1947b. *Shakespeare's Use of the Arts of Language*. New York: Columbia University Press. Republished 2013. Mansfield Center, CT: Martino Publishing.
Kennedy, George A. 1994. *A New History of Classical Rhetoric*. Princeton: Princeton University Press.
Kennedy, George A., trans. 2003. *Protogymnasmata: Greek Textbooks of Prose Composition and Rhetoric*. Atlanta: Society of Biblical Literature.
King, D. and H.D. Rix, eds. 2007. *Desiderius Erasmus on Copia of Words and Ideas*. Milwaukee: Marquette University Press.
Lanham, Richard A. 1991. *A Handlist of Rhetorical Terms*. Los Angeles: University of California Press.
Lynn, Raphael. 2011. *Shakespeare, Rhetoric and Cognition*. Cambridge: Cambridge University Press.
Plutarch. "Demosthenes." *The Parallel Lives*. 7.1. http://penelope.uchicago.edu/Thayer/E/Roman/Texts/Plutarch/Lives/Demosthenes*.html
Sherry, Richard. 1550. *A Treatise of Schemes and Tropes*. Project Gutenberg, 2009. www.gutenberg.org/files/28447/28447-h/28447-h.htm
Whigham, Frank and Wayne A. Rebhorn, eds. 2007. *The Art of English Poesy by George Puttenham: A Critical Edition*. Ithaca: Cornell University Press.

Erasmus Writes Colloquies

Baldwin, T.W. 1944. *William Shakespere's Small Latine & Lesse Greeke, Volumes I & II.* Urbana: University of Illinois Press.

Clark, J. 1800. *Erasmi Colloquia Selecta: The Selected Colloquies of Erasmus.* London: R. Raikes.

Cordier, Mathurin J. Clarke, trans. 1788. *Corderii Colloquiorum Centruria Selecta, A Select Century of Corderius's Colloquies with an English Translation as Literal as Possible; Designed for the Use of Beginners in the Latin Tongue.* London: Booksellers.

De Vocht, H., ed. 1928. *The Earliest English Translations of Eramus' Colloquia 1536–1566.* London: Oxford University Press.

Johnson, E., ed. 1878. *The Colloquies of Erasmus.* Translated by N. Bailey. London: Filiquarian Publishing, LLC.

Smith, Preserved. 1927. *A Key to the Colloquies of Erasmus.* Cambridge: Harvard University Press.

Stritmatter, R. and L. Kosisky, M.A. 2006. *Pale as Death: The Fictionalizing Influence of Erasmus's "Naufragium" on the Renaissance Travel Narrative.* Discovering Shakespeare. A Festschrift. http://shakespearestempest.com/articles/pale_as_death.pdf

Thompson, C.R. 1965, ed. *The Colloquies of Erasmus.* Chicago: University of Chicago Press.

Vives, Juan Luis and F. Watson, trans. 1908. *Tudor School-boy Life: The Dialogues of Juan Luis Vives.* London: J.M. Dent & Company.

Woodbridge, L.T. 1983. "Shakespeare's Use of Two Erasmian Colloquies." Notes and Queries. Oxford Journals, Vol. 30, No. 2, pp. 122–123. http://nq.oxfordjournals.org/content/30/2/122.extract#

The Little Eyases: Professional Boy Actors

Chambers, E.K. 1923. *The Elizabethan Stage Vol. IV.* Oxford: Clarendon Press.

Gibson, Joy Leslie. 2000. *Squeaking Cleopatras: the Elizabethan Boy Player.* Stroud, Gloucestershire: Sutton Publishing Limited.

Gunther, Anke L.B., Nadina Karaolis-Dancke, Anja Kroke, Thomas Remer and Anette E. Buyken. 2010. *Dietary Protein Intake throughout Childhood Is Associated with the Timing of Puberty.* http://jn.nutrition.org/content/140/3/565.full.

Hillebrand, Harold Newcomb. 1964 (first published 1926). *The Child Actors.* New York: Russell & Russell, Inc.

Joseph, Bertram Leon. 1964 (first published 1951) *Elizabethan Acting.* London: Oxford University Press.

King, Ross. 2001. *The Works of Richard Edwards. The Revels Plays Companion Library.* Manchester University Press. https://books.google.com/books?id=eLesSrzp6-AC&pg=PA2&lpg=PA2&dq=Richard+Edwards+1550s&source=bl&ots=L0uhZRysi7&sig=rkUMIb2dAQsPOLjUFPGK5Z_-0uo&hl=en&sa=X&ved=0ahUKEwiSotbVg6POAhUQ02MKHdCuBScQ6AEIHDAA#v=onepage&q=Richard%20Edwards%201550s&f=false

Shapiro, James. 2015. *The Year of Lear: Shakespeare in 1606.* New York: Simon & Schuster.

Wallace, William Charles. 1912. *The Evolution of the English Drama Up To Shakespeare.* Berlin: Georg Reimer, Publisher and Printer.

The Lego Snap of Learning

Baldwin, Patrice. 2012. *With Drama in Mind: Real Learning in Imagined Worlds*. Second edition. London: Continuum International Publishing Group.
Booth, Eric. 1999. *The Every Day Work of Art*. Naperville, IL: Sourcebooks, Inc.
Carr, Nicholas. 2011. *The Shallows: What the Internet Is Doing to Our Brains*. New York: W.W. Norton and Company.
Catterall, James. 2009. *Doing Well and Doing Good by Doing Art: The Effects of Education in the Visual and Performing Arts on the Achievements and Values of Young Adults*. New York: Anchor Books.
Damasio, Antonio R. 1999. *The Feeling of What Happens*. New York: Harcourt Brace & Co.
Dewey, John. 1916 (Updated 2018). *Democracy and Education*. Gorham, ME: Myers Education Press.
Dewey, John. 1938. *Experience and Education*. New York: Touchstone.
Eisner, Elliot. 2004. *The Arts and the Creation of Mind*. New Haven: Yale University Press.
Feinstein, Sheryl. 2004. *Secrets of the Teenage Brain*. Thousand Oaks, CA: Corwin Press.
Fiske, Edward B., ed. 1999. *Champions of Change: the Impact of the Arts on Learning*.
Gardner, Harold. Updated 2006. *Multiple Intelligences: New Horizons in Theory and Practice*. New York: Basic Books (Perseus Group).
Immordino-Yang, Mary Helen. 2016. *Emotions, Learning and the Brain: Exploring the Educational Implications of Affective Neuroscience*. New York: W.W. Norton & Co.
Jenson, Eric. 2005. *Teaching with the Brain in Mind*. Alexandria, VA: Association for Curriculum and Development (ASCA).
Lehrer, Jonah. June 5, 2012. *The Virtues of Day Dreaming*. The New Yorker, Condé Nast.
Lynn, Raphael. 2011. *Shakespeare, Rhetoric and Cognition*. Cambridge: Cambridge University Press.
Newman, Eric A., Alfonso Araque and Janet M. Dubinsky, eds. 2018. *The Beautiful Brain: The Drawings of Santiago Ramón y Cajal*. New York: Abrams.
Siegel, Daniel J. 2013. *Brainstorm: The Power and Purpose of the Teenage Brain*. New York: Penguin Group.

Miscellaneous Reading Regarding the Context of Shakespeare's Life and Education

Ackroyd, Peter. 2005. *Shakespeare the Biography*. New York: Random House.
Altman, J.B. 1978. *The Tudor Play of Mind: Rhetorical Inquiry and the Development of Elizabethan Drama*. Oakland: University of California Press.
Berry, Cicely. 1973. *Voice and the Actor*. New York: Wiley Publishing, Inc.
Chambers, E.K. 1923. *The Elizabethan Stage Vol. IV*. Oxford: Clarendon Press.
Dowden, Edward, L.L.D. 1880. *Shakespeare: A Critical Study of His Mind and His Art*. New York: Harper & Brothers Publishers.
Greenblatt, Stephen. 2016. "How Shakespeare Lives Now." *The New York Review of Books*, April 21, 2016. www.nybooks.com/articles/2016/04/21/how-shakespeare-lives-now/
Honigmann, E.A.J. 1985. *Shakespeare: The 'Lost Years'*. Trenton: Barnes & Noble Books.
Kastan, D.S., ed. 2006. *The Oxford Encyclopedia of English Literature*. Oxford Reference.
Kay, Dennis. 1992. *Shakespeare, His Life, Work, and Era*. London: Sidgwick & Jackson Limited.

Murray, Tessa. 2014. *Thomas Morley, Elizabethan Music Publisher*. Woodbridge: The Boydell Press.

Palmer, Donald. 1988. *Looking at Philosophy: The Unbearable Heaviness of Philosophy Made Lighter*. Mountain View, CA: Mayfield Publishing Co.

Roach, Joseph R. 1985. *The Player's Passion: Studies in the Science of Acting*. Newark: University of Delaware Press.

Rodenburg, Patsy. 2000. *The Actor Speaks*. New York: St. Martin's Press.

Shapiro, James. 2006. *A Year in the Life of William Shakespeare:1599*. New York: Harper Perennial.

Shapiro, James. 2010. *Contested Will: Who Wrote Shakespeare?* New York: Simon & Schuster.

Shapiro, James. 2015. *The Year of Lear: Shakespeare in 1606*. New York: Simon & Schuster.

Van Laan, Thomas F. 1978. *Role Playing in Shakespeare*. Toronto: University of Toronto Press.

Venezky, A.S. 1951. *Pageantry on the Shakespearean Stage*. New York: Twayne Publishers.

INDEX

Abbot Ælfric 118
abecedarian 27, 80
Act of Succession 50, 69
actio 85, 98–100, 104, 112
Adagia ix, 58, 64, 71
Adventure of English: The Biography of a Language, The 55, 232
Aesop 33–34, 41, 71, 131, 144
affect 172–173
Agricola, Rudolph 61
à Kempis, Thomas 61
Alleyn, Edward 44
Amphitrio 148
amygdala 179
anacoenosis 98
anadiplosis 97
antanaclasis 98
anthimeria 96
Antioch Shakespeare Festival 174
Antony and Cleopatra 104, 108
apoplanesis 98
aporia 97
aposiopesis 99
Apostle's Creed 27
Appius and Virginia 145
Apuleius 34, 85
Aquinas, Thomas 63–64
Archbishop Cranmer 47
Aristotle 35, 50, 52, 63, 67, 69, 76, 85, 101–103, 117; Lyceum 101
Arraignment of Paris, The 148
Arts Education Partnership 166

As You Like It 105, 115, 125–126, 132, 157, 189
Ascham, Roger 79, 229
Asperger's Syndrome 174
assessment 2, 78, 167–168, 170, 185, 189
At Freddie's 140
Aubrey, John 28, 36, 123
Augustine 64, 69
axons 177

Bailey, Nathan 12, 191, 232, 233
Baker, Sir Richard 44
Baldwin, Patrice 163
Baldwin, T.W 15, 29, 54–55, 57, 137
Bate, Jonathan 14, 122, 229
Blackfriars 90, 146–152
Bonæ Litteræ 49–50, 52; *see also* New Learning
Booth, Eric xiii, 8, 114, 158, 171, 175, 234
Bracciolini, Poggio 52, 104
Bragg, Melvyn 55, 232
Brinsley, John 29, 41, 44, 76, 116, 129
Broca 178, 181
Brotherhood of the Common Life 61
Bruegel 14
Bruno, Giordano 67
Bulwer, John 44, 232
Burbage, James 147, 151
Burbage, Richard 44
Bussy D'Ambois 152

Index **237**

cacosistation 98
Caesar 35, 86; Caesar's *Commentaries* 34, 85
Cajal, Santiago Ramón y 176–177, 180, 234
Calvin 52, 63, 119
Cardinal Wolsey 34, 40, 47, 146
Carr, Nicholas 179, 234
Castiglione 34
Casting of accounts 27, 51, 83
Catechism 27, 71
Cato 34
Catterall, James *xii*, 165–166, 169–170, 234
cerebral cortex 176, 178
Champions of Change 165–166, 234
chantry schools 49, 51, 56
Chapel Royal 18–19, 142
Chapman, George 143, 152, 154
Chaucer 57, 144
chiasmus 97
Child Actors, The 37, 140, 229, 233
Children of Saint Paul's 140–141, 145–146, 149–150
Children of the Chapel 19, 140–143, 145, 150–151, 155
Children of the Queen's Revels 151
chirologia 44, 232
chironomia 44, 232
Cicero 6, 31, 34–36, 52, 67, 85, 98–99, 104, 107, 108, 112, 123, 232
Clifton, Henry Esq. 151
Cloister and the Hearth, The 60
Cloridon and Radiamante 145
Colet, John *ix*, 34–35, 56, 58–59, 63, 69–70, 81
Colloquia familiaria ix, 12, 15, 60, 121, 123, 137, 145
Compaspe 148
confirmatio 35, 103
confutatio 35, 103
Connie Covert 39
Conspiracy and Tragedy of Charles, Duke of Biron, The 154
Corderius, Maturinus 41, 119, 124, 233
Cornish, William 142–143
corpus callosum 178
Cotham John *ix–x*, 28, 91–92, 124
Council of Trent 63
Council of Worms 68
Cox, Leonard 81
Creed of the Apostles 65
Critical Evidence 166

Critical Links 166
Cromwell, Thomas 20, 47
Culman, Leonard 33

da Feltre, Vittorino 52
Damasio, Antonio 171, 233
dame schools 27, 80
Damon and Pythias 145
Daniel, Samuel 152, 154
Darby, Ferdinando Stanley, Earl of 88
Darrow, Clarence 104
Day, John 152, 154
De copia ix, 36, 58, 67, 96, 104, 106, 106–107, 110, 121, 144, 175, 7273
De inventione 98, 104
deMolen, Richard 76, 87, 231
Demosthenes 103–104, 232
dendrites 177
De ratione studii ix, 30, 58, 123, 176, 356, 712
Desainliens, Claude 18
Deventer 61, 62, 70
Dewey, John *xi*, 84, 175, 234
diacope 97
Dido, Queen of Carthage 144
Diet of Worms 137
dispositio 98
divisio 35, 103
Doctor Greasepaint 171, 174
Dragicevich, Milan 99, 232
Drama for Learning 161
Dream of Reason, The 101
Dutch Courtesan, The 152

Eastward Ho 152, 154
Education of Children in Learning, Declared by the Dignitie, Utilitie, and Method Thereof, The 41, 230
Edward VI *x*, 26, 56
Edwards, Richard 142, 145, 146–147, 233
Eisner, Eliot 166, 234
ekphrasia 97, 99
Elegantiae 34
Elementarie ix, 40, 78, 80, 87, 91, 232
Elizabethan Renaissance 47
elocutio 98
Elyot, Sir Thomas 76, 87, 230
enargia 99
Endymion 148
English Reformation vii, 47, 50, 56, 230
Enterline, Lynn 38, 172, 230
enthymeme 106
epimone 97, 160

238 Index

Epicoene, or the Silent Woman 152
epizeuxis 96, 105
Erasmus of Rotterdam 59, 231
Esquith, Rafe 76, 78
Essex, Robert Devereaux, Earl of 88–89, 154
Ethopoeia 99
ethos 103
Evans, Henry 151
Evolution of the English Drama up to Shakespeare, The 140, 233
exordium 35, 72, 103
eyases 90, 139, 153

fast processing 179–180
Fatal Discord: Erasmus, Luther, and the Fight for the Western Mind 47, 59, 230, 231
Ferrant, Richard 143
Fitzgerald, Penelope 140–141
Flecknoe, Richard 44
Florio, John 89
free will 68–69, 122
Froben, Johann *ix*, 64
frontal lobes 178–180
Froude, James Anthony 65–66, 231

Gallathea 148
Geneva Bible 48
Gentleman Usher, The 152
Girl of Andros, The 148
Gismunda 149
Globe Theatre 17, 43, 56, 110, 140, 156–157
Gonzalez, Emma 160
Googe, Barnaby 145
Gorboduc 149
Gorgias 102
Gosson, Stephen 42
Gottlieb, Anthony 101, 230
Grammer Gurton's Needle 149
Greene, Robert 89, 143, 148
Grocyn, William 81
Gunpowder Plot 155
Guy Fawkes Day 155
Gyles, Thomas 151

Hamlet 44, 90, 95, 98, 137, 152
Heath, Shirley Brice 166, 176
Heathcote, Dorothy 161
Hegius, Alexander 61
hendiadys 97
Henry VIII x, 48, 50, 56, 65, 69, 86, 88, 141–144, 147

Hesketh Plot 88
Heywood, John 86, 143
Hillebrand, Harold Newcomb 140–142, 154, 229, 233
History of Mutius Scevola, The 147
Holofernes 34, 42, 79, 87–91
Homer 94, 100, 107, 118
Homo mensura 101
Hoole, Charles 29, 41, 76, 183, 230
Horace 34, 107, 116
hornbook 27, 87
Hughes, Langston 112
humanism 2, 12, 502, 57, 64–65, 70, 122, 137; humanist education 2, 15, 578; humanists 2, 35, 502, 56, 72, 58, 81, 86, 100, 120, 104
Hunnis, William 143, 147, 149
Hunt, Simon 28, 31, 92, 124
Hurston, Zora Neale 112
hyperbaton 97
hypophora 98
hypothalamus 179

idolopoeia 99
imitatio 99
Imitation of Christ The 61
impressment 19, 140, 150–151, 153
inkhorn terms 95
Inns of Court 49, 55, 100, 149
In Praise of Folly 69, 231
Institutio Oratoria 99, 104
interluders 43, 143
in utramque partem 36, 45, 168, 183
inventio 98
Isle of Gulls, The 154
isomorphic match 171, 176

Jack and Jill 145
Jack the Juggler 148
Jacobean Age x, 150
James I *vi*, 90, 151, 154, 156
Jenkins, Thomas ix, x, 27–29, 34–35, 91–92, 124
Jocasta 149
John the Husband and Tyb the Wife 145
Johnson, Christopher 41–42
Jones, Emrys 57, 231
Jonson, Ben 43, 55, 57, 82, 96, 110, 143, 151–152, 154
Joseph, B.L. 44
Joseph, Sister Miriam 97, 232
Julius Caesar 34, 36, 104, 108
Justin 34

Index **239**

Kempe, William 41, 76, 230
Kerr, Dr. Sherry 164–165, 177
King's Men 154
King's Revels 155
Kyd, Thomas 55, 91

La Giocosa 52
Latin accidence 27, 30, 40
Lehrer, Jonah 186, 234
Leicester, Robert Dudley, Earl of 43, 56, 91
Lily's Latin Grammar, De Constructione 31, 71
Limbic system 178–179
Livy 34, 85, 107
lizard brain 179
Lodge, Thomas 91
logos 103
Looking Glass for London and England, A 148
Lord Leicester's Men 147
Lord of Misrule 142
Love's Labor's Lost 34, 90, 94
Loyalty and Beauty 145
Lucian 35, 70–71, 73, 107, 116, 118
Ludus Literarius or the Grammar Schoole 29, 41, 44, 82, 229
Luther, Martin 47, 52, 59, 63, 66–69, 71, 122, 146, 230–231
Lyly, John 89, 143, 145, 148, 150

Mad World My Masters, A 152
Magnetic Resonance Imaging (MRI) 177
Malcontent, The 152
Mantel, Hilary 20
Mantuan 34
Manutius, Aldus 64
Mark Antony 97, 104, 108
Marlowe, Christopher 57, 80, 89, 108, 143, 149
Marprelate controversy 150
Marsden, John 143, 152
Martial 34, 107
masque 48, 144, 149, 152, 156
Massing, Michael 47, 230–231
May Day 152
meiosis 98, 105
memoria 98
Merchant Taylors' School *vii, ix, xi*, 2, 20, 27–28, 34, 56, 73, 76–80, 88, 90–92, 124, 141, 146, 231; Merchant Taylor's Guild 17
Merry Wives of Windsor, The 31

Midas, and Love's Metamorphosis 148
Middleton, Thomas 55, 143, 152
Midsummer Night's Dream, A 38, 106, 127
Miles Gloriosus 148
mimesis 99
miracle play 143
mirror neurons 180–181, 184
Misogonus 149
Monsieur d'Olive 152
morality plays 144
More, Thomas ix, 47, 56, 59, 63, 69–70, 81
Mulcaster, Richard 67, 73, 75–83, 85–92
Munday, Anthony 143
mycterismus 99
Mystery plays 48

narratio 35, 103
Nash, Thomas 54, 89, 149
neologisms 95
neurons 177, 180–181, 184
New Learning 49–52, 61, 70, 181; *see also* BonæLitteræ
Nowell, Alexander 37, 76

occipital lobe 179
Office of the Revels 144
ominatio 99
oratorical performance 7, 15, 105
Origins of Shakespeare, The 57, 231
Orlando Furioso 148
orthopoeia 99–100
Othello 97, 129, 136
Ovid 6, 20, 31, 35, 86–87, 107, 112, 116, 122, 140, 163
Oxford, Edward de Vere, Earl of 147–148

Palaemon and Arcyte 145
Palingenius 42
Paraclesis 65
paranomasia 98
Parasitaster 152
Pardoner and the Friar, The 145
parietal lobe 178
Parmenides 102, 171
partitio 103
Paternoster 27, 120, 226
pathopopoeia 99
pathos 103, 144
Peele, George 55, 89, 143, 148–149
Pelagius 69
peroratio 35, 103
Persuasive Actor, The: Rhetorical Power on the Contemporary Stage 99, 232

Petrarch 50, 52, 64
petty school 27, 80, 83, 87
physical rhetoric 15, 37, 73, 112, 124, 139
Pierce, Edward 151, 155
Plato 52, 67, 72, 83, 92, 101–102, 104, 117, 132, 158, 161, 169, 171, 175; Plato's Academy 116
Plautus 6, 34, 37, 45, 86, 107, 144–145, 148, 149, 189
Pogue, Kate Emory 29–30, 230
Pope Adrian VI 68
Positions ix, 40, 75, 78–80, 87, 175, 231
Potter, Ursula 37, 45, 230
praepositore 28, 30, 45, 182
Predor and Lucia 145
Progymnasmata of Aphthonius 35, 104
Project Zero 166
prosodia 39
prosopopoeia 99, 144
Protagoras 101
Puttenham, George 95, 105, 232
Pythagoras 84, 102, 132, 171

quadrivium 28, 49, 230
Queen Elizabeth 31, 46, 89, 91
Quintilian i, 36, 38, 67, 85, 96, 99, 104, 107, 116, 139

Radcliffe, Ralph 42, 85
Raleigh, Sir Walter 89
Ralph Roister Doister 149
Reade, Charles 60
REAP Report 166
Reggio Emilia 185
rhetor 94
Rhetorica ad Herennium 36, 96, 103
Roscius, Quintus Gallus 104

Saint Jerome 65, 107
Saint Paul's ix, 18–20, 34, 37–38, 58, 70–71, 76, 78, 85, 88, 90, 94, 140, 152
Sapho and Phao 148
Sapphire 112
Satyrus 101
scholasticism 63
Schoolmaster, The 79
Scottish History of James the Fourth, The 148
Scotus, Duns 64
Seidel Steve 166
Seneca 34, 104, 107, 112, 116, 148, 166, 189
Sententiae pueriles 33

Shakespeare's Schoolroom: Rhetoric, Discipline, Emotion 38, 230
Shapiro, James 155, 233, 235
Sherry, Richard 95, 232
Sir Clyomon and Sir Clamydkes 145
slow processing 179–180
Socrates 12, 101–102, 107, 115–116, 122, 132
song schools 19, 38, 49, 51
sophist 64, 101–104, 196, 220; sophism 102; sophistry 100
Sophister, The 39
Soul of the Age 122, 229
Southampton, Henry Wriothesley, Earl of 56, 88–89
Spenser, Edmund 55–56, 91
Squeaking Cleopatras 157, 233
Staple of News, The 43
STEAM 184–185
stichomythia 99
Stratford Grammar School x, 43, 91, 123–124, 138, 189
Susenbrotus, Joannes 35, 96

tables 4, 30–31, 35, 108
The Taming of the Shrew 12–13, 88, 92, 94, 136, 138
Tancred 149
tasis 99
Tempest, The 17, 133–135, 155–157
temporal lobe 178–179
Terence 6, 20, 34, 37, 41, 43, 45, 61, 86, 140, 144–145, 189, 197
thalamus 178–179
Theatre, The 147–148
Thereof, The 41, 230
Thompson, Craig R. 12, 191
Thrasymachus 101
Trick to Catch the Old One, A 152
Tridentine Index 123
trivial schools 28
trivium 28, 49, 52, 58, 94, 188
Troilus and Pandor 143
Twelfth Night 134–135; the holiday 86, 144, 147
Tyndale, William 42, 48, 50, 55, 65, 67

Udall, Nicholas 78, 81, 86, 141, 148
Utopia 55

Valla, Lorenzo 52
Virgil 6, 107, 40; Eclogues 41
Vives, Juan *xi*, 76, 81, 119–120, 124, 233

Vulgaria 30
Vulgate Bible 48

Wallace, Charles William
 140–141, 143–144,
 147–149, 229
Watson, Foster 116, 230, 232
Webster, John 143
Westcote, Sebastian 142, 145
Westminster Boys' Choir 18
Westminster School 42
Whitefriars 155
Whittington, Robert 39
Widow's Tears, The 152

*William Shakespere's Small Latine and Lesse
 Greeke* 15, 229
Wilson, August 112
Wilson, John Dover 88, 232
Wit and Will 145
Wolf, Dennie Palmer 166
Wyatt, Thomas 47, 55

Your Five Gallants 152

Zanti, Kim *xii*, 165
zeugma 97
Zouch, Richard 39
Zweig, Stefan 59, 231

For Product Safety Concerns and Information please contact our EU representative GPSR@taylorandfrancis.com
Taylor & Francis Verlag GmbH, Kaufingerstraße 24, 80331 München, Germany

www.ingramcontent.com/pod-product-compliance
Lightning Source LLC
Chambersburg PA
CBHW051354290426
44108CB00015B/2012